ATHENIAN TRAGEDY

ATHENIAN TRAGEDY
A STUDY IN POPULAR ART

BY THOMAS DWIGHT GOODELL

882.
09
G 61

KENNIKAT PRESS
Port Washington, N. Y./London

ATHENIAN TRAGEDY

First published in 1920
Reissued in 1969 by Kennikat Press
Library of Congress Catalog Card No: 75-86018
SBN 8046-0612-9

Manufactured by Taylor Publishing Company   Dallas, Texas

KENNIKAT CLASSICS SERIES

PREFACE

THE aim of these pages is to clear the way to a
better understanding of Greek tragedy. They
are intended for any who are reading the plays
with serious interest; for those who read them only in
translation all Greek terms are fully explained, and the
few quotations are given in English. As these plays constitute the earliest drama of the world, outgrowth of
another society than ours, a certain remoteness is what
first impresses one, even if one feels, beneath what is
antique and strange, a peculiar freshness and power. I
should like to aid in clearing away that sense of remoteness, to aid in revealing the perennial beauty and vigor.

Prominence is given to a side which it is often taken
for granted needs little or no elucidation. Dramatic art
includes much besides text; it is largely in what we have
to add in imagination that the remoteness of Attic
tragedy lies. The earlier chapters therefore include some
pages on the nature of drama and on the peculiarities of
Attic drama. Some may think too much space is given
to theory, and again too much to elementary matters.
I hope those to whom such matters are elementary and
familiar will have patience, for the sake of others who
may be grateful for a statement of some of the foundations of criticism. All too few are in fact familiar with
those foundations. Where can one more fitly make their
acquaintance, or review them, than in studying masterpieces of the earliest dramatic school? But one can
easily begin with Chapter II, coming back to these
general discussions later, if one likes.

Since the book is not intended as a contribution to

philological science, only complete plays are considered. Restoring a play from fragments and allusions involves much hypothesis and conjecture. The professional scholar knows where to go for this; what other readers care for is the plays we have, not those we have lost. So, too, inferences about the direct reflections of current events in contemporary plays, enticing as they often are, are far too uncertain for use here. It is credible, for example, that the revelation of Athenian ruthlessness in the affair of Melos inspired the "Trojan Women," as Gilbert Murray thinks; this would be most interesting if proven. But too much has been put forth as fact which can be no more than plausible conjecture.

How to transfer Greek proper names to English is a troublesome problem. Only a pedant can be consistent; and usage is changing. They first came to us through Latin, in Latin transliteration or in what were regarded as Roman equivalents. But for a century or more the tendency has increasingly been to approach Hellenic art, letters, and life directly, removing the Roman twist wherever possible. Archeologists, handling the actual objects,—sculpture, pottery, inscriptions, and the rest,— have led the way in this; they can never go back. And museums are now the chief popularizers of Greek studies. Sharing the same impulse, other scholars and men of letters have followed in the same line, breaking with the Latin tradition more or less boldly. When Bryant issued his translation of Homer, less than fifty years ago, he thought the Greek names of Greek gods were quite out of the question, Jove, Juno, and other Latin forms were alone admissible. But immediately there followed the admirable prose version of Butcher, Lang, Leaf, and Myers, which is more widely read, and which transfers most names letter for letter. Robert Browning's transcripts from Euripides pushed the direct method much too far; yet they are excellent versions and have had great influence. Many poets and prose writers of all degrees, and even newspapers, have familiarized the public with the Greek forms, while the Latin forms continue to be widely used. In short, usage is divided and is changing. Latinists, quite naturally, are among those who in this matter adhere to tradition, and underrate the forces that are making for more direct contact with Hellas, ancient and modern.

I have always followed in this regard the honored teacher who inducted me into Greek tragedy, and to whose memory this book is dedicated. But for the present purpose it seemed wise to let the unavoidable inconsistency go a little farther. Names that have taken an English form, like Athens, Corinth, Helen, are of course so written. Others, like Aeschylus, Achilles, Oedipus, Plataea, are given in the common Latin spelling. For others the current Latin forms contain medieval blunders which offend scholars. The Romans wrote and said Aiax for Aias; must we therefore keep the ugly form Ajax? Or the *n*, unknown to antiquity, that has been foisted upon Klytaimestra? To insist on the spelling Clytaemnestra is like stickling for the unmeaning *h* in naming the immortal city of the Remi which the French write Reims. Are we to sit forever, in the bonds of emotional inertia, helpless before the mere mistakes of our ancestors? Again, since *k* is as good an English letter as it is Greek, why put *c* for it in Greek names? We accept *k* in other words from Greek, like skeptic and a host of modern formations, and even in such Latin words as Mark (Marcus) and Greek (Graecus). Another set of comic inconsistencies have arisen with innocent *i*. Jason for Iason is held sacred; why not Jonians and Jon and Jo? But we need waste no more words on a matter which is really trivial, except as partisans of a recent past resent a closer approach to the Greek. Readers of the sort for whom this book is written will be grateful, rather

PREFACE

than otherwise, for being brought in this little detail a trifle nearer to the original.

A note on page 284 mentions a few of the available translations of the three tragedians. No bibliography is attempted; the footnotes refer merely to books or articles from which a passage or an idea is taken, or with which I do not agree.

I wish to thank especially my colleague, Mr. Jack Randall Crawford, for helpful criticism and suggestions on the earlier chapters, and my friend, Professor Clarence H. Young of Columbia University, for like assistance on the entire book, which he was good enough to read or listen to at different stages.

THOMAS DWIGHT GOODELL.

Yale University.

CONTENTS

I. ART, THE ARTS, DRAMA

I

TRAGEDY is a very complex art, with close relations to many other arts. If therefore we would understand its nature and those relations, we need first of all a clear notion of what art in general is—a notion of that common element in all the arts that differentiates them from other modes of human activity. Starting from this common basis we shall then readily see what differentiates them from one another, and how they fall into two groups, to both of which drama belongs.

But we will not, in search of that notion, enter the obscure jungle of esthetic theory. We will go rather to the workmen themselves, whose works we enjoy and whose activity we would comprehend. Artists are apt to be impatient of theory; their business is not to theorize but to create. But they are pretty well agreed in their understanding on one point; the mainspring of their activity is the love of beauty and the desire to produce it. They feel themselves to be above all else craftsmen of beauty. Art in the active sense is to them the creation of beautiful things. A work of art is accordingly a beautiful thing made by man, in distinction from the beautiful things produced by nature, or the forces that are not man. The terms of this definition imply a certain degree of contrast between the works of nature and of art, a difference that goes deep and reaches far, and to which we shall presently return.

One might fill pages with quotations from artists to justify the assertion that they are pretty well agreed in thus understanding their own activity. We will content ourselves with four such quotations, reminding ourselves that, as I said, artists rarely talk or write about theory. John La Farge, whose little book, "Considerations on Painting," is most illuminating to a sympathetic reader, speaks frankly of "the unaccustomed position which the artist takes when he attempts to give explanations in words of what he thinks without words." Still some have taken that to them unwonted position, and with great skill; when they consent to do this, we who need words for our thoughts are grateful to them. So Mr. Kenyon Cox* in a paper on Saint-Gaudens calls him "essentially the artist—the artificer of beauty—ever bent on the making of a lovely and significant thing." Similarly Elihu Vedder:† "As one definition more or less can do no harm, I also will venture to make one. Art is a beautiful body for a beautiful thought." One of Whistler's friends, Mr. Otto H. Bacher, says‡ that Whistler called art "the science of the beautiful." There is indeed a Whistlerian turn in his use of the word science, but he meant about the same thing that the others do. And to come nearer to our special subject, Sir Henry Irving in his lectures on "The Drama" says:§ "Finally, in the consideration of the Art of Acting, it must never be forgotten that its ultimate aim is beauty."

*_Atlantic Monthly,_ March, 1908, p. 303.
†_Atlantic Monthly,_ Sept., 1910, p. 404.
‡_Century Magazine,_ Dec., 1906, p. 213.
§P. 199.

These quotations are enough for our purpose. It is true that Tolstoi does not agree. In his heretical book, "What is Art?" the artist in him is sadly jostled and perturbed by the social reformer. He insists that art is simply the means of transmitting feeling. Yet what else can he mean than essentially what Elihu Vedder means, when he says, later in the paper before cited, "After all, the artist is only expressing his delight in something, and striving to share his delight with another; at least I think that is what I was made for"? His delight in something beautiful, something beautiful in nature or in human life, is what the artist desires to express and to share with others. In striving to do this he expresses himself—his vision, his thought, his personality—in a work that shall reproduce, in a sense we shall have to consider later, that whose beauty was a joy to him.

We must look a little closer, however, at the undoubted fact which was the starting-point of Tolstoi's view. Art does deal with emotion or feeling; the artist desires to express, to communicate to others, emotions which he has deeply felt, whether they be the childlike joy in a beautiful thing, love for a person, or the complex of emotions, eluding exact analysis, that one feels, for example, in a great national crisis. These varied emotions in the stream of consciousness are the heart of life. The endeavor to express and communicate this best part of our life is a fundamental characteristic of man. The artist has, above his fellows, the power to do this. Those who do this best are among our greatest benefactors, and have always been highly honored, even though the particular benefaction may not be fully recognized by his fellows until the benefactor is beyond reach of their honor.

But the artist, in so far as he is artist, cannot detach

those emotions from beauty. In particular he does not feel that he has properly expressed them unless that expression, by which he desires to communicate them, is itself a thing of beauty.

But perhaps at this point we should stop a moment for a word on certain other fundamentals. Just what beauty is no one has been able to define. Like some other things of undoubted reality and of the utmost importance to us, it probably does not admit of scientific definition. That need not trouble us however. Some things, when seen, please normal human beings in such a way that we call them beautiful. We apply the same term to certain sounds because of a subtle likeness in the effect upon us. By a farther transfer, a more subtle analogy, we speak of moral beauty, beauty of ideas, and the like. These familiar facts are all we need at present.

Also, by a force that is part of his life man is impelled to create. This force acts imperiously from early childhood. To make something—to make anything—is one form of self-expression; the thing made and the act of making, when conditions are normal and healthy, give pleasure to the person so acting. Still greater pleasure is given, both to the maker and to others, if the thing made is beautiful.

Accordingly, from as far back as we can follow man toward his origin the impulse to create beauty in visible forms, and probably also in audible forms and in the realm of conduct and ideas, has been active in all races. The cave dwellers have left their drawings on bone, their paintings on the walls of their caverns; savages decorate their tools and weapons; everywhere rules of social conduct and of religious ceremonial are in part based on the like innate craving for what is simply pleasing, whether useful in material ways or not. Whatever the differences of endowment in this regard, between races as between individuals, from the Eskimos to the ancient Athenians, from South Sea Islanders to the most machine-ridden factory-workers, and however crude may be the conception of beauty, the same impulse is there in some degree, and its exercise yields a peculiar satisfaction.

A distinction is often drawn between "fine arts" and "useful" or "industrial" arts, and this is sometimes convenient. But it is using the word art in two senses; and to call some modes of producing beauty fine in contrast with other and less fine modes of producing beauty is apt to mislead and has an unpleasant air of condescension. The arts collectively are the various modes and processes (as music, painting, landscape gardening, play-acting, poetry, sculpture) of creating beautiful things. Every mode or process of creating beauty, whether separately named or not, is properly called an art. Even of things made primarily for everyday use—house, boat, lamp, dish, tools, garments—the normal and uncorrupted human being wishes them to please by grace of form and by appropriate ornament. In so far as it does so please, the useful thing is a work of art also. Anything beautiful produced by man is in so far a work of art. Beauty—in differing spheres and kinds, it is true—is the common element in all the arts and their products. At the same time we must recognize degrees, and should avoid applying grandiose terms to the lesser degree.

Here we must guard against a misconception which confused so clear a thinker as Plato and has always been very common. Starting from such arts as painting and sculpture one may imagine that imitation of nature is an important, or even essential, element in art. People who are far beyond the stage of admiring photographs above painted portraits, as being more perfect likenesses, may still retain a vague inclination to make success in imitation a criterion. Does not a play imitate an episode or a series of events, an actor imitate a person in real life? The landscape architect, using material that is a part of nature, disposes trees, rocks, lawns, water, and the like to produce a real landscape that in a way imitates a natural one. The Greeks went farther, applying the words which we render by imitate, imitation, imitative, to music, and apparently to all arts of which they discussed the theory. Plato, I say, was undoubtedly confused by this; he made it part of his condemnation of the arts, not only that they sometimes imitate actions which on moral grounds we condemn, but that the finest works of painting and sculpture are mere copies of natural objects, which are themselves transient imitations of the eternal "ideal" forms.

Aristotle, however, though no artist as Plato was, understood the matter better. When he speaks of lyre- and clarinet-playing as imitating human emotions; when he speaks of dancers as imitating, through the rhythms embodied in their movements, both characters and emotions as well as actions, it is clear that he means by imitating what we should call expressing them. Lyre and clarinet and the dancer's movements express character and emotion by virtue of that subtle kinship whereby they recall and reawaken the mental attitudes and moral sentiments concerned.

If now we look more closely at the arts which at first glance appear to be purely imitative, we find that the case of music is after all more typical and significant than that of painting, sculpture, or acting, and will help us to see

these latter more truly. To obtain the tones of music,—
its material and special language,—sounds that nature
nowhere gives in purity, but only hints at, have been
freed from disturbing elements and put into combinations
that nature nowhere hints at and that no creature but
man ever thought of. The same may be said of the forms
of architecture, which are nowhere furnished by nature,
but have been devised and combined by man alone. It
is true we speak of the songs of birds and vainly try to
record them in our notation, recognizing their exquisite
beauty. We speak, too, of the architecture of certain
nests and other animal constructions. But all these
belong to the world of nature; they have no more to do
with the world of art than tree-forms and the sunset have.
They may surpass in certain ways all work of man; but
only in the latter does the human spirit appear, without
which there is no art.

Now these human combinations—a symphony, for
example, or a temple—do not imitate or copy anything.
Yet they express—that is, they recall, suggest, and
reawaken—a wide range of sentiments and emotions, and
do this with a distinctness and a force that will of course
vary with the sensitiveness of the person who comes
under their influence. If the range of expressiveness of
architecture is narrower than that of music, yet within its
range the mutilated Parthenon, the Taj Mahal, or a great
cathedral affects the sensitive observer profoundly by the
emotions it awakens. Turn now to the most imitative
arts as applied even to portraiture, and consider how little
of real imitation there is. How can living flesh be reproduced or copied in dead paint, an active being of three
dimensions be put on flat canvas? How much actual
likeness is there between a living person and his statue in

bronze or marble? Or between a human face and an etching of it, mere black lines on white paper? The change of material sets an impassable barrier. The child imitates, trying to do what he has seen another do; the processes of an art or trade are learned by imitating the action of one who practises it. But an artist's imitation of nature is of quite another sort, involving a complete transformation. Instead of repetition or duplication there is and can be only a re-presentation in another material, subject to laws of its own that strictly condition the new creation. The truth is, we are so wonted from childhood to the whole series of changes that effect the transformation, that we forget their existence.

Then another force is brought into play by the simple fact that the re-presentation is isolated, as nothing in nature can be,—cut off from the rest of the world and bounded, the statue by its own surface, the painting by the rectangular limits of the canvas. Laws of composition emerge. Things combine well in this way and not in that. The new material insists on being handled according to its own nature, and isolation makes these demands the more imperative; to disregard them is to make an unpleasing instead of a beautiful thing. Selection and convention are unavoidable. Selection means the rejection of everything, even in the outward appearance, that the new material does not take readily; with this goes a certain emphasis on whatever the new material does readily express. Convention means a tacit agreement—since the material cannot really express certain things—that such and such lines, colors, forms, very little like what they stand for, shall be understood to stand for just those untransferable things. Thus arises a kind of shorthand, of like character with picture-writing or hieroglyphics, though not carried so far. Every art makes large use of such tacit understandings.

By this complex process of selection, omission, and conventionalization systems of geometrical designs have grown up, in some cases clearly traceable to their origin in the re-presentation of natural forms, as flowers, leaves, or shells. Gradually some lines were eliminated, others developed or combined, without reference to the original, in obedience to some new law in the decorator's mind, until a pattern, a series of patterns, a style, had arisen, in which there was no thought of imitation. There is a fair probability that the countless tribal systems of geometrical ornament all arose in a similar way, though in most cases the clue is lost.

But these processes are all akin. Even when the first impulse was simply to re-present in another material something in nature that pleased, the workman, noting the inadequacy, and also the peculiar capabilities, of the new material, slowly learning its laws and special advantages, guided not less by the laws of his own mind and by the impulse to express himself than by this desire to re-present an interesting experience, developed in the course of generations the special language of each art that he practised. Words constitute one of the materials which the Greeks very early employed as a medium for re-presenting life in a form more beautiful than the original experience; and words are of course peculiarly adapted to expressing many things that cannot be expressed otherwise. On the other hand they are incapable of expressing what music or the graphic or the plastic arts can say best. It is by an obvious transfer that we speak of the language of color, of form, of line, of gesture, of rhythm, and the like. A special point to notice is that each medium employed in art, each separate language in this figurative sense, has its peculiar capacities and its own grammar, or system of natural laws that determine how it may and how it cannot produce what will please. Hence what is said impressively in one art-form can never be translated fully, often cannot at all be translated, into another. Particularly we should get rid of the notion that any other language of art can be translated into words, the limits of which are as strict as of any other language, even though they be wider. To illustrate this we need go no farther than the very word imitation, whose ambiguity and inadequacy have made so much trouble.

Still it is clear that music and architecture and purely geometric design are farther removed from nature than, for example, sculpture and painting. It is sometimes convenient, and does no harm if the facts are understood, to group together under the term imitative arts those which use as an essential part of their language forms or colors that at once remind us of the natural forms and colors from which they are derived.

II

To the Greek Aristoxenos, of the generation next after Aristotle, we owe the earliest statement we know of a principle which Lessing, over two thousand years later, rediscovered in essence, and in his "Laokoön" made the basis and starting-point of modern criticism in these matters. The principle may be put as follows.

The arts fall into two classes, according as their products occupy space or time. In architecture and painting, for example, the product occupies space; it is contemplated at rest; it is perceived as a whole (not in detail, perhaps), all at one view; it is more or less permanent; it is complete in visible form on leaving the workman's hand. Finally, it reaches the sense directly, without intermediary. In contrast with these a song, for example, occupies time but not space; it is presented to the sense through motion; its parts are perceived in succession; it is felt as a whole only after it is ended, by the exercise of the memory; its parts and the whole do not wait for scrutiny, but are fleeting. And it requires a performer as intermediary between maker and public, to present it to the sense.

The former class includes all the arts of form or arts of design, whether in two dimensions or in three—all the graphic arts as well as painting; wood-carving, gem-cutting, and so on, as well as sculpture in marble or bronze; landscape gardening as well as architecture. The latter class includes all arts of motion—music, dancing, poetry, in all varieties. In the dance, it is true, the persons dancing occupy space, and so are subject to the general laws of the other class as well. But time, the time of representation through motion, is so dominating a factor that it places the dance in the same class with music, even though the laws of design exercise a condominium. It should be remembered also, with particular reference to Greek drama, that the dance includes much more than our current social dances; these are but a poverty-stricken remnant of an art once rich and fine, which now gives good promise of renewed life among us.

In all arts of form the law of symmetry takes precedence. That is, a design in two dimensions or in three, to satisfy the eye, must show due proportion of parts in relation to one another; grace, expression, the

25

essential value of the work, reside largely in the manner in which space is filled and spaces are related to one another by the parts of the design. The space-relations may be very simple, as in a geometrical pattern like a rosette or a meander, or may be very complex and subtle, as in a fresco by Michael Angelo or a Pheidian pediment group. In like manner the dance, poetry, music, are subject first of all to the law of rhythm, which is in the broadest sense due proportion of parts in time. Evidently rhythm and symmetry are but two aspects of one law, that of proportionality, acting in time or space according to the material concerned. In the arts of time, then, beauty, expression, the essential value of the work, reside largely in the manner in which time is divided and its divisions are related to one another by the parts, longer and shorter, of the dance, the musical composition, or the poem. As in the other class the space-relations, so here time-relations may be very various. In fact, even a simple dance or song exhibits much complexity of time-relations, from the single step or measure up through its various clearly marked divisions of the larger whole.

But important differences flow from the nature of space and time. As the parts of anything in space may be contemplated at leisure, complex relations there are readily apprehended. But where the successive parts are fleeting motions, each can be observed but an instant, and the whole must be unified in memory. Here, then, the large divisions must be clearly marked, if they are to catch the attention enough to be noted and remembered. Also much repetition, with or without minor variations, is needed for the same purpose. In a simple song, for example, stanzas are clearly separated, and in successive stanzas the same rhythmical forms are repeatedly im-

26

pressed on the ear. A parallel in the other class of arts would be perhaps an egg-and-dart molding, a strip of lace, the border of an Oriental carpet. A rather simple form of symmetry would thus correspond to an elaborate piece of rhythm. As this aspect of rhythm is more to the front in music, verse, and the dance, a better definition of rhythm in these arts is that of Aristoxenos,—a definite arrangement of time intervals, *temporum inter se ordo quidam.* This is a bit of Greek science that is as final, for verse in all languages and for music, as the simplest proposition of Euclid's geometry.

It is now time to show how these general and rather abstractly stated principles apply to drama and enable us to understand better the nature of Greek tragedy and comedy.

It is evident that increasing the number of people who must cooperate to produce a thing complicates the matter. A painter, once supplied with canvas, paints, and brushes, may conceive and execute his work quite independently and invite people to look at the completed painting. The architect, however, having completed his design, must then get workmen to assemble the materials and put them together under his directions. To construct the cathedral, workmen of a high degree of skill in many contributory arts are requisite, though the architect's one mind has originated every part of it. But the relation of these workmen and their skill to the designer's work is one of complete subordination. They are but his instruments, an extension of his mind and will. The whole is complete and lasting when he, as thus extended, calls it complete and leaves it.

For the arts of motion the case is far more complex. Subordination indeed there is, in that the intermediary must follow the plan of the artist. But a symphony, when completed by the composer, exists only in his imagination, and is merely indicated by elaborate notes on paper, which only experts can interpret. In one sense they may be said to correspond to the architect's plan, rather than to the cathedral. That the symphony may exist objectively, players of stringed and wood instruments must unite and under guidance of a conductor translate the notes into sound; and when they have done so the composition again ceases to be until the whole process is repeated. The executants are joint creators. They must be highly gifted and highly trained. For some kinds of music the situation is almost comical; pianist and singer are more in the public eye than the composer, and their larger honorarium measures the higher esteem in the public mind. Very similar is the relation of actors to the play. They are partners and joint creators with the playwright. The technic of performance requires talent and long study; it is wholly unlike that of the playwright or the composer. The great actor, like a great pianist or singer, is recognized as possessing a semi-independent art; he is rare and must be highly paid.

Let us look for a moment in the arts of motion at the subject—the original experience which constitutes the starting-point for the artist's impulse—and at the nature of the transfer to the new material.

For instrumental music the subject would seem to be the sentiment or emotion connected with an experience; this is re-presented in musical tones. Now musical tones in their great variety of quality and combination have a peculiar vitality of their own. In the present development of music their language and its grammar are very rich and full; perhaps a composer becomes fully conscious of a new subject only when it has already begun to embody itself in a theme, which is the smallest fully significant element in a composition. The first theme associates with itself another and another, which develop and combine in ways that are a marvel to the uninitiated. We have already recognized that no thought of imitation is here admissible. And we have noted the importance of the performer.

It is not easy for an outsider to enter into the consciousness of the original composer of an expressive dance; but his subject would seem to be very like that of the composer of instrumental music—sentiments and emotions that accompany an experience. These he represents in graceful bodily movements, which may be more or less reminiscent of movements that were connected with the original emotions. The ancient Greeks, like the modern Japanese, were familiar with dancing of a distinctly mimetic nature, in which the dancers also re-present the experience itself with which the emotions were connected. The incident is reproduced somewhat as in pantomime, yet not so literally,—always in graceful, rhythmical, highly idealized bodily motions, for which we have no other name than dancing. This form of the art we had wholly lost; a serious endeavor is under way to revive it. That even this mimetic dancing is a different material from the original incident or story is plain enough. The persons are not the same. The movements are not the same; selection, abstraction, conventionalization have been applied to elaborate a special language. The subjection to rhythm is one element of the idealizing process; all is omitted that cannot be imbued with grace; and always the emotions rather than

29

the incident itself are kept to the front. The movements merely suggest, to the initiated, the original incident. That there are strict limits to the range of this art is even clearer than in the case of music; it is no less clear that both are highly expressive within those limits.

In poetry may be expressed or suggested a wider range of life than in any other art. Any significant experience may be the subject, which the poet re-presents in words. Now words are at bottom nothing but a most elaborate and complex system of conventional signs, having practically no other relation to what they signify than that which convention has given them. True, in any given case the history of the convention has been long; at the earliest date at which we catch a language it is already old, rich in accumulated associations, full of anomalies that are surviving fragments from stages already ancient. To every race its own language seems to be natural and unchangeable, though the speakers of it are continually changing the conventions and the associations that alone give meaning to each combination of spoken sounds. No material could be more unlike the experience which they somehow express. All our familiar types of poetry, essentially, the Greeks developed; our very names for them are largely Greek—as poem, epic, elegiac, lyric, bucolic, idyl, dramatic, tragic, comic.

A special distinction of words, compared with any other medium of art, is that they can express thoughts and not merely feelings,—propositions and judgments, not merely emotions. This it is which vastly enlarges the range of their use in art. At the same time, as was said before, for certain purposes words are inadequate and vague; colors, lines, tones, actions, are clearer and better; the limitations of words must not be forgotten.

And words are also the common means of communication in everyday life—about trivial daily needs as well as on business, mathematics, biology, and metaphysics. How the poet can make this daily drudge, this instrument of science, also serve the ends of art, is an interesting subject of study in itself; the methods of doing it are part of the poet's technic.

Without entering into the modern discussion as to whether a poem can exist in prose, I merely note that the whole discussion is modern. To any Greek of the classical age it would have seemed a symptom of degeneracy to raise the question—a breaking down of inherent divisions. It is really a question of definitions. Literature as a whole, expression in words as an art, of course includes prose as well as verse; but no Greek would have called anything poetry that was not in verse, though he did in the earlier period accept verse in uses for which later, as with us, prose was thought more appropriate. And Greek drama, both tragedy and comedy, was always in verse. And verse implies rhythm, the same kind of rhythm—there is but one kind—that we hear in music. This observance of rhythm is one element of many that mark poetry as idealized language, in so far not "natural," since no one in fact talks in meter.

The situation in regard to the intermediary who reproduces the poem is singular, now that writing and printing are universal and everyone can read. Strictly a living voice is the intermediary that re-creates the poem and is in some degree partner with the poet, whose writing corresponds exactly to the musician's notes and the choregraphic notes of the deviser of a dance. Only, in the two latter cases, few can read the notes and very few can execute elaborate music, while everyone can read plain

31

writing or print, and all who can speak can reproduce verses in some fashion. Not only that, but in the course of our era (apparently not in antiquity) the habit of reading silently has also become universal, though young children, and adults who read little, still find it difficult, like the ancients, to read without at least moving the lips. While our eyes follow the lines we pronounce them internally, and in imagination hear our own voices,* and may be almost as sensible of the rhythm and harmony as if one read the lines to us. Whoever possesses a printed copy of the poem may be himself the intermediary who re-creates it. But there is no poem, in the full intention of the author, unless it is thus in one way or the other re-created and made audible.

III

What, finally, is drama?

A play is a story, not told by someone outside of it, but enacted by people who are for the time being the persons of the story. The subject is a bit of life, commonly fictitious. This is re-presented in other persons than those who have lived it, or are supposed to have lived it, and in another setting than the original one. The actors are not the persons of the story,—Macbeth, Juliet, or whoever; they only pretend to be for the time

---

*With easy prose some do not do this, but read with the eye only, taking in the ideas without this internal voice. But no one can have any sense of the style of what he thus reads. If anyone so reads poetry, it is all lost on him as poetry. No one can write even a letter with any sense of a style in what he writes, unless in imagination he hears every phrase as he writes it. But no doubt some do so write.

being. Their emotions are not those of the original persons, but only simulated; their actions, their outward form and dress, are those which the story imposes, perhaps quite unnatural to them outside of their rôles. It is a re-presentation of a selected portion or aspect of life; only such fragments of life as are adapted to effective and interesting portrayal in this medium may be selected, under penalty of failure; a playwright must know how to select. He must also know how to recast and adapt to the new physical conditions. For the scene of the story is changed. Not only is it now isolated, cut off from life as a whole,—from all that would, or did, precede and follow,—so as to receive a unity and completeness of its own; but it is presented in a theater, which is unlike any other part of the world, in an artificial setting and before a throng of people, who must be enabled to see and hear all that goes on. What a transformation this implies for, let us say, a private interview between lovers, or between conspirators.

In view of all this it is clear that drama is one of the most complex of arts. It is conditioned in time, and doubly so, since the medium includes both speech—in the Athenian drama always verse—and bodily movement. But it also occupies space, precisely as sculpture does, and must conform, if it is to please most fully, to all the laws of space. The executants, the actors, are not only essential, the major part of the new material in which life is re-presented, but their art is even more than in the case of music an independent one, requiring special talent and long training. They are in the fullest sense joint creators with the author, who indeed may often learn from them how to improve his play. In any case the *dramatis personae* of a good play admit of different interpretations; the common phrase, by which one who first acts a part in a new play is said to create the character, is a just recognition of his importance.

The history of this complex art is extremely interesting, and especially now, when it is perhaps entering on a new phase with renewed vitality. First brought to maturity, in a form adapted to their civilization, by the Athenians of the fifth century before Christ, gradually degenerating with the slow decay of ancient culture, for several centuries lost, born again in Elizabethan England and contemporary Spain, flowering in another form in the France of Louis XIV, its condition has been a fair index, from age to age, of the state of European civilization. So high was the development which tragedy attained in Athens that it has profoundly influenced all later types of drama in the Occident. Yet the Attic drama was of another type than ours, a natural growth from its own soil; a wonderful flowering of Athenian life, yet in form so alien to us that it requires interpretation to reveal its full charm and its kinship in spirit with our own life. Though in essence the drama has always been one, Athenian conventions were not like ours; a different historical background, another social setting, require study before we can fully enter into our inheritance.

II. CONDITIONS AND CONVENTIONS

I

HOW is a selected bit of life adapted to presentation in a play, and what do the physical conditions of such presentation, the new material,
and the new setting, require in the way of reshaping?

First, the mere isolation is a radical departure from
the facts as we see them. "In life there are no groups of
human beings detached from their fellows, sufficient unto
themselves and uninfluenced by the rest of humanity."*
In a play the characters must constitute such a group;
we expect the dramatist to cut away from them the
tangled web of relations that bind every one to the rest
of mankind—all threads of relation, that is, which do
not clearly bear on their relations to one another and to
the incidents of the story. So of the sequence of events.
"Every work of literary art must have a beginning, a
middle, and an end; and here is where art sharply sepa-
rates itself from life, which is all middle with an end that
no man may see, and with numberless beginnings lost in
the dark backward of Time. . . . Many things must
have happened before [the dramatist] lifts the curtain;
and out of all these he has to make his choice, so that he
can center attention on these special things which he
knows the audience must have in mind for the full comprehension of his action. He suppresses rigorously all

*B. Matthews, "Study of the Drama," p. 198.

the rest, however tempting they may be in themselves. He must supply the spectators with exactly the information they will need to apprehend the movement of the plot, no more and no less."* He must also provide in a converse way for the end of the play, so that, however tense the listener's interest has been, he will not ask what followed, and miss the sequel. The series of events that interested him must have reached a natural close; if nothing has been said or done to raise question of a sequel, the spectator will not raise the question. In essence this is like the painter's way in his realm of space; nothing is placed near the edge of the predetermined field that would direct attention too far beyond it, nothing that is not in some way tributary to his subject. It is indeed the plan we all follow on a small scale in telling a story with a point; we mention what is needed to explain the point, and nothing more. Making such constant use of this convention of the fictive beginning and end, we forget the real nature of it.

Again, since the parts of a play succeed one another, and one after another vanish into nothingness as they pass, each part must be made so clear, must while passing be so impressed on the spectator's mind, that it will be recalled when a later part, dependent on it and prepared by it, is in progress. Only so can the relations of successive parts become intelligible. This requires a sharpness of outline, a degree of emphasis on significant details, that rarely appears in life. Our daily experience flows on in unbroken stream; we do not perceive till later, perhaps years afterward, what the real crises were. Even in lives of exceptional and striking character, suitable perhaps with little change for dramatic treatment,

*O. c., pp. 179 f.

this is the rule. But the dramatist must make sure that an alert listener shall not miss, while it is passing, the incident or utterance that is to have a dramatic consequence; that he shall not fail, when a dramatic result arrives, to recall its dramatic antecedent and the relation between the two. This we may call the convention of significant emphasis.

And the time of the play is limited, two to three hours at most. When Wagner demands four hours for an opera, do not all but musical enthusiasts feel that his work would have been stronger had he conceived it on a less generous scale? The action must be condensed and simplified by omitting all that is not significant and contributory, and must be reorganized into a whole, duly articulated, well-rounded, complete. This is a wide departure from reality. If occasionally a single crisis of brief duration is so crowded with life, so pregnant with great issues, that it might, so far as that goes, be transferred almost entire to a play, that is certainly very rare; and even in such a case the antecedent train of events that led to the crisis, and without which the crisis cannot be understood, must by narrative, if not otherwise, be made part of the play. But this is only one of many ways in which the action is condensed. Unless everything trivial is ignored—the things that make up the bulk of life, but do not explain the crises—time will fail for what is significant and does explain them. To explain and rationalize the apparent confusion of life is just one of the things we demand that serious drama shall do for us.

Also, a play must be heard; if possible, every word must reach everyone's ear in a large audience, and this necessity has far-reaching consequences. If the actors

37

are to be heard to the farthest corner, they must speak with a perfection of enunciation, a purity of tone, which are unfortunately rare. They are much more common in French than in English, and there are grounds for believing that ancient Greek was spoken with equal precision and delicacy. Verse, a measured metrical structure, favors that kind of utterance. But the actor must add thereto a deliberateness and a degree of force that would be in ordinary intercourse unnatural, affected, and offensive. And not only this; a playwright must compose his sentences in such a way that when so spoken they will be effective under the conditions of the theater. Many sentences that are perfectly suitable when silently read are feeble to the ears of an audience. To be effective on the stage a sentence must be transparent in structure and must end strongly, with emphasis on the last word, preferably on the last syllable. These are elementary requisites of a good dramatic style in English. But the matter is far more complicated than that. A competent playwright knows all this and writes accordingly; a competent actor, from his familiarity with the conditions of his art, may sometimes improve in this respect the work of a far abler writer than himself.

But a play appeals to sight as well; the attitude, gestures, and facial expression of the players (in Athenian drama the mask) must be clearly visible from the auditorium under the conditions of lighting that prevail in the theater of the time. This brings with it departures from the scale and manner of ordinary life that correspond to those in the management of the voice. Action has to be enlarged after it is condensed. But the matter goes deeper, determining much of the inner structure of the play. Alteration in the arrangement of the theater and in the circumstances of representation have led to corresponding alterations in play-construction, as plants and animals are slowly modified by changes of environment. Mr. Brander Matthews has called attention to changes brought about by the introduction of electric lighting, which has done away with what was known as the apron, the curved extension of the stage in front. Conditions of sight and hearing alike are not the same when the stage, or place of the actors, projects out among the audience and when, as at present, the actors remain always back of the line on which the modern curtain descends. Conditions of sight are not the same in a closed building by artificial light and in the open daylight. In the evening illumination of the modern theater illusions can be effected, or can be attempted without too obvious failure, that would have been quite impossible in Athenian sunshine. The directors of pageants find that some good theatrical usage cannot be transferred to the open air, which on the other hand offers opportunity for telling effects that cannot be attained indoors. The scale is different, as well as the lighting; the size of the audience, the distance from the players, are factors that may determine the success or failure of a play. Adaptation to conditions of sight involves a variety of practices that need not be separately named; but the actor's whole "make-up," by which colors are heightened and natural lines exaggerated, is obviously determined by conditions of distance and lighting. The use of the mask in the ancient theater was perhaps due originally to other motives; but when audiences became large the mask was the only means of making at least a general average of facial expression visible. The modern "make-up" would have been insufficient, and of course all minor play of facial expression would be wholly lost on most of an audience of ten to twenty thousand.

And one convention, whether named or not, is inexorably demanded by the presence of any considerable audience,—that whereby the actor, whomever the dialogue requires him to address, and whomever therefore he seems to address, must ever bear in mind that his first duty is to the audience. Never addressing them directly he must take good care that they hear him. In recent years there has grown up a decided tendency to relax this rule. In the effort to keep near to nature (that is, in this case, to everyday life) an actor allows himself to speak with his back to the audience. This may be quite right in an " intimate" comedy and in the small theater demanded by such a play. If, however, the theater is larger, the first effect is that many people may lose the action as well as the words. The actor's naturalness does not console them, if what was lost was important for the play; and if it was not, it might better be omitted. Of course conformity to the good old rule, which can never go long out of fashion for serious drama before large audiences, requires especial skill. The actor must conceal his artifice, must so speak to the audience as to seem still to be addressing the other character in the play. The conditions of Attic tragedy must have required a close observance of this principle.

Unlike the novel, the surviving member of the epic family, drama has no other means of presentation; what the actors say or sing, their bodily forms, at rest or in expressive motion—these are the bulk of a play. Add to these the scenery, lighting, and stage properties, and any audible outside sounds, as thunder, bells, music, and you have the total material that the playwright can use. He cannot in his own person give explanations of this or that. What cannot be given directly by the actors or suggested by the setting cannot be given at all.

Out of this fact, so self-evident that one may wonder at so much emphasis upon it, arises a convention that is fundamental in the drama. However strange or absurd it may appear when looked at by itself, we accept it without hesitation, without any thought about it at all, because we could have no play—at least no tragedy or serious drama—without it. It is simply that, as Hamlet puts it, "The players cannot keep counsel; they'll tell all."

In other words, all that passes in the soul of the persons in the play is freely exposed to the public; there is no concealment of thought or emotion. It is tacitly assumed that everyone is in all circumstances not only ready but able to expose his inmost being completely—as completely, that is to say, as the playwright desires for the purposes of the play. On occasion he may judge that a character will express most—or most for the immediate purpose—by remaining speechless for a moment. Taciturnity and silence may be eloquent with dramatic expression. Not infrequently also an appeal to sight may be more to the purpose than words—a gesture, an attitude, withdrawal from the scene—an appeal, perhaps, of a sort that will not appear in a printed text. Such cases do not contradict the principle, but merely extend its application; every character has always at command all the resources for self-expression that his creator deems adapted to his ends, including verse and song and that perfect presence of mind which enables one to choose instantly the mode of utterance or the movement that will tell most. Caliban not only speaks the language of Shakspere, which he has learned marvelously well from Prospero, but he has the imagination and poetic faculty of Shakspere, which he displays precisely so far as Shakspere thought best. In Attic tragedy poetry is the common speech; the chorus and the leading personages can sing, and often do sing—whenever the poet so wills. In the world of Wagner everybody always sings, the chief characters pouring out their souls with the combined resources of Wagner and the greatest opera stars. How far removed this is from the reality of tongue-tied, stumbling humanity, the more civilized the more severely schooled in self-repression. Such humanity can have great drama only by accepting for the mimic world a very different humanity, freed from those other conventions of society that command rigorous emotional self-control, and endowed with the powers that none but a creative genius can have, and that even he cannot in his own life at all times and instantly command. Even his imaginary world of supermen he cannot extemporize, but must construct it slowly and with the effort of his happier hours. In moments of deep emotion, such as correspond to the crises of tragedy, silence or mere broken exclamation is apt to be the most natural outward manifestation. But this will not do for dramatic art. The fact that some people can sometimes utter intense emotion in eloquent word and speaking action is taken by the artist, enlarged, idealized, made universal.

Corollaries to this convention are the soliloquy, the aside, and the stage whisper.

In the soliloquy a person supposing himself alone thinks aloud. In real life we sometimes do this to a limited extent. An exclamation of impatience or surprise, a scrap of a fancied conversation, a sentence or two of deliberation—these are frequently spoken unconsciously aloud, or half aloud. This fact is taken as a basis and elaborated. A personage is made to go through, at length and in detail, in good resounding verse to reach the remotest seat, his most secret thought—say the train of emotions and of reasoning that carries him on to crime or to suicide. Shakspere, as we all remember, made large use of this; the French classic tragedians less, because they made so much of the confidant—the friend with whom a prominent character is always provided, and with whom everything of which the audience are to be informed can be talked over. The Greeks employed the soliloquy with much restraint. Unequivocal and famous cases in the extant tragedies are those of the watchman who opens the "Agamemnon" and of Aias in the Sophoklean play before his suicide. Just now dramatists writing in prose are excluding it almost entirely. It will never again, probably, be employed so freely as it was by Shakspere; but in moderation the device is perfectly legitimate, and will surely be readmitted if we ever again have great tragedies. It is perhaps more congruous with that degree of idealization which demands verse, but we shall presently notice an extended and striking case in prose.

The aside seems more suitable to comedy. It is quite natural in some circumstances, though hardly compatible with good manners, to release one's feelings in a side remark which the speaker whom you interrupt does not hear, absorbed as he is in his own affair. In lively French conversation this is more common than with us; national habits vary. In English and French comedy the practice has been carried to great excess and is now tabu. Aristophanes does not shrink from it; any absurdity is legitimate for him if it makes sport. In Greek tragedy the choral odes occasionally have a little of this character and Euripides has one clear case in dialogue. In "Hecuba" (737-751), when the queen is considering whether she shall entreat Agamemnon to assist her plan of vengeance, she turns her back upon him and deliberates aloud in four passages of two and three lines each; meanwhile the king, in three intervening couplets, wonders what is going on in her mind, not hearing what the audience hears.

The stage whisper is much like the aside. Something is whispered in the ear of one character, that another may not hear; meantime the whole audience, such is the actor's elocutionary art, hears every syllable. We find two unmistakable examples in Greek tragedy, one in Sophokles and one in Euripides. In "Philoktetes" (573-577) the pretended merchant begins to tell Neoptolemos how Odysseus and Diomed have set out to fetch Philoktetes, but breaks off and furtively asks who this third man is. Being told that it is Philoktetes, he begs Neoptolemos to question no farther but sail away at once. Whereupon Philoktetes inquires what the seafaring merchant has been saying "in darkness." It is hard to believe that a real whisper could be made audible to that great audience, but the convention is the same if the tone was merely lowered. In the other case Ion, in the play of that name, several years earlier in date, says to his mother (1520 f.), "The rest I wish to say to you alone. Come hither; I would speak in your ear and wrap the matter in darkness." He hesitates to admonish his mother openly, before the chorus, not to put off upon the god a fault that perhaps was her own. But the privacy

44

is only pretended; or rather, it is only conventional. Chorus and audience hear every word.

A play of David Belasco's had a successful run a few years ago by virtue, chiefly, of two bold conventions of the kind we have been considering. A certain Peter Grimm dies at the end of the first act, and then longs to "return" from the other world in order to undo a mistake of his that seriously affects people whom he loves. And this he does. When in the second act he reappears, unchanged, we know he must be what he claims to be, a departed spirit. He mingles with his friends and they remain unconscious of his presence, though to the audience he is as real and visible as anyone. And audible as well; for he tells all that is going on in his mind, his emotions at their situation and plans, his wishes for them. They speak of him as dead and gone, are unaware that he is among them, yet in some mysterious way his mind, as revealed to the audience by his words, moves them to see reasons for doing what he wishes them to do. Here is a very modern ghost, appearing and talking as in life, affecting action rather more than the ghostly king of Denmark; he soliloquizes at length and in prose, yet is quite unseen and unheard by everyone else in the play—except a dying boy. Even a present-day audience is quite ready to use its imagination, on fair reason being given, and enjoys taking an active part in a piece of childlike—that is, natural—make-believe.

II

One factor in the reshaping process, a formative principle of it, has already been taken for granted, but requires a further word. The familiar term idealize has been applied to the artist's procedure in re-presenting nature or reality in the material chosen. What do we mean by this? The term is much employed, as we are all aware, very loosely, with but hazy notions of its meaning. Can we attach to it a clearer and more definite significance? Just what do we mean by saying that a portrait is properly an idealized representation of a person, a play an idealized fragment or section of life—that any art which, like serious drama, re-presents life in beauty, idealizes life? In one sense, the primary one, which Freytag* emphasizes, to idealize is simply to reshape the subject, in the artist's handling, according to a single and unifying idea. This of course the artist does. But this definition does not, I think, quite cover what we include in the word. We want, if possible, a clearer conception of the nature, and perhaps of the source, of the idea by which, in conformity with which, the reshaping process is guided. We certainly ought not to mean that the artistic remodeling *mis*represents, or in any proper sense falsifies. In some modern plays written to support a thesis or a doctrine, the playwright does, reshaping facts according to an idea, to enforce his lesson, really misrepresent life. This criticism has been made of M. Eugène Brieux—that life does not in fact teach some particular lessons which he would enforce, that the dominance of his moral has distorted his picture. We should not call that idealizing, though it conforms to Freytag's definition.

To idealize is not, in a proper sense, to add an alien element, to remodel according to an idea imported from without; it is not even to add beauty to a dull or repellent

*"Technik des Dramas," p. 17: Einen Stoff nach einheitlicher Idee künstlerich umbilden.

46

reality. It does not mean placing a pretty screen before the ugly facts to hide them. That is not what Rembrandt or Whistler did in etching a landscape, a river scene, a view in Venice. Rather, the artist sees, and reveals to others by his representation, the beauty that is already there in the real scene in spite of, underneath, and vastly transcending in import, any trivial or repellent details that conceal it. To one lacking the artist's eye those trivial or repellent details are too prominent. They obscure the beauty, hide the true significance of the whole. It is to bring out that inner significance that the painter or the playwright omits, or at least puts into their true relations as regards beauty and real import, those discordant details. That is the proper function of the artist, in all arts that can be fairly called in any sense imitative—to see and reveal the inner truth, beauty, and significance of things. Just what he will see depends on his personality, which therefore his work will express. *His idea of the beauty and significance in the subject is what guides the process of remodeling.*

The poetic form of the entire Greek drama, as of the Elizabethan mostly and of classic French tragedy, is one element in the idealization. "The language of verse," says Freytag,* "lifts the characters to a higher plane. It keeps ever awake in the spectator the feeling that he is in the presence of art, that its influence is withdrawing him from reality into a different world, whose relations the human spirit has freely ordered." When Matthew Arnold called poetry the most perfect speech of man, he meant, among other things, that in verse the essence of life, the heart of it, its real relations with the universe, the truth of it underneath our imperfections and our petti-

*"Technik des Dramas," p. 279.

ness, can in poetry find better utterance than in any other style. The personages in serious drama, with the resources of the poet at their command, can express themselves—such selves as they must by hypothesis be—better in verse than in prose. The habitual assumption of the Greek, Elizabethan, or French public that a tragedy should be in verse, held the playwright to the constant necessity of a suitable degree of idealization, in the sense described—idealization of the whole drama, and not merely of the separate utterances of individual characters. The danger of occasional bombast, of a content below the level of the form, is outweighed by the steady lifting power of the form. If the drama ever rises again to the height of its great historic periods, the greatest playwrights will be poets.

Granted there is a wide gulf between the idealized utterance of the poetic drama and the speech of real life. Of course we do not and cannot speak in verse, much less in song, when we would in ordinary life utter even our best thought, our purest and finest feeling. But would it not be a good thing, if, in our best moments, our brief intervals when life is on the highest plane, we could do that? Would it not be well if our lives could move, for brief intervals at least, on the plane presented to us in the best plays of Sophokles and Shakspere? Such mimic re-presentation of life in beauty is an elevating influence by showing what life, the tragic suffering apart, might be; by showing how life might be broadened, deepened, ennobled. The tragic criminal, even, is not a vulgar, sordid criminal. A Lady Macbeth or a Klytaimestra is a great nature gone astray; but she is a part of life on a higher plane than is apparent in the life we see about us. The poet's picture of her is a truer picture of her real self; it enables us to see that, though a murderer, deserving her fate, she is also something else, a rich and complex personality, that still commands admiration and sympathy, while we condemn her. The poetic speech of that mimic life is not alien to us; it is true to our inmost nature; our lack of technical skill and our imperfections alone prevent our rising to that style.

When now to this idealization are added the conventions we have described, the total effect is to remove the drama very far from a transcript of real life, and to create a paradoxical world, that conveys inner truth by a combination of outward falsities—by exaggerations, distortions, pretenses. The reminiscences of actors are very instructive about this, and especially when they allow themselves to speak of the principles of their branch of theatrical art. The late Sir Henry Irving in his lectures on "The Drama," after speaking of dramatic elocution, adds:* "And I should tell you that this exaggeration applies to everything on the stage. To appear to be natural you must in reality be much broader than nature. To act on the stage as one would in a room would be ineffective and colorless." For the actor, like the painter, aims first of all to produce a natural *appearance;* he wishes to seem, not be, natural. Real cloth of gold on the stage is found to look less real than a cheap imitation, staring stage jewels more real than diamonds.†

What then did Shakspere mean when he made Hamlet say to the players, "Anything so overdone is from the purpose of playing, whose end, both at the first and now, was and is, to hold, as 'twere, the mirror up to nature; to show virtue her own feature, scorn her own image, and

*P. 74.
†Bram Stoker, "Personal Reminiscences of H. Irving," I, p. 115.

the very age and body of the time his form and pressure"? Of course Hamlet is warning the players against
overdoing; but none knew better than Shakspere that the
playwright and the actor are far enough from simply reflecting as in a mirror nature's external features. The
words are sometimes so applied as to make him ignorant
of that fact, so elementary in Shakspere's business. He
can only refer to the inner truth which the drama does
indeed reflect with peculiar vividness. The fact I am insisting on is indeed so elementary that Shakspere must
have felt it needless to explain it to his audience, habitu-
ated as they were to the drama. "It is by theatrical
means," as Ellen Terry puts it,* "not natural means,
paradoxical as it may sound, that a play is made to hold
a mirror up to nature."

Before turning now from general principles to their
exemplification in the drama of Athens a word of warning
is needed. We have ever to keep in mind that a printed
play is no more the play itself than the score of the composer is the symphony—no more than the architect's
plans are the cathedral. From the score a conductor and
his band of players can always create the symphony anew,
but the symphony is always the performance itself. The
intermediaries are always indispensable; the work of art
is the great structure of blended musical sounds, and it
dies as fast as it falls upon the ear. From the score only
the expert musician can more or less reproduce it in
imagination. The Greek plays that have survived in
manuscript, a handful out of many hundreds, are not
even the musician's score, for they contain only the
words; the music and the dance, integral parts of the
plays, have vanished without leaving a trace. The words

*McClure's Magazine, Jan., 1911, p. 291.

have been handed down through a series of historical accidents, the selections being made in part on considerations that had little to do with them as primarily plays. Literary, rather than dramatic merit, and adaptation to educational purposes in the centuries when Greek culture was dying, and when those who understood the immensity of the loss were struggling to preserve, through the schools, at least the ancient language and such of the literary monuments as were helpful to that end,—such appear to have been the primary selective influences, outside of pure chance. If now we are to gain any comprehension of these plays we must continually make vigorous use of imagination, supplementing the words by what knowledge we can glean of the manner of presenting them in the theater, and so doing what we can to read the words as a competent musician reads a score. I do not say that this is quite as difficult, or requires as much expert knowledge, as reading a score; but it does call for effort—effort to acquire the requisite knowledge of a bygone age and of a phase of life that, though our own is rooted in it, has become with time more subtly foreign to us in externals than any life in the Europe of today. And above all, it calls for effort to vivify this knowledge. In acquiring the language one slowly acquires a little of the Greek point of view. If one must rely on translations, a still more vigorous call must be made on imagination to make an alien mode of expression live. Lose no opportunity to witness a Greek play tolerably acted; continually, while reading, think of yourself as in the Athenian theater, and ask yourself, "What do I see?"

After this rather long preliminary we will take up the historical and social background out of which Greek drama grew.

III. THE ATHENIAN BACKGROUND

I

ARISTOTLE'S account of the rise of the drama is this.*

"It [tragedy] certainly began in improvisations—as did also comedy; the one originating with the authors of the dithyramb, the other with those of the phallic songs, which still survive as institutions in many of our cities. And its advance after that was little by little, through their improving on whatever they had before them at each stage. It was in fact only after a long series of changes that the movement of tragedy stopped on its attaining to its natural form. (1) The number of actors was first increased to two by Aeschylus, who curtailed the business of the chorus, and made the dialogue, or spoken portion, take the leading part in the play. (2) A third actor and scene-painting were due to Sophokles. (3) Tragedy acquired also its magnitude. Discarding short stories and a ludicrous diction, through its passing out of its satyric stage, it assumed, though only at a late period in its progress, a tone of dignity; and its meter changed then from trochaic to iambic. The reason for their original use of the trochaic tetrameter was that their poetry was satyric and more connected with dancing than it now is. As soon, however, as a spoken part came in, nature herself found the appropriate

*"Poetics," 1449 a. b., Bywater's version mostly.

meter. The iambic, we know, is the most speakable of meters, as is shown by the fact that we very often fall into it in conversation, whereas we rarely talk in hexameters, and only when we depart from the speaking tone of voice. (4) Another change was a plurality of episodes or acts. As for the remaining matters, the superadded embellishments and the account of their introduction, these must be taken as said, as it would probably be a long piece of work to go through the details.

"As for comedy, it is (as has been observed) an imitation of men worse than the average; worse, however, not as regards any and every sort of fault, but only as regards one particular kind, the ridiculous, which is a species of the ugly. The ridiculous may be defined as a mistake or deformity, not productive of pain or harm to others; the mask, for instance, that excites laughter, is something ugly and distorted without causing pain.

"Though the successive changes in tragedy and their authors are not unknown, we cannot say the same of comedy; its early stages passed unnoticed, because it was not as yet taken up in a serious way. It was only at a late point in its progress that a chorus of comedians was officially granted by the archon; they used to be mere volunteers. It had also already certain definite forms at the time when the record of those termed comic poets begins. Who it was who supplied it with masks, or prologues, or a plurality of actors, and the like, has remained unknown. The invented fable, or plot, however, originated in Sicily, with Epicharmos and Phormis; of Athenian poets Krates was the first to drop the comedy of invective and frame stories of a general and non-personal nature, in other words, fables or plots."

In this account by Aristotle we need to know the meaning of several unfamiliar terms—dithyramb, phallic songs, the satyr-play.

Dionysos was the god who gave the fertility that ripens in the moist fruits of earth, especially the grape, as Demeter the fertility manifested in grain and the dry fruits. To the early Greeks, as in Palestine, and to the mass of the inhabitants of Greece today, bread and wine were really the double staff of life, constituting the bulk of their food. Our use of the two elements in the Mass and the Lord's Supper, in all branches of the Church, is a survival in ritual, a direct inheritance, of what was in antiquity a central fact of daily life. And as is still the case in Syria and among other people of simple habits, the humble sense of direct dependence on divine bounty for these blessings was ever present and active. Hunger was never far away; accumulation of wealth and multiplication of its forms had not yet diversified food and by augmenting human resources dimmed men's consciousness of the divine. Demeter and Dionysos were associated gods to be propitiated and acknowledged with gratitude, especially in spring and after the harvest.

The dithyramb in the early seventh century before Christ was a choral hymn, or ballad dance, performed by the peasants as part of the spring festival of Dionysos, when the previous autumn's wine, made and preserved by primitive methods, was ready for drinking. This ballad dance, partly traditional, partly extemporaneous, was a lyric narrative of the birth or one of the numerous adventures of the god, sung and danced by the band of worshipers, to the accompaniment of the clarinet.* The

*The Greek αὐλός, Lat. *tibia*, is traditionally rendered flute, but this is quite misleading. It was a reed instrument, rather shrill and exciting, not soft and soothing like our flute.

dance was no less mimetic than the words and the music, an integral part of the hymn, the three together forming a natural unit. Though our more complex civilization has pretty nearly lost this triune art, we know that it was, in the simpler stages of culture, nearly universal, in work, play, and religion—which were never far separated.* The songs (chanteys) by which our sailors regulate and coordinate their movements in performing a common task, and some childish games, are perhaps the analogues nearest to us in two of the three spheres of activity, which are now wholly divorced from that of religion and reduced to a simple type.

The phallos was a figure of the human male member, which in many nature-religions has been a symbol of fertility, widely displayed and familiar to everyone from childhood in this religious significance; in Greece it was a common symbol of Dionysos. At the winter festival in his honor a big phallos was carried in procession, while the band of revelers, known as *kōmos*, in the so-called phallic songs made coarse jests and scurrilous but good-natured attacks on whomsoever they pleased. Perhaps the English-speaking peoples of the present day are less able than any other race at any other period to connect with such usages any vestige of religious sentiment. But it is the Greek background that we are seeking. In a nature-religion, which makes little of the line between secular and religious, of which we commonly make too much, a religion in which gods and worshipers are on very easy terms, the fertility of the earth, of animals, and of the human race is recognized as at bottom one; and in such religions all doings of nature have their due place. Fertility is one of God's greatest gifts, and wine that

*See Karl Bücher, "Rhythmus und Arbeit," 3d ed. Leipzig, 1902.

maketh glad the heart of man is to be accepted and used with joy and thanksgiving. What Aristotle tells us, then, is that the kōmos-song (κωμῳδία) was developed from these extemporaneous phallic songs, though the intervening steps were forgotten, and tragedy was developed from the dithyramb. Both continued to be associated chiefly with the same Dionysiac festivals of winter and spring respectively. Comedy we now leave for the present, noting, however, that the last sentence quoted from Aristotle refers to the transition from the Old Comedy, of Aristophanes and his rivals, to New Comedy, which in Aristotle's time was alone living, and which is best represented to us by Menander and his Roman imitators, Plautus and Terence.

The first steps in the development of tragedy we learn from other writers, partly later, but no doubt drawing their information from earlier sources. We are told that Arīon, of Lesbian birth but domiciled in Corinth, first gave a more regular and more literary character to the dithyramb. The chorus, disguised as satyrs (attendants of Dionysos, personifying the animal tendencies that wine favors), was fixed in number at fifty, singing and dancing in a circular *orchēstra* (ὀρχήστρα) or dancing-place. Song and mimetic dance were made to correspond in strophe and antistrophe, the latter repeating the rhythm of the former; and some suggestion of dialogue was introduced, the leader sometimes separating himself from the rest of the band for question or response. In this form the dithyramb was called also *tragoedia* (τραγῳδία) or goat-song, probably because *tragos*, goat, was a common term for satyr. This type of satyr-song was taken up in Attica, a slight Doric tinge in its language displaying perhaps a trace of its Doric origin. In the country

56

district of Ikaria, still known as Diónyso, among the northern foothills of Pentelikon, Thespis made the next advance. To the chorus of satyrs with its leader he added one who was not costumed as a satyr, called the ὑποκριτής (*hypokritēs*), which Bywater on plausible grounds would render interpreter or speaker, rather than answerer. His office was to appear as Dionysos himself or some character in the story, and in that guise to carry on (speaking in trochaic verse, according to Aristotle) conversation with the chorus or the leader. Here is the beginning of real drama—personification, and the acting of a story, instead of narrating it, which is epic, or reflecting upon it, which falls under lyric. *Hypokritēs* remained the regular word for actor. That he might more readily change his disguise, part of which was a mask, we are told that Thespis, who himself played these parts, one after another in the same story, had a temporary booth set up, for which the common word was σκηνή (*skēnē*), beside the dancing-place. The goat-songs of this new type were popular, attracted visitors, called out rival poets, were exhibited in other places. Thespis is said to have exhibited in Athens before 560 B. C., on which occasion the aged Solon expressed hearty disapproval of the deception, much in the spirit of Plato some five generations later.

In 535 B. C. Peisistratos, now firmly seated in Athens as benevolent tyrant, either established or enlarged and made more magnificent the greater Dionysia, which for centuries continued to be the most important spring festival of Dionysos at Athens. Contests in tragedy were made a chief attraction in this festival, and Thespis contended, though he must have been very old. Of his immediate rivals no name has been handed down; from the period just after his death we hear of Choirilos, Pratinas, and Phrynichos, all of whom lived to be defeated by Aeschylus, who was born in 525. Of Pratinas we shall speak presently; the lyrics of Phrynichos, now lost, were long highly praised, and Aeschylus took from him the subject of one play, the "Persians," which we have. It was Aeschylus, Aristotle tells us, who by adding a second actor created at last full-fledged drama. Two actors, with a company of minor participants, even though the latter sing as one, can enact a great variety of stories.

Meantime the range of stories had been widened, being now no longer confined to the Dionysiac cycle. With this went another advance, in that the more serious kind of story received the preference, the tale that included suffering. The chorus were no longer always satyrs, nor always represented males; in the earliest Aeschylean play we have, they are the fifty daughters of Danaos, who have fled to Argos to escape the hated marriage with their cousins, the fifty sons of Aegyptus. No woman ever took part; as in Shakspere's time, female parts were filled by boys or men. This play, the "Suppliants," is still prevailingly lyric; and though it requires two actors, all but a small part could be played by one actor with the chorus. The goat-song had before the death of Thespis completely emerged from the satyric stage.

But by becoming what we also can call tragedy, sloughing off the satyric element, it had sacrificed precisely that which was more peculiar to Dionysos. Religious conservatism was offended. Alongside of the new tragedy, therefore, Pratinas, who came to Athens from a region where the old dithyramb was still popular, developed this along another line in the satyr-play, which retained the satyr chorus, but added the actors of tragedy. For this combination only lighter stories were suitable. In effect a bifurcation, a natural biological division, had taken place. Thus from the seventh century goat-song arose both Aeschylean tragedy and the satyr-play as we know it. To the latter there is no modern parallel. Of the hundreds composed, only one, the "Cyclops" of Euripides,* has come down to us entire; a third or more of another has been lately recovered, the "Trackers" of Sophokles. The satyr-play was evidently light and romantic in tone. Only those myths with which a band of satyrs could somehow be connected could be put into this form; but a good deal of freedom was allowed in making the connection. This was part of the romantic tone. The choral parts of course were suited to the characteristics of satyrs—who were sensual, cowardly, but not wholly unattractive children of nature; the dialogue was sober, if light, the metrical coloring of it essentially like that of tragic dialogue, not admitting the licenses of comedy. The humor lay partly in the contrast of serious form with light content as well as with the coarse humor of the satyrs; there was none of the personal attack which came to Aristophanic comedy from the phallic songs.

Not only did these two dramatic types develop from the old dithyramb, but the original choral type of dithyramb continued to live, retaining for a time something like the form which Arion gave it; Pindar and Simonides in the early half of the fifth century handled it with distinction. But it, too, lost connection with Dionysos and his satyrs, ceased to be choral and became a solo

*Translated by Shelley, with softening or omission of the coarser jests.

performance, and finally became a synonym for high-flown nonsense, for virtuosity in language and in music with emptiness of content.

We must not ignore the fact that this traditional account of the origin of tragedy, as here repeated, has been vigorously attacked by a school of English Hellenists, who make out a different pedigree. But it seems highly improbable that Aristotle in the fourth century B. C. should have been quite ignorant of the evidence for matters which he puts down as undisputed, in the same passage where he confesses ignorance on other points and speaks of opposing claims on yet others. For our purpose, the understanding of Greek drama as we have it, the Aristotelian account not only appears more probable than the inferences of the recent school, but it is satisfactory as offering a reasonable explanation of those peculiarities that from our point of view need explaining.

II

We have seen that contests of tragedies were introduced by Peisistratos in 535 B. C. as part of the greater Dionysia, the spring festival of Dionysos in the city of Athens. That implies—what we know was the case throughout the following century—a preliminary selection of the contestants by some state authority as well as some way of deciding on the victor among them; details of the sixth century are all unknown. But the custom of arranging all such exhibitions in a contest, with prizes for the victors, at a festival in honor of a god, and under state supervision, is distinctive and significant. These are outstanding features of theatrical production in Athens: first, the religious atmosphere—that of a polytheistic nature-religion, it is true, not of Semitic mono-theism, but none the less a sincere recognition of dependence on divine power, a feeling shared by a whole people, so that its manifestation is part of the state worship; second, in close connection with this worship, shared by the whole community, the best literary talent stimulated to offer each year its best products for popular approval; third, a goodly number from the community giving their time and effort and submitting to a lengthy training, or else paying the expenses, as befitting a citizen's duty to the god and to his fellows, that new works of art might be brought out in a manner worthy of the god and of the state. This combination grew quite naturally out of the community life; it was highly favorable for the growth of a great art, and it has never recurred elsewhere. The conditions in which the medieval miracle and mystery plays arose were indeed similar in many ways, only there was no succession of great dramatic poets—a fatal difference. When the Elizabethan playwrights were developing great drama from those medieval antecedents, the connection both with the state and with religion was cut; dramatic performances were merely a private business, purveying public amusement for pay, as at present in England and America. The court of Louis XIV again offered quite other conditions, another background. In combination the Athenian conditions have never recurred.

And of course these conditions and the antecedents out of which they grew were determining influences, laying down the main lines of Athenian drama, of whose three branches tragedy was the most important in its own time, as it has been since Greek letters were rediscovered. The poet's individual genius might discern within these lines this or that opportunity hitherto unexploited, and so might create new varieties under the inclusive type, but it could not remake the type. The three great tragedians illustrate both propositions—that the type continues to be essentially one, while they created distinct varieties within its limits. So in the great age of Italian painting, for example—without at all pressing the comparison in detail—Michael Angelo, Raphael, and Titian. As these painters—we leave out of view for the moment other sides of their activity—took their subjects from the Bible stories and glorified with their art the walls and ceilings of churches, working really for religion and for the whole public, whoever was their immediate patron, so the Athenian tragic poet drew from the old mythology the stories which he presented at a popular religious festival, in the dramatic form consecrated by his predecessors. The type was susceptible of enormous variety, yet the careless reader sees only the main lines and may fancy it very simple.

We have seen that the tales to be dramatized began early to be drawn from quite outside of the Dionysiac cycle, rich as that was. Phrynichos attempted even to use recent history in the same way. The Ionian cities of Asia Minor, revolting from the rule of Persia, were again reduced to subjection. The Athenians had assisted their Ionian kinsmen. The recapture of Miletus by the Persians in 494 B. C. was so tragic that Phrynichos dramatized it. The result illustrated a dramatic law that he had not learned; the Athenians fined him for reminding them of their sorrows.

The law against which he offended may be put in several ways. The aim of every art is to give a complex kind of elevated and ennobling pleasure. This does not exclude a modicum of instruction, if duly subordinated, and sympathy with ideal suffering is of the essence of our pleasure in tragedy; our sympathy may even be the keener from some remembered suffering of our own. But our personal suffering, while it may be idealized into a work of art that will give the right pleasure to others, cannot be so re-presented to us. Our pain will be so keen as to overpower the pleasure. In more general terms: If a story when dramatized will cause pain of a kind and degree that will banish the artistic pleasure, the play is sure to fail. On the other hand, when Phrynichos drama-tized in a second attempt the defeat of the Persians at Salamis, in a tragedy entitled "Phoenician Women," it was successful enough to lead Aeschylus shortly afterward to take the same theme, in the "Persians," which is ex-tant. This will engage our study later. We hear of but one other exception to the rule that the plots of tragedies were drawn from the great store of old myths; Agathon's "Antheus," for which he devised the entire plot, quite in modern fashion, has left no trace in dramatic history.

As these myths were known to everyone, simple curi-osity about the outcome of the story could have no place in the dramatic interest; at the most a spectator at the first performance might wonder how the playwright would manage details, which everyone who retold the story might vary. Occasionally a play, like "Oedipus at Kolonos," might be based on such local or non-Attic legends that some would be unacquainted with them; yet in general the Athenian before a new play would be more nearly in the mental attitude which we take when a new actor plays Hamlet.

This raises the question of curiosity and interest—

how far, that is, curiosity about what is to follow is an element in dramatic interest on the part of the audience.* Not far, I think. The young child likes to hear the same story told over and over; when it is known by heart the repetition still delights, and any variation is resented. Mr. Archer compares the case of a great piece of music, of which our enjoyment grows with repetition, after every vestige of curiosity is gone. One might maintain, perhaps, that in the arts of time some faint ghost of curiosity survives after many hearings, enough to perform the function of the original curiosity at the first hearing. But we find the situation the same in the plastic and graphic arts, where every inch as well as the whole may be enjoyed as long as one will, and so be imprinted on the memory. One still returns to it with the same delight, if the work be great enough. Mr. Archer also points out that nothing palls more quickly than the appeal to mere curiosity; though it may secure a first success, no play can hold very long that makes much of this. In short, we want good construction, natural articulation; the Greek playwright could secure this in dramatizing old tales that everyone knew. If that be present, and the play is good enough otherwise, dramatic interest will be as keen at the tenth hearing as at the first, though the whole audience from the first knows just how it is all coming out. There is indeed a dramatic value in the spectator's foreknowledge, as Mr. Archer says, far superior to the dramatic value of the ignorance on which curiosity depends. It puts us in the position of higher intelligences, who know what the persons in the play cannot know. This enables us to follow with still deeper interest the inner experience, at each turn, of the charac-

*See William Archer, "Playmaking," Chap. IX.

ters whose fortunes we are following, whose hearts we are by the dramatist's art permitted to read.

Another slight advantage the old tales had for the dramatist. The initial step in the reshaping has been taken for him, in that the fictive beginning and ending are already made by previous tellers of the story. He may see reasons for changing these in some way; but in most cases by the very fact of their being old, often re-told, an effective version has long since been found, which in that one particular, at least, he does well to adopt.

III

Aristotle's brief sketch of the origin of tragedy makes clear why the chorus, which we at first view take as an excrescence, was by every Greek felt to be the very center of the play. Not only was it the root out of which the whole grew; we have to remember that the taste for choral dancing was highly developed among the Greeks. It requires effort for us to realize their superiority to us on this point. Most of us grew up with associations that connect dancing primarily with social amusements; and by social amusements we mean mostly forms of play between the two sexes. No such associations existed in Greece. To the present day among the country people there, as in antiquity, women dance by themselves; at the most one man may lead a dance of women, holding the hand of the woman next to him. A man and woman tip-toeing about in a mutual embrace would have seemed to them utterly scandalous. The Greek separation of the sexes in social life had indeed melancholy results, which were far worse than our promiscuous dancing. We are not now concerned, however, with these. But the entire absence from the dance of all thought of sex, together with the high development of mimetic dancing, made their enjoyment of choral dancing a purely esthetic pleasure of a peculiarly refined sort. Of course we must not think of the modern ballet, in any of its varieties, as a parallel. Acrobatic agility, the development of special muscles by years of professional training, was no less alien than every sort of sex-appeal. The tragic chorus was always of men, even if representing women. The spectator's pleasure had in it no element less appropriate to a religious festival than is our organ music.

Plays were often named from the chorus—as the "Suppliants," "Libation-pourers," "Eumenides," "Women of Trachis," "Bacchants," "Trojan Women." The archon "granted a chorus" to the contesting poets. That is, from the body of wealthier citizens, on whom fell by turns in accordance with a regular system this direct taxation, he assigned one as *chorēgos* (χορηγός) who was to pay the expense of selecting, costuming, and training a chorus. The members of this were always amateurs, citizens younger or older, with good voices and sufficient musical and orchestic gifts, who underwent the requisite course of training. To them and the actors the poet—to use the technical term—"taught" the play. About the movements of the chorus we know little enough in detail, different as they must have been for every play; but there seems to have been a combination of regularity with a great variety of graceful steps and postures, which would require much instruction and long practice.

The number of the chorus, which was at first fifty, was reduced, early in the career of Aeschylus, to twelve, which Sophokles raised to fifteen. The reduction to twelve has been plausibly, but purely on conjecture, connected with the rule requiring each contestant to present four plays. Twelve bands of fifty each might make too heavy a demand on the community; to require all fifty to learn four plays, relieving that difficulty, would lay too heavy a burden on each member; forty-eight distributed over four plays would be manageable. What esthetic or other considerations had weight we can only guess, just as we have no hint as to why the comic chorus was fixed at a different number, twenty-four. The increase from twelve to fifteen by Sophokles no doubt was connected with some improvement in choral evolutions. But the Greek dance is wholly lost; the scanty hints gathered from vase-paintings and sculpture can be but hints, because it is forever beyond the capacity of the arts of rest to express incessant motion. Our mechanisms for making light impress on the film and reproducing ten thousand successive momentary positions, thus simulating motions, of course no one had dreamed of.

To each contestant with his four plays a whole day was at first given. The fourth play in each set was commonly—not by absolute requirement—a satyr-play, apparently a little shorter than a tragedy. Aeschylus repeatedly, not always, connected the three tragedies in a trilogy, treating in each a single stage of a longer myth. For example, in the one extant trilogy the "Agamemnon" portrays the king's murder by Klytaimestra, the "Liba-tion-pourers" the vengeance of Orestes on the murderer and her paramour, the "Eumenides" the pursuit of Orestes by the Furies for killing his mother, with his final acquittal by the Athenian court. Such an arrange-ment was like three long acts of one great tragedy; in this and in some other trilogies the third brings the tragic story to a close in peace and reconciliation. But Sophokles and Euripides, so far as we know, did not so connect their tragedies; it cannot have been required. In harmony with this practice of the younger tragedians, of making the single play and not a trilogy their unit, the distribution of the plays over three days was changed. To assign to each contestant a whole day was thought to carry an unfair advantage to that poet to whom fell the last day. Accordingly one tragedy of each contestant was put on for each day. This would of course discourage the composition of trilogies, and incline the dramatist to make each play stand firmly on its own feet. Whether the result was a gain or loss to dramatic art we have too little material to enable us to decide. Certainly the one trilogy we have is a masterpiece. The satyr-play at the close of each day might or might not deal in a lighter way with some bit of the same story as the trilogy, or as some single play of the author's three tragedies.

If this appears like a strenuous day for spectators, we may recall the Passion Play at Oberammergau, which is in several ways an instructive parallel. This, too, is a religious festival, preceded, for the performers and for such of the audience as will participate, by a religious service in the church; thousands gathered from all over the world sit with absorbed attention through an eight-hour performance, broken by one intermission. Most of them, whether they fully share the faith of the performers or not, easily take an attitude of sympathetic acceptance for the occasion. And interpretative singing by a chorus, enhanced by the harmonies of carefully studied costumes, though lacking the animation of motion, fills long intervals in the dramatic action. Finally, though the spectators are sheltered by a roof, the stage is open to the sky, and all is performed by daylight. The most significant features were all paralleled in the Dionysiac theater at Athens.

Thespis, as we have seen, was his own actor (or *hypokritēs*) and Aeschylus took a rôle in his own plays; but as the art developed and much higher demands were made, the actors became professionals—in the latter part of the fifth century paid by the state. In the earlier half, for a time, they seem to have been selected by the poet and paid by his *chorēgos.*

In the costuming there was no thought of realism, still less of historical precision in representing, for example, Homeric personages. The aim was first to remove the figures from everyday life, suggesting the heroic and the antique, and secondly to meet the conditions of the theater. The latter motive is the same which leads our actors to assume a make-up, as it is called, that under such conditions of distance, lighting, relative positions, will produce an appearance, not the reality, of naturalness, and will be effective toward the end in view. This make-up has been not a little changed by the substitution of full electric lighting for the old footlights, first candles, and later gas. The Greek theater was open to a southern sun in a nearly cloudless sky; the audience appears to have numbered from fifteen to twenty thousand. This would call for a make-up quite unlike ours. Aeschylus gave great attention to the subject; and we may be sure that the taste of the most artistic of races was not content with crudeness or absurdities. Paintings or statuettes of any theatrical make-up, seen close at hand, are totally misleading; all was planned with a view to distance and sunshine. The Greek actor was increased in size by thick-soled shoes, padding, and by an upward extension of the mask, which covered not only the face but the whole head. The mask could be changed, if there was occasion, at every appearance of a character; but no change or play of feature was possible during a scene. Change of expression would in any case be invisible to half or more of such an audience. The actor must have relied for expression on attitude, gesture, and modulation of the voice. That the voice might not be impeded, the mouth of the mask had to be always wide open. This minor convention, I venture to say, any audience today would in like conditions quickly accept and think no more about, if the play were well done. When the students of a men's college present a play, how long does it take us to accept the convention that for the time being all the women will speak with men's voices? We are always quite willing to forget nature for the nonce, if the art is good. This last convention, too, the Greek audience were accustomed to, since all actors were men. Brilliant colors in the ample garments were softened and blended by a sunshine like that of southern California, precisely as were the gilding and the brilliant blue and red masses on the marble temples. To convince one of this blending and softening effect of light, a look at fresh modern buildings in Athens, of marble painted in imitation of the ancient temples, will suffice; the effectiveness of the mosaics on the façade of St. Mark's in Venice may suggest it.

IV

The theater itself as a structure offers problems about which archeologists are still disputing, and which we cannot wholly ignore. The word ($\theta\acute{\epsilon}\alpha\tau\rho o\nu$, *theātron*) meant primarily the place of viewing, and was applied to what we call the auditorium, or place of hearing, that is, the seats of the spectators. But the main thing was really what they looked at, the circular dancing-place, the *orchēstra* of the chorus. The existing Athenian theater of current photographs must all be thought away, if we would arrive at the structure of the fifth century, of which traces of the orchestra have been uncovered beneath the larger but later remains.

In the precinct of Dionysos Eleuthereus, just below the Acropolis, where the southern slope approaches the more nearly level ground, stood the temple, a building of very modest size. In front of this, but a little to the north and higher up, was the orchestra, not quite seventy feet in diameter, pretty certainly unpaved, merely smooth-trodden ground, probably inclosed by a low curb. Around and above this the people sat on the hillside, occupying all the space of the precinct above the orchestra, and wholly unsheltered from the sun, which in March may be very hot. As a practical people the Athenians utilized all the available space, though it was irregular. When some of the wooden substructure of the seats broke down in 499 they resolved to build new seats of stone. What they apparently did was to fill in with stone and earth the space where a substructure was needed, but they continued to use wooden seats till the great productive age was over. This constituted nearly the whole theater as Aeschylus, Sophokles, and Euripides knew it. The really troublesome problems concern the *skēnē*, which was originally the temporary booth of Thespis. Where did the actors stand? What was the *skēnē* in the fifth century?

Reading with open mind the extant plays of that period one finds many indications of free intermingling of actors

and chorus, if not on the same level, at least not divided
by any barrier of height or otherwise that was not easily
crossed. Also, there are no architectural traces of any
raised stage of that period. This lack of evidence can
have no weight, as all remains are so scant; but the other
evidence, that in the text of the plays, is positive and in
my judgment conclusive. And yet von Wilamowitz-
Moellendorff, for example, in his recent edition of Aeschylus postulates, from the text alone, a high stage in
the "Suppliants," "Prometheus," and "Seven against
Thebes." I cannot find in the text what he does; his
interpretation seems to me impossible. The assump-
tions, rather than arguments, of Eugen Petersen* in a
like direction are to me no more convincing. On the
other hand, there is convincing architectural as well as
literary evidence for a high and rather narrow stage in
the Hellenistic period and for a somewhat lower and
wider stage in the Roman period, after the chorus has
ceased to have any vital meaning or any part in the
action. Such changes are not easy to account for, but
they are not incredible. We are so wonted to a stage in
the modern theater that scholars have found it hard to
drop the Hellenistic and Roman tradition and read Greek
tragedy with a fresh view, keeping in mind the other conditions that we know existed, and which modern pageants and stadiums and "Greek theaters" and the Yale
"Bowl" are again enabling us to realize. None of these
modern developments, I believe, have had any place in
Germany. If the lowest row of spectators, around say
two thirds of the dancing-place, sit with their heads
near the level of the shoulders of the chorus, and all
other spectators sit still higher, everybody back of the

*"Die Attische Tragoedie als Bild. u. Bühnenkunst"; Bonn, 1915.

first three rows looking down on the heads of everybody in the orchestra, surely fifteen to twenty people in a circle over sixty-five feet in diameter need not get in one another's way for even the lowest row. Moreover the action often gave occasion for a speaker to stand on the steps of the temple or palace before which the incident is placed, or on the steps of an altar, or on a rock, part of the setting. In short, in none of the tragedies we possess is clarity gained by supposing an elevated stage, other than such steps or natural objects.

The *skēnē* was necessarily temporary, set up to suit the need of each play, or at least of each festival, because otherwise it would have blocked the entrance to the temple, which was built before theatrical exhibitions demanded the space. Later, when permanent "stage-buildings" were thought necessary, a new temple was built lower down, to obviate that difficulty. Until after 400, then, the *skēnē* was a temporary structure representing the background which the play required—the king's dwelling, a sacred grove, a rocky shore, the mountain-side against which Prometheus is bound, the front of a temple. Its use as a dressing-room was incidental; it was primarily a piece of the "property" of the play.

IV. CONVENTIONS OF ATTIC TRAGEDY

I

BEFORE examining the special conventions of the Athenian type of tragedy we must consider for a moment how the Athenian conception of tragedy differed from ours—what sort of stories they accepted as suitable, intrinsically, to be cast in tragic form. Our Elizabethan ancestors took over the Greek word tragedy, but not the thing. Out of their own life and history grew a drama no less rich, briefer in its period of bloom, in no one of its named varieties quite the same in character as its closest Greek parallel. The French a little later in like manner developed a tragedy and comedy, on the whole of not unequal worth, but again unlike, so far unlike that English-speaking people do not easily become at home in them. Particularly the merits of classical French tragedy are seldom fully appreciated by those who have been brought up on Shakspere, unless fortune has brought them into familiarity with it in early life.* The transformation of the Greek word τραγῳδία in English and in French mouths matches the difference in the thing signified.

A tragedy of Elizabethan type presents† "a story of exceptional calamity leading to the death of a man in

---

*Emile Faguet, "Drame Ancien, Drame Moderne," is an interesting study of the three types from the French point of view.
†A. G. Bradley, "Shakespearean Tragedy," p. 16.

high estate." A peaceful ending, a cessation of suffering on the part of the hero or heroine otherwise than by death, would have seemed to Shakspere's audience to remove the play from the tragic category. On the other hand a Greek tragedy, while it presents, in Aristotle's phrase, an action that is serious and complete in itself, having a certain magnitude, does not of necessity lead to the death of hero or heroine. That is the first striking difference. Elektra and Orestes succeed in their enterprise; only their enemies are slain. Not only that; in the "Eumenides" Orestes is acquitted and the Furies are appeased, the woes of the family are brought to an end; Iphigeneia escapes from the Taurians with her brother, the Taurian king is reconciled, no one is slain. Yet the plays are great tragedies. By "magnitude" no doubt Aristotle in his definition meant primarily length; the story dramatized must not be long enough for an epic, but must exhibit enough of life and include enough change of fortune to render the action serious and important. In a later and explanatory passage the specific word length is used. But magnitude, not length, is the word used in the definition, in close connection with the word serious; in the passage quoted above (p. 52), where magnitude is first mentioned, the remark soon follows that tragedy was late in assuming a tone of dignity. Elsewhere, too, Aristotle couples magnitude with dignity. I agree with Bywater that this is "at any rate by implication the sense in the present passage." In the Greek conception a tragic story must exhibit suffering, of immortals or of mortals in high estate, which may, however, end without a catastrophe. Yet it must not lose the tone of seriousness and dignity. We shall see later that Euripides, enlarging the range of tragedy on that side, strained the type and violated the Greek sense of fitness.

In choice of stories Elizabethan tragedy was broader as well as narrower. Narrower, by the limitation mentioned; the tale must be one of calamity ending in death. But broader, because it might be taken from any source— history, myth, existing narrative fiction in prose or verse, or the dramatist's own invention. Often one simply took an older play and made it over, retaining or changing freely what he would. The religious associations of the mysteries and moralities were dropped; there was no thought of church patronage or of state patronage, and hence no limitation by authority on the range of stories from which the desired sort of public amusement might be drawn. In contrast with this freedom Greek tragedies were made, as a rule, on tales from the old myths, tales of gods and heroes, in which existing poetry and local legend were so rich.

Yet in spite of significant differences, the likeness goes deeper and justifies the common term. In all periods and among all nations that kind of play which we should now call tragedy presents, through people personating the characters, a serious story of action and of suffering connected therewith, of which we can predicate dignity and completeness.

II

This brings us to those pure conventions in which the types disagree, in part very widely. First, as we have before noted, Attic tragedy was always in verse, of varied rhythms in the several parts. And the verse was sung and accompanied by mimetic dancing where melody and dance were thought appropriate as expressing enhanced emotion. Although Shakspere's characters mostly speak in language idealized by poetic diction and rhythm, they descend to prose freely when thought is on the lower level; and song, like dance, is never more than an occasional ornament, an interlude in the action rather than an integral part of it. A tragedy wholly in prose, which we today take as normal for a new tragedy, was to the Greeks unthinkable. For all their tragic characters the ordinary speech is poetry, in the rhythms demanded by the sentiment or the action; all sing to express heightened emotion, for a large group of them mimetic dance is no less natural. In fact, the form of Attic drama in its three divisions was established before any kind of prose literature, of prose that could seem in any way an art, was thought of as possible. Solon put even his political pamphlets into verse; philosophy, if it was to have wide circulation, had to assume a poetic garb.

And a Greek tragedy could not exist without a chorus, the historic beginning and ever the heart of drama to the Greeks. A unified group of participants in the action—fifty, twelve, finally fifteen—had to be provided, whether the story naturally called for them or not. The first business of the playwright was to shape the story so that it would call for them. In a way they may be compared to the minor characters in Shakspere—lords and ladies named or unnamed, the Roman populace in "Julius Caesar," and the like. But with the subtle difference, to our fancy quite artificial, that the group commonly sings as one, occasionally dividing into halves or smaller sections, or recites in unison, when it enters, the anapestic systems that were the regular march measure; it speaks as one, when it does speak, through the leader alone. Hence the group refers to itself now in the plural, now in the singular, indifferently, passing freely from one to the other on no apparent ground but metrical convenience.

A few myths provide suitable groups of major participants of whom to make a chorus. The fifty daughters of Danaos in the "Suppliants" of Aeschylus are the multiple heroine; the Furies in the "Eumenides" are no less important than Orestes; they are the attacking party and represent the ancient law. But more often the chorus are minor participants in the action, though in another aspect central in the drama as an art-form. The council of elders gathers for consultation with the king or regent— Atossa, Klytaimestra, Oedipus; the Salaminian soldier-sailors of Aias come to his tent to learn the truth about the dreadful rumor they have heard about their leader, and remain to sympathize and to defend him and his from the hostile chiefs; soldiers of Neoptolemos go with him and Odysseus to fetch Philoktetes to Troy; the men of Kolonos hasten to defend the sanctity of their sacred grove, are struck with the dignity of the stranger, old and blind, but speaking with more than mortal authority, and accept him as an honored guest; the suppliant women of Argos come to entreat Theseus to obtain from Thebes the bodies of their sons for the burial which Thebes had forbidden; the temple-attendants of Iphigeneia are her natural assistants; the handmaids of Creüsa—who must be just fifteen in number—accompany their mistress to Delphi; the Theban women, terror-stricken at the approaching battle, flee to the acropolis and beseech the gods and King Eteokles for protection; the female slaves of the royal household are sent with Elektra to pour libations at the grave of Agamemnon, and they help her and Orestes at a critical point; Trojan women, fellow-captives with their queen, pour out their sympathy and help her

78

inflict vengeance on the treacherous Thracian who had murdered her son; bacchants were no less traditional attendants and celebrants of Dionysos than were satyrs; the friends of Hippolytos were naturally hunters, and might have been made a chorus, but for the purpose of making Phaidra prominent the women of Trozen were more suitable. When other motives for producing a chorus were lacking, there was always that of sympathy or of curiosity. Women cross the narrow strait from Chalkis to the camp at Aulis to see the Greek army, though blushing at their own temerity; the ocean nymphs hasten to offer sympathy to Prometheus; neighbors come to condole with Deianeira, with Elektra, with Medea. Here is a wide variety, but a thousand plays might exhaust the possibilities. Perhaps this was a factor in the decay of the type. Yet Sophokles and Euripides could still find new variations for the "Oedipus at Kolonos" and the "Bacchants," their latest tragedies, each a masterpiece.

With this conventional requirement of a chorus goes a convention that embodies one of the sharp contrasts between the ancient type of tragedy and the modern. In our theater the scene of the action may be placed anywhere. If a closed room is chosen, an impossibility is tacitly assumed to be an everyday occurrence; the whole auditorium is supposed to be a part of that room. The wall that would in reality hide from the spectators what goes on inside is removed and we all imagine ourselves inside, each quite undisturbed by the bodily presence of hundreds of others, whose imaginations have wrought the same miracle and placed them in the same little room. No one is crowded; it's all make-believe. The Greeks never took this bold step. The nearest approach to it that we can trace in the tragedies themselves, disregarding later commentaries, is this: the wide double doors of a royal dwelling or a temple are opened and part of the interior is disclosed. Aristophanes ridicules Euripides for using a machine called the *ekkyklēma*, by which the interior was somehow "rolled out" through the open door; and the commentators of later centuries invoke the contrivance rather often. I can only say that in the extant plays I find no occasion for it, and cannot imagine it in operation. In any case it is not like our convention. It is rather turning a room inside out than putting the audience into the room. If, however, when one is asked to open the doors, a farther step is taken and the front wall of the structure is drawn back a few feet, as would seem natural at some points, this would be a momentary approach to our usage.

But such moments are comparatively brief. In Greek tragedy the scene is always out of doors, in some place where in fact many people might be present—a place by the seashore, a mountain-side, near a sacred grove, the open space before a temple or palace. The limitation was really narrow. The Greeks lived much on shipboard; no shipboard scene occurs in tragedy. The deliberations of a council would in the fifth century take place indoors; in tragedy they are always held outside. It is true that such limitation was less violent than it would be for us, because so much more of Greek life did go on out of doors—public worship in the form of sacrifice, popular assemblies, many domestic operations that we confine to the house. Still, by virtue of this convention an action is often made to occur in public that would in real life nearly always be private. In constructing the plot a playwright was obliged to manage that the whole action should center in such a series of incidents as could without too violent distortion occur in a public place. What could not so occur could be used as part of the plot only by the narration of someone. In Racine and Corneille, on the contrary, the commonest location of the action is a palace; it is what takes place out of doors that must be narrated.

The reason in each case is the same, however unlike the effects. It is the influence of the place where the plays were ordinarily first given, in one case the court of Louis XIV—and if not there, at least in a closed room— in the other case the precinct of Dionysos at Athens. The realities of open sky and sunshine and blue Saronic Gulf in plain view, with Mt. Hymettós on the other side and the Acropolis above, on whose flank they were seated— these were too insistent; to imagine oneself shut in by walls and a roof was too difficult. Hence the king meets his council in the square before his palace, not within. Kings may well have done so in the heroic age, as the assembly of the people was always held under the open sky. Antigone leads Ismene out of doors for a moment of privacy; Medea bewails her woes and reveals her schemes of vengeance to her friendly Corinthian visitors in front of her house; a dying person is brought out to the street to greet the sun for the last time. In such cases convention rather forces the action, that everything possible may be in the open air where the main scenes are placed; on the other hand, reasons are found and easily accepted why a character or the chorus shall not go inside when such withdrawal would be natural, except that it would spoil the play.

There is indeed a peculiar intertwining of convention and reality about the location and the chorus. This round plot which we look down to, between sixty-five and seventy feet across, is, in the play, the mountain-side, or the seashore, or the edge of a grove, or the square before a temple or before a royal house. At the same time it is really a dancing-plot in the precinct of Dionysos, whose temple is there below on the western side. The chorus are a group of people having a part in the story that is being enacted; at the same time they are Athenian citizens, not professionals, piously singing and dancing in honor of the god the newest form and representative of the old dithyramb. It is all religious, in the spirit of a natural and popular religion, not of a foreign and exotic one. The service—curious name for a ritual!—is a joyous festival, not sorrowful, though it began with a solemn sacrifice and the festival includes nine new tragedies with much sorrow in them. It is March, and the god is making the sap flow to the vine-buds in promise of a new vintage.

A change of scene under these conditions involved such difficulties that it was not often attempted. After the chorus entered it ordinarily remained in the orchestra till the close, tying all action to the same spot. Hence arose the modern notion of a dramatic law requiring strict unity of place throughout. But there was no such law.

In the "Aias" the scene at first is before the hero's dwelling, later in a lonely place outside the camp. Aias withdraws "to baths and meadows near the shore," that he may purify himself and bury the sword, Hector's gift, that has brought him only misfortune. The chorus and Tekmessa, warned that his absence just now portends danger, go in search of him, leaving the scene vacant. Aias now reappears and proceeds to bury the hilt of the sword that he may fall upon the point. He is therefore in such a place as he sought. According to the uniform custom of Greek tragedy, whereby violent death never occurs in full view, the sword must be so behind a bush or rock that his body disappears when he falls. Tekmessa, reentering with the chorus, after some search finds his body there. We have to judge from the text alone how the change of scene was made possible; for I do not believe that the theatrical practice of later centuries has more bearing on that of Sophokles than the practice of the later eighteenth century has on that of Shakspere in the early seventeenth. Possibly the light structure that served for the dwelling of Aias was taken away when all were gone. But in view of other cases I think another method about as probable. Suppose the dwelling to have filled not over half of the background, which was not less than the diameter of the orchestra, and that it remained unchanged, while the other half was set with the suggestion of bushes or rocks; the whole camp was near the shore, and in the "Iliad" the tent of Aias was at one end of the Greek line. Previous to the change of scene this open field was ignored, tacitly assumed as beyond the camp. If the later action was all in and in front of this field, while the dwelling of Aias was ignored, the spectators would readily follow in imagination the suggestion of words and action.*

The case in the "Eumenides" is more complicated. The first scene is before a temple front, of which the great double doors are closed; the words of the Pythia, who has come in at the parodos, make clear that this is

---

*Mr. Jack Randall Crawford tells me that his experience in outdoor theaters proves that a modern audience in such a theater readily accepts a change of scene made by this simple means.

Apollo's temple at Delphi. She enters the temple, leaving the door, perhaps, just enough open to admit her easily. This would be natural with a door so large. She soon returns in terror and tells in detail what has driven her out—a suppliant, his sword and hands wet with blood, and before him the strange company of Furies, seated in chairs, asleep and snoring. After a rather minute description of what the audience presently will see, she hastens away to her own dwelling. Now the doors are opened wide, by silent people who may be taken for temple servants. They, in performance of their routine, have noticed nothing strange within; but the spectators, informed beforehand precisely what is there, see enough to enable them to imagine the rest. From the dim interior Apollo now comes forward, and from the doorway, where he is visible to all, encourages the suppliant Orestes, telling him to go to the city of Pallas and sit in supplication with arms about her ancient image; there trial and acquittal shall be found. Hermes is called, appears from within, and is directed to guide and guard Orestes. They come out past Apollo at the door and depart—toward the city of Pallas, of course. The ghost of Klytaimestra appears within the temple, reproaches and rouses the Furies, and Apollo drives them out, assuring them that Pallas herself will preside at the approaching trial and that he will help and rescue the suppliant. Apollo disappears within, the scene is vacant, and the doors are closed.

Attendants now bring from outside the rude image of Pallas and place it just within the orchestra, on the side toward the temple, which is unchanged. When now Orestes, guided by Hermes, enters the orchestra by the parodos, and embracing the Palladium entreats Athena to save him, can anyone fail to understand that we are now in the city of Pallas, that is, on the Athenian Acropolis, and this temple is now that of Athena? The ancient image of the goddess was in fact in the temple, as everybody knew; but since dramatic necessity required it to be outside, outside it was, that the play might go on. And the temple itself is henceforth ignored and so disappears from the play. The chorus now make their regular entrance, hunting for their victim. The change of scene is complete, and things take the course that had been promised by Apollo at Delphi.

These two shifts of location, in the "Eumenides" and the "Aias," are so clearly described in the text that no reader can overlook them; the chorus leave the orchestra and return. Others may have been made in silence, the chorus remaining all the while. First perhaps in the "Eumenides"; for there is room for division of opinion about this. After hearing Orestes' plea and the opposing claims of the Furies, Athena goes out to select the foremost citizens as a jury. A choral song of eight stanzas proclaims the ancient functions of the Furies, and the danger of allowing those functions to fall into abeyance. Then Athena returns, leading the jury, for whom seats and the other properties of a court have meanwhile been brought, and a body of other citizens come with them as spectators of the trial. She bids the herald make proclamation; the Furies, Orestes, and Apollo in simple forms carry on the accusation and defense. Then Athena, as president of the court, sums up, sets forth the future law of trials for bloodshed, and casts her own vote for Orestes.

Where was the trial held? Not a word is spoken that implies a shift of scene. As Athena is here instituting the court of the Areopagos, some suppose that the trial must have been imagined by the playwright and the audience as held where such trials were held in the fifth century. But does that follow? The same demonstrative pronoun, "this" (τόνδε, τήνδε), is applied in the same sentence by Athena, in her instituting address, both to the hill of Ares and to the Acropolis, as if the poet were declining to indicate on which hill they are. The law required in historical times that the jury should not vote on the same day on which they heard the evidence and the pleas. That law is ignored in this trial. So, in my judgment, was the law touching the place. On sound principles of art the trial is idealized, reduced to its essence. What would not serve the ends of dramatic art is omitted and disregarded; the inner spirit is glorified, by the presence of gods and by the poetic language, as the heart of their ancient court. I conceive the jury and Athena in the drama to have been seated between Orestes at the image and the nearly forgotten temple, in such way that Orestes without moving—dramatic expression of the fact that he remains under Athena's protection—is conveniently placed for the trial, and the spectators fill the space at the sides without obscuring the chorus. At the close of the play, when the additional escort and the torch-bearers form the procession that conducts the Furies, henceforth named the Kindly Ones, to their future shrine, they cannot be imagined as clambering down the rude steps of Mars' Hill. The path from the ideal scene, westward from the temple on the Acropolis, blends with the actual path out the western entrance of the theater toward the well-known shrine. I think there was no change of scene imagined for the trial.

In the "Libation-pourers" the case is clearer. The play begins at the grave of Agamemnon, on which Orestes places his offering of a lock of hair, and to which Elektra and the chorus come bringing the drink-offering which Klytaimestra has sent. The chorus expressly say that they came from the house. After the mutual recognition and joint petition for the ghostly help of their father, Orestes' plan is explained, Elektra is directed to go into the house to assist them there, and Orestes and Pylades withdraw to perfect their preparations. A choral song ends the scene and prepares for the next. Orestes with his attendants then enters and knocks for entrance at the house, which now, full halfway through the play, is found to constitute the background. It was the background of the preceding play, the palace of Agamemnon, and must have been there from the beginning. To it Elektra must have returned, though she came from outside the theater, the assumption *then* being that the house was at a distance. The grave of Agamemnon, then, must be thought of as in the orchestra—a mound of earth, hitherto neglected and dishonored. The tomb was the center of the action in the first half, while the palace was ignored, and the tomb is ignored for the rest of the play, which goes on in front of the palace. As choruses regularly enter from outside by a parodos, the entrance of this chorus from outside with Elektra raised no question. This is an illustration of the freedom with which space is treated conventionally; the two centers, actually a few yards apart, are assumed to be at the distance which would in fact separate the royal dwelling and the royal tomb; nothing contrary to that assumption occurs, except the silent passage of Elektra from the tomb to the house. Reality is not obtruded to disturb the imagination.

Very similar is the situation in the "Persians," fourteen years earlier, but with a slight addition. First the councilors appointed by Xerxes before his departure come to an "ancient building" (στέγος ἀρχαῖον) as they call it, as if to hold a council, and seat themselves, or propose to seat themselves. To them, however, before they are seated, comes the queen-mother, telling them that she has left her palace and come hither because of an ominous dream. Her palace, then, is not the ancient building before which they stand. She comes from outside the theater by one of the main entrances. After the messenger has reported the battle of Salamis and the plight of Xerxes she goes out, promising to return with drink-offerings "from her dwelling." Lyric reflections of the chorus give her time for this, and at her return she bids them accompany her libations with a hymn, calling to their aid the sainted Darius. Standing "near the tomb" they invoke him, and he appears "above the crown of the tomb." Informed of what has happened, he predicts farther woe, warns against renewed aggression, and bids the queen go home and get new garments for Xerxes, who is now in rags. She obeys, promising to try to meet her son before he reaches the palace. Darius and Atossa both disappear now from the play, and from this point no farther mention is made of either tomb or council-house. Xerxes soon appears, and joins with the chorus in lyric lamentation for some minutes, till Xerxes bids them go home (ἐς δόμους), and they reply, in their final line, "I will accompany thee." By implication, then, we seem to have three locations, though the last is not by a word differentiated from the second. The first is in front of the "ancient building" which is regarded as a senate-house; the second is about the tomb of Darius, which is in the orchestra, as was the tomb of Agamemnon. No tomb would in reality be so near the senate-house;* space is condensed, distance ignored. While they are supposed to be in one location, no allusion is made to the other, nothing calls attention to their nearness. Xerxes might, it is true, come upon them by the senate-house, but not without being first seen by many others; but that fact is ignored. If, in accordance with contemporary Greek custom, the tomb was outside of the city, he might more naturally come upon them there, but nothing has indicated that the tomb was outside. And in fact the tomb of a hero or a founder of a city was often in the market-place, within the city; the early kings of Mycenae had a sacred burial plot inside of the Lion gate. Discreet silence about distances and anything like a city plan leaves all inconvenient details floating in ideal space. No similar shifts of location, either assumed or plainly indicated, occur in our extant plays after the date of the "Aias," somewhere about 440 B. C.

III

One other convention is very curious, though we are so wonted to it in novels and the modern drama that we seldom think of it. The absence of a curtain in the Greek theater forces it on the attention. I mean the double standard of time, which nearly every play illustrates. There is a good example in our earliest tragedy, the "Suppliants" of Aeschylus. At line 523 the king goes to consult his people as to whether the state shall receive and defend these suppliant women; the chorus while he

*It should be noted, however, that in the "Helen" Euripides expressly locates the tomb of Proteus close by the entrance (ἐπ' ἐξόδοις) of the palace.

is gone sing five short strophes and antistrophes, seventy-seven lines in the traditional numbering. This might take fifteen minutes, twenty at most. At line 600 their father Danaos returns and reports that the people have accepted their petition. There has been time for the king to reach Argos, call together the assembly, present the case, and take the vote; and time in addition for Danaos to walk from the assembly place to the scene of the play. How long would it take to assemble by public crier the voters of even the smallest state, offer the requisite sacrifice and prayer, and transact the business? Ten times as long, at least, as to perform the choral dance and song. A still more striking case is in our latest tragedy, the "Oedipus at Kolonos." During a choral song of fifty-three lines Theseus and his men have pursued the kidnappers of Antigone and Ismene for some miles, as the chorus conceive it, and after something of a fight have brought the girls back in safety. The needless rehearsal of details is precluded by a more pressing topic, but an hour or two is the least we must assume for events out of the theater that filled the interval of ten or fifteen minutes within it. In "Oedipus King" during the interval of one strophe and antistrophe a messenger goes from Thebes to Cithaeron, say two hours away, finds a wandering shepherd and brings him to the king's presence.

The principle is quite clear. Conventionally, in the matter of time, a choral ode has one of the functions of our curtain lowered between acts. During that interval, longer or shorter, any time that is required by the story is assumed to have elapsed for events outside; only, the Greek play was continuous, while with us the lowered curtain breaks the play by certain minutes subtracted from it. Our wait between acts is time lost—given up unwillingly to mechanism; the choral ode was a portion of the play, a relief from dramatic tension, but filled with interest of another and calmer sort. Its time was real and counted in the play; alongside of it, however, existed another time, an ideal time, that which was required for occurrences essential to the play but unsuitable, on whatever ground, for ocular presentation. The two kinds of time coexist in the spectator's mind without interfering with each other; as no allusion to incongruity is made, he is not likely even to think of it.

The parallel in fictitious narrative is familiar; the instance in Plato's "Protagoras" will serve as example. The youthful Hippokrates in his eagerness to begin lessons with the famous teacher comes to Sokrates' house and wakes him at daybreak, while it is too dark to see, and begs his elder friend to take him at once to Protagoras. Sokrates calms his impatience; they go out together to the courtyard and talk awhile, walking about till sunrise. The conversation as reported word for word is supposed to occupy an hour or so; it really takes perhaps ten minutes. But the parallel is incomplete, because the talk is only narrated; reading it makes no such impression of time as the combined report of our own eyes and ears in the theater.

The boldest instances of the convention appear in two plays of Aeschylus. The case in the "Agamemnon" is well known. A watchman on the roof of the palace descries the beacon-fire, last in the prearranged line, which announces the capture of Troy. It is then, of course, still night. In the theater it was broad sunlight, but early in the day. The chorus immediately enter to learn the meaning of the sacrifices that are already being offered on altars everywhere. Even before their songs begin, then, in the interval between two lines, which no doubt is prolonged by the dumb show of sacrifice on the altar before the palace, the queen has had time to order these rites, the chorus time to learn of them, rise from bed, assemble, and come to the palace. Their entrance ode is the longest extant, it is true; no definite allusion is made to time, but at its close, when the queen appears, it is clearly daylight, at least two hours after the beacon was seen. After the interview between chorus and queen, followed by another song, a herald from the army, that, on the farther side of the Aegean Sea, has just reported by the line of beacons the capture of Troy, comes to announce the near approach of Agamemnon. His narrative tells of a disastrous storm on the voyage; *several days have elapsed since the play began*. The herald sailed with the king; one more choral song and Agamemnon enters. From this point there is no separate outside time.

In "Prometheus Bound" the lapse of outside time is very skillfully hidden; unless forewarned the reader is unaware of it. But did the poet mean us to suppose that the Titan, who with such dramatic emphasis was fastened in the first scene to the Scythian cliff, remains there but two hours before the rock is shattered by earthquake and hides him for ages in the earth? That is impossible. Indeed in that first scene Hephaistos says to him:

>   —"Thy beauty's flower,
> Scorched in the sun's clear heat, shall fade away.
> Night shall come up with garniture of stars
> To comfort thee with shadow, and the sun
> Disperse with retrickt beams the morning frosts:
> But through all changes, sense of present woe
> Shall vex thee sore."

All the characters but Io are immortals, to whom time is naught; we are in an almost timeless world. Silences, when Prometheus is first left alone, and again at the close of the choral song in which is painted the sympathy of all mankind and all nature for the suffering Titan, are made to suggest the boundless leisure of immortals. Until Io appears, however, there seems to be no distinct suggestion that time has passed. True, the detailed account of the benefactions of Prometheus implies a long development of human civilization under his guidance— at least proceeding from the instruction which, after the gift of fire, he had imparted. If this be somewhat inconsistent with the obvious presumption that his punishment followed not long after the gift of fire, the inconsistency is in the myth; Aeschylus is not responsible for it, and neither spectator nor reader thinks of it till he has become critical to a degree quite unknown to any contemporary of the poet. Still the thought of a long period of human history since the play began is vaguely raised. But Io, though daughter of a river god, is mortal. Divine beings are kinsmen and associates of hers; she is not surprised at meeting ocean nymphs and Prometheus. But she is a mortal woman who had been wooed by Zeus; the historic oracles of Delphi and Dodona had been consulted by her anxious father to learn the meaning of her tormenting dreams. And she knows, apparently, the story of the great benefaction of Prometheus to mankind, though she wonders what he is being punished for. The choral song that follows her departure laments the woes that come from unequal unions, particularly between gods and women. It is in harmony with this thought that Prometheus proceeds to tell them that Zeus is even now meditating the step which, if he is not saved from it

93

by learning in time from Prometheus its sequel, will hurl him from his throne. No word of a definite lapse of time is let fall; yet the event which, when first vaguely referred to, was imagined as in a distant future, is now nearer. The catastrophe that closes the play is now quickly brought on. By slight hints these beings to whom time is nothing have suggested the lapse of ages in the course of what to us has been two hours.

Here then are the facts in regard to that unity of time which once made so great stir as a supposed law of Greek tragedy; and we have seen what were the facts in regard to unity of place. As we are concerned with realities of the ancient art, not with modern theories about it, we will not retrace the rise of a doctrine that has no basis in those realities. In fairness, however, it should be noted that Aristotle began it—set the error going—by observing that a tragedy, contrariwise to the epic, "endeavors to keep as far as possible within a single circuit of the sun, or something near that." No doubt this was true in his day, a generation or two after the death of the great tragedians; the tendency toward restriction in that regard was strong even in Sophokles and Euripides. It may have been connected with improvements in material means of representation; as a general law the closer the approach to realism or to ocular illusion the less active the imagination. Aeschylus did not hesitate to make the heaviest demands on the cooperation of the spectator's own creative faculty.

Plots drawn almost wholly from the ancient store of religious myth, the poetic language of all participants in the play, song and expressive dance for a group—the chorus—who are evidently a continuation of the old

94

dithyramb, the atmosphere of a popular religious festival, the infrequency of the celebration, and the feel of spring in the Athenian air—all these factors joined forces with the poet's genius to stir men's imagination to its utmost activity. But poetic and dramatic genius was the originating force; when this failed, the art decayed. Aristotle could only analyze and tabulate, for the guidance, and occasionally to the misleading, of the later non-Hellenic world.

V. EXTERNAL FORM

I

THE division of a play into acts and scenes, which our practice inclines us to regard as normal, has no application to Greek tragedy. The modern connotation of the terms misleads if one tries to fit them to the ancient form. Often, it is true, the action does fall into two or three larger sections, which one is tempted to call acts. But that term implies an outward break and pause, and there was no such break and pause in the Greek theater. We may, for certain purposes, apply the French and German conception of *scène* or *Eintritt*, which is really inherent, marked by the entrance or exit of a character. But the Greeks like ourselves had no name for this; having observed the reality of it as a minor division we may appreciate its effect, as in our own drama, without naming it. It is indeed disputed, I believe, how much of the systematic chopping into scenes that our current texts of Shakspere exhibit would have seemed to the poet himself appropriate. Each act was probably continuous; a shift of location on his front, middle, or back stage made but the slightest pause.

The Greek chorus, even after it ceased to play an important rôle in the plot, continued, as we have seen, to be felt as the core of the play. This double aspect of the chorus is rather paradoxical. The future development of drama lay implicit in the dialogue; vaguely this was recognized in the great century of tragedy; in the New Comedy of Menander it was openly acknowledged. Yet the form of tragedy to the end of the fifth century was dominated by the chorus, as containing for the Greek more of the religious, more of the spirit of Dionysiac worship. This in spite of the fact that only one song in the extant plays—barring the "Bacchants," in which the god himself is a leading character—otherwise only the famous prayer in the "Antigone" is wholly addressed to Dionysos.

We have seen that in the "Suppliants" of Aeschylus the chorus was really the leading character, the multiple heroine; we may suppose that earlier this was often the case. But thereafter, in the plays now extant, this recurs only in the "Eumenides." As regards action in a narrower sense, elsewhere the chorus was subordinate.

And we must distinguish the chorus-leader as a speaker in dialogue, in so far virtually an actor, from the company of singers as a whole. The former may expostulate, or give advice when appealed to; he often endeavors to mediate, to allay a quarrel. In those angry debates, word-duels, which Athenian audiences enjoyed, a couplet, perhaps four lines, of well-meant commonplace may be expected from the chorus-leader as transition between the longer speeches. So in various ways he may influence leading characters and their action without making himself too prominent by displaying initiative. Or again, as the chorus commonly remain on the scene from their entrance to the close, they are present at all consultations and hear all revelations made to anybody. So the leader must on occasion keep secrets and not reveal what would spoil the plot. When it will help the plot, it is true, the secret is told, as in the "Ion." Xuthos bids Creüsa's women, under threat of death, not to reveal to their mistress the fact that the oracle has given him Ion as a son. Loyal to her mistress, the leader disregards the threat, thus bringing on dramatic complications that are desired. But more often it is the other way. The temple-attendants of Iphigeneia, entreated to keep her secret, brave the anger of Thoas; their leader tells him a downright falsehood to delay pursuit. In the "Hippolytos" if the chorus had told what they knew, the father's curse would not have been spoken, the tragic outcome would have been impossible. The leader keeps her oath of secrecy. The women of Corinth guard the secret of Medea's purpose, and through their leader become accessory to the murder of their own king and his daughter. The convention is allowed to excuse a highly improbable course.

But set choral songs, except in the two plays named, never affect the action. After the entering song, which has in part another function, they are the emotional reflex of the action. They express the sentiments and reflections natural to the chorus as a whole in the situation as thus far developed. The members of the chorus are by no means neutral bystanders; they are not "ideal spectators," whatever that may mean. They are a part of the group of people, isolated from the rest of the world, who are living the story, men or women who are deeply interested, whose lives will be affected by the outcome. This is no less true for Euripides than for Aeschylus and Sophokles; there is no deterioration in that respect in the surviving plays from the fifth century. Their personal influence on the course of events may be more or less, but emotionally they are always fully within it.

Their sentiments and emotions are therefore part of the dramatic subject; their expression of them, even for the modern reader, who cannot readily take the Greek view that the chorus are the heart of the play, is at once a relief from the dramatic tension and an enrichment of the dramatic theme. The musical and orchestic sides of their expression, lost for us, enhanced both the relief and the enrichment.

So highly was the choral element appreciated that an extra chorus was sometimes introduced. As that involved extra expense, the consent of the choregos, who had to pay it, was perhaps requisite. The hunting companions of Hippolytos sing with him, at his entrance, a short hymn to Artemis; when he is setting out for exile they alternate with the regular chorus of Trozenian women in a musical farewell. In the Euripidean "Suppliants" a company of boys, children of the dead warriors, join with the regular chorus, the warriors' mothers, in the dirge over the dead. But this is no innovation of Euripides; Aeschylus has it in the "Eumenides." A band of women who guard the sacred image of Athena, which has been prominent in the play, sing in honor of the Kindly Ones as the whole people escort them to their new shrine. This band probably consisted of those who had been the regular chorus in the "Libation-pourers," which had just preceded, now differently costumed. That means of providing the personnel of an extra chorus was always at hand.

II

The twelfth chapter of the "Poetics" defines the divisions of a tragedy in relation to set songs of the chorus. It is doubtful whether the chapter came from the hand of

Aristotle; but the names are ancient and are convenient, even if not so strictly applicable to the earliest plays. They are certainly more fitting than our modern terms.

The entering song of the chorus, with any recited march-anapests that went with it, was known as the *parodos* (πάροδος), which was also the name of the two main entrances to the theater by way of the *orchēstra*. By one or both of these entrances the chorus appeared, reciting or singing, ordinarily in a close formation of rank and file. Before Aeschylus probably the play always began with the *parodos;* his "Suppliants" and "Persians" begin so, and there are indications that the fifty suppliant Danaïds sang their anapests as they marched in, though the Persian elders recited theirs—in unison, therefore in a formal manner not far from song. The only other play that so begins is the "Rhesos," which has come down under the name of Euripides. If not his, then it is the work of a fourth tragic poet, otherwise unknown, and is the more valuable for that reason. It is interesting also as the only one remaining to us whose plot is taken directly from the Iliad. Certain peculiarities of its *parodos* have led to a belief that the beginning of the play is lost. The grounds adduced for that belief are in my opinion insufficient, allowing too little play for the ingenuity and fondness for variety that belonged to Euripides, that may equally have belonged to his unknown fellow-playwright. It was quite in the Euripidean manner to revive an antique method, with changes that made it novel. That after only ten lines of march-anapests, in which Hector is by name called from his bed (it is in the night), the chorus-leader and Hector continue the anapests awhile in dialogue—this in itself is just such a novelty as one might expect from Euripides. The anapestic dialogue that opens "Iphigeneia at Aulis" in our text is closely akin.

But only in these three plays does a chorus enter first. When they became subordinate in the plot it was more natural that other characters should begin the exposition; to a situation already partially known the chorus could come without assuming too large a place in it. All that preceded the entrance of the chorus was called the *prologos* (πρόλογος). Prologue, our form of the word, has been narrowed to the most detached form of exposition, a speech preliminary to the play rather than integral with it. The old form of the word is therefore better for the Greek *prologos*. This might be a true soliloquy, as in the "Agamemnon"; in the seven plays of Sophokles it is always a dialogue, and is often so in Euripides; yet the latter inclined to the semi-detached speech, frankly narrating to the audience the essential antecedents of the opening situation and clearly foreshadowing the outcome. Only the extreme form of the Euripidean *prologos* accords with our concept of prologue, which is quite inapplicable to the dramatic exposition. All types were alike *prologoi*.

An *epeisodion* (ἐπεισόδιον) included all the dialogue, even if part of it were lyric, that intervened between two entire choral songs. Again our modification, episode, has taken on a different meaning, this time a greatly enlarged one. It includes the *epeisodion* as well as a dozen other things; it is not distinctive enough, diluting too much the definite conception of the original word.

A *stasimon* (στάσιμον) is a complete song of the chorus, following an *epeisodion* and marking a pause in the action in the narrower sense of the word, the action as carried by the actors apart from the chorus. To the *stasimon* preeminently the remark is applicable which I made before; it offers relief from dramatic tension, in an interest of another and calmer sort—in portraying through music and dance added to lyric verse the reflections and emotions called forth by the preceding *epeisodion* in people who are in the story, though not the center of it. As a rule, at the end of the *epeisodion* the other characters have withdrawn, or, if one remains, he has become in one way or another oblivious of their song. Virtually the chorus is alone; they think over what has happened, try to fathom its meaning, draw from it a warning, forecast dimly what it portends. Or at most, if the situation forbids open declaration of such thoughts, they sing of some situation in myth which resembles it and may suggest similar thoughts. The most loosely adherent *stasimon* has at least so much of dramatic fitness and a plausible dramatic reason for an apparent lack of cohesion.

The number of alternating *epeisodia* and *stasima* may be two, three, or even four; three is the commonest number of pairs, but all details are governed by the nature of the story. In place of a *stasimon* a lyric dialogue, between chorus and actor or between actors without the chorus, may better suit the development of the story. Song from the *skēnē* ($\mu\acute{\epsilon}\lambda os$ $\mathring{a}\pi\grave{o}$ $\sigma\kappa\eta\nu\hat{\eta}s$) was the technical name for a lyric passage by an actor, *kommos* ($\kappa o\mu\mu\acute{o}s$) for a lyric bit of dialogue between chorus and one or more actors. A *kommos* was usually, but by no means always, a lamentation; a *parodos* is called kommatic if chorus and an actor make it a dialogue.

Finally the *exodos* ($\mathring{\epsilon}\xi o\delta os$) was all that followed the last *stasimon*, the last entire choral song. The catastrophe commonly falls within the *exodos*, with the excitement and expressions of sorrow occasioned by the catastrophe. Thus the *exodos* is likely to be the most agitated in movement, in language, in metrical and musical expression. In the "Persians" the entire *exodos* is filled with an Oriental dirge led by Xerxes, whose return is the signal for beginning it. The catastrophe has been related previously. The agitation usually calms down before the end, closing in a bit of commonplace from the chorus as they march out by the parodos with a short song or recitative known as the *exodion* (ἐξόδιον), or exit-piece.

Besides the set lyric forms already described, the chorus may at any point in the dialogue, if the action calls for it, sing instead of speaking a response—a brief choral song that is not a *stasimon*, simply an instant of higher emotion in the dialogue where speech rises to song. The *kommos* is at bottom only an extension of this; one or more actors join with the chorus in the enhanced emotion and therefore in its natural expression through song. Lamentation is in tragedy the most common sort of emotion that so finds expression, but not the only sort.

No form of violent death or of bodily mutilation was allowed to occur in sight of the audience. As events of that nature are a prominent feature in many tragic stories, they had to be narrated. Moreover, from the difficulty of changing the scene, whatever took place elsewhere than in the public place that the orchestra for the time being represents must also be narrated. Hence the formal messenger and his narrative are in many plays rather prominent. He is a subordinate character, often a servant or a man of the people, reporting to the chorus or someone else outside of the house a suicide or murder done inside, or something important to the story done elsewhere. For instance, in the "Women of Trachis" an unnamed man, loyal to Deianeira, and also hoping for a tip, hastens from the market-place that he may be the first to bring to Deianeira the news from her long absent husband, which Lichas has just brought thither. Later in the same play Deianeira's son Hyllos reports at length the tortures which her fatal gift, sent as a love-charm, has inflicted on his father Herakles while offering a sacrifice of thanksgiving, and his father's consequent killing of Lichas. In the "Persians" again, as the scene is at the Persian court, a messenger reports at some length, before the *exodos,* the great catastrophe of the play, the Greek victory at Salamis with the destruction of the Persian host. These are typical cases, but there is great variety in them as a class. Both in spirit and in language these narratives retain a certain epic tinge. On the other hand they are much more highly colored than the epic; aiming to paint vividly some horrifying occurrence for people who had not seen it, the excited eyewitness has none of the epic calm, as of one who tells of suffering long gone by. His part demands peculiar skill: an incompetent messenger may nearly spoil a representation.

Why deeds of blood were banished from actual sight of the audience it may not be easy to say; but the contrast with the floods of gore in Elizabethan tragedy is striking enough, and is significant. I see no reason for supposing that the Athenians were less cruel or bloody in real life. Hand-to-hand fighting, sack and massacre, the slaughter of prisoners, bloody vengeance—all were familiar and not severely reprehended. It is true, however, that bodily mutilation was not, as in Persia and in Elizabethan England, a common form of punishment; beheading was not, as it was for centuries in western Europe, a

public spectacle; execution, for freemen, was by a pain-
less poison; more savage methods were reserved for
slaves and the worst of miscreants. Probably these last-
named facts have some relation to theatrical practice.
I incline to believe that this rested chiefly on esthetic
considerations, in which the Athenians were certainly
more advanced than Londoners of three centuries ago.
In this matter of bloody deeds on the stage we today are
happily nearer in feeling to the Greeks. No new tragedy
would admit them; we do not like that side of such a
close as the final scene of "Hamlet"; we merely accept it,
if it is not emphasized, for the sake of that which makes
the whole so great, and because it is outweighed by our
veneration for genius. We do not nowadays accept on
the stage any "tragedy of blood" by a contemporary of
Shakspere. In their case the pain, the disagreeable of
such scenes, outweighs any pleasure the rest might give.
That seems to have been the basis of Athenian objection.
Perhaps Horace, who was familiar with bloody gladiatorial fights as an amusement, got from some Greek the
true doctrine, which he put in the two words *incredulus
odi*. Such scenes make too severe a strain on the imagination; the sight of them calls forth as an involuntary
and immediate reaction the feeling that they are all pre-
tense; there is no illusion. And they are disagreeable.
A vivid narrative is painful enough; sight would be too
much.

Besides narrative, a more direct reflex of such deeds
was often highly effective. The immediate result was
shown, after a narrative or along with it. The death cry
of Agamemnon is heard, followed by silence, then by the
excited debate of the chorus of elders. Then through the
open door we see Klytaimestra with her bloody weapon

standing over the corpse, proudly acknowledging the deed. Again, the messenger describes how Oedipus has blinded himself with the brooch which he had snatched from the robe of his mother-wife, dead by her own act; then the king comes forth, groping his way, his face marred and bloody. The mask is enough for our imagination; since we know it to be a mask it is less painful than a modern actor's make-up, imitating the reality more closely. In comparison with these methods, the direct exhibition of murder, suicide, or mutilation is crude and barbarous.

A suicide could also be so arranged that the act was visible, the effect hidden. Aias firmly plants the hilt of his sword, as he describes in his soliloquy, and falls upon the point. The scene in which the body is discovered shows that sword and corpse were hidden behind something—a rock or bush. We see the fall, but not his death. So, too, we must understand the case of Euadne in the Euripidean "Suppliants." She throws herself from a high rock upon the pyre where the corpse of her husband is burning. The pyre must therefore be behind the scene, indicated perhaps by rising smoke; into this Euadne can safely throw herself. A peaceful death, like that of Alkestis, the dramatist does not hesitate to show.

In addition to the reports of messengers there is, as in every type of drama, a good deal of other narrative. Any tragedy of Shakspere will illustrate the point; even his freedom in shifting localities did not suffice to enable him to present through action every incident of the story. So in the "Philoktetes," for example, Odysseus tells Neoptolemos, as part of his argument to induce the young man to follow his wiser companion's guidance, all the circumstances that led the Greek expedition to abandon the wounded Philoktetes on this lonely island; later Philoktetes narrates the course of his solitary life. While the audience by this means learn facts essential to the story, the emotional effects on Neoptolemos are highly dramatic; subsequent action is determined thereby and characters are portrayed. In "Oedipus King" the drama consists largely in the gradual revelation of acts completed before the tragedy opens, and in the slowly accumulating effects of this unfolding. The king and queen, the seer Teiresias, the shepherd of Laïos, and the messenger from Corinth, the latter in addition to his primary function as messenger, all by straightforward narration out of their own past supply their several parts of the revelation. It is the fitting together of these parts, each highly dramatic in its place, that slowly builds up the overwhelming whole of revelation. The real action, that which the poet and we also most care for, is internal, in the souls of Oedipus and of Iokaste.

Within each *epeisodion,* and in *prologos* and *exodos* as well, as I said, the French and German conception of *scène* or *Eintritt* is as applicable as to the plays of Racine or Schiller. That system of division rests on daily experience. If two people in conversation are joined by a third, inevitably the talk changes; the tone or the subject is adjusted to another element. If now one of the original pair withdraws, another readjustment follows. Entrance or exit of any significant character makes a division that is not the less real because neither we nor the Greeks have named the minor sections thus produced. Except as it helps to clarify our own perception it is perhaps not important to notice such divisions in Greek tragedy. There is no rule about their number. One scene, in the French sense of the word, may fill an entire *prologos* or *epeisodion;* there may be two or more; the *exodos* often has four or five. The nature of the action and the playwright's judgment alone determine.

III

The rule about two actors, later three, is easily misunderstood if stated from the wrong end. We are told that the state furnished and paid only that number; therefore not more than three could appear in the same scene, and each actor was expected to take, if necessary, two or more successive rôles that would not interfere with one another. Masks made that easier than it would be in our theater. But we know neither when such rules were adopted nor what was their scope. In later times, when the drama was more of an amusement, such a practice was economical for traveling companies. But we know that Thespis and Aeschylus and other playwrights acted in their own plays; probably Sophokles did in minor parts, his voice not being strong enough for heavier ones. There was no reason why non-professionals might not help out, if available, and if the choregos or someone else was willing to pay whatever cost was entailed. In "Oedipus at Kolonos" either a fourth actor was employed or one rôle was divided between two actors. And in the second *epeisodion* of "Andromache" Peleus enters to a group of three actors; Andromache and her child have just sung a duet of entreaty, which Menelaos has repulsed. The rule was not without exception, then.

But the matter has a different aspect when viewed from another and more significant side. The restriction, so far as it was real, was probably the observance of an artistic law, and not at all the result of economy. When Aeschylus added a second actor he extended greatly the scope of his art; a wider variety of incidents was brought within reach, and the direct clash of personalities with one another as well as with the chorus. To add a third was characteristic of Sophokles with his deeper interest in personality; it enabled him to display the differing reaction of two natures to the influence of a third. The drama as an instrument for the portrayal of humanity was now complete; a fourth person besides the chorus in the same scene would complicate and confuse more than would be compensated by possible extension of range. Accustomed as we are to the entire freedom of modern drama in this regard we may at first blush incline to doubt this. We are not so sensitive to values arising from restraint in art as were the Greeks. But in practice the great modern dramatists have not wandered far from the same restriction, when this is properly stated. More than three distinct persons and points of view in one scene, besides that of the chorus, would rather detract from clarity and dissipate interest; two or three clearly presented are more effective, and especially is this true when the audience is large.

The practice, in fact, only follows common experience. Among a company in high spirits about a dinner-table, for example, a dozen people may carry on a rapid cross-fire of light repartee; two or three may speak at once and no harm is done. But let the talk become serious, on a topic that interests all, and there is a change. The discussion is slower, two or three carry the talk awhile, with a tendency toward longer speeches; one drops out and another takes his place, while at any of the successive stages the majority merely listen. This even when there is no larger audience to be reached and influenced. Shakspere, under no outward constraint on this point, is surprisingly near to Greek usage. Let one read "Hamlet" or any tragedy with this in mind, remembering that minor characters take the place of the chorus and the chorus-leader. Looked at in this light the rule of three actors is found to be not artificial and not a mark of poverty, pecuniary or artistic, but a recognition, in true Greek fashion, of paramount dramatic law.

And then it must not be forgotten that there was no known restriction on the number of "mute characters" or supernumeraries—a silent Pylades in the Sophoklean "Elektra," the maid-servants of the Danaïds, attendants on a king or queen, the band of suppliants at the opening of "Oedipus," the citizens of the court of Areopagos in the "Eumenides," the escort and the torch-bearers at the end of the last-named play. A brilliant spectacle of that sort was always a joy to Athenians; few speakers need not imply a meager scene.

Such is the general scheme, externally, of a Greek tragedy: a chorus, singing and dancing, as the formal center, few speaking characters, rarely over three appearing at once, alternation of speech and song, the plot drawn from old and familiar stories. The description may appear like that of a rather meager and limited drama. The superficial reader is apt to find it so, however he may be impressed by some passages. So people who have not seen Doric temples, but only pictures of them, and have given no study to Greek architecture, may imagine that Doric temples are simple buildings and much alike, in contrast with the boundless variety of the Gothic cathedral. That is a grave mistake that grows naturally out of our antecedents—our history and perhaps our race. Most of us require special training to get

rid of the prepossessions bred in us by centuries of northern civilization, with so many roots in the Middle Ages.
We who have been brought up on Shakspere, while we
take readily to Goethe, require long habituation before
we feel deeply Racine or the French lyric of the last century. Rembrandt and the Gothic masterpieces speak to
us at once; for Giotto and Pheidias longer acquaintance
is needed before they yield us their meanings. We have
to enlarge our boundaries, learn languages of art that are
new to us; whether finer or inferior to our own is wholly
beside the point—a question we have no right to ask and
are incompetent to answer until we are equally at home
in both.

A fundamental character of Athenian tragedy, as of
Greek art universally, is relative simplicity and perspicu-
ity in the larger masses with exquisite proportion and
minute variation in details, which are never made so conspicuous as to withdraw attention in the least from the
larger masses. Subordination of every part to its whole
of the next higher order, and the utmost charm and perfection in each order—this is the dominating principle.
Therein resides the union of majesty and grace in the
Parthenon. The proportions of the whole were for the
architect the final issue of the most successful previous
experiments of predecessors and of himself; outer colon-
nade, alternating triglyphs and metopes, are in their
grouping not unlike the grouping of the chorus—the units
more effective when thus disposed in a mass; all vertical
and horizontal lines beautified by slight and subtle curva-
ture; echinos and molding and every ornament delicately
studied, the mason's workmanship throughout as fine as
our cabinetwork; and all combining to make a worthy
setting for the sculptured frieze and pediment groups of

Pheidias. The "Agamemnon" and "Oedipus King" may without incongruity be compared to such a masterpiece.

I would emphasize the point that there is no set scheme of *prologos, parodos, epeisodia, stasima,* and *exodos,* which the playwright must follow. The elements we have considered were combined in endless variety. No two plays were alike; each plot and the poet's genius determined each combination. Wonder at the flexibility of the form which at first we thought so limited is one's final sentiment about it. Unity of type, endless variation! The same story was used over and over, a new reading, a new point of view, sufficing for a new tragedy. This persistence or continuity of type is a mark of the greatest ages in every art. How simple a subject is that of Madonna and Child in Italian religious painting; yet centuries of repetition and scores of great successes left room for Raphael to paint a Sistine Madonna, which breathes a new life into the old conventions. Simplicity of type is no defect. In our music no doubt the symphony, employing a hundred instruments, brass and cymbals among them, attracts more people than the string quartette; yet the great masters have chosen to write, and have written some of their greatest music, for the four quieter stringed instruments. Three or four human souls of tragic mold in the grip of tragic circumstance may suffice for a microcosm of life that shall move us profoundly. The genius of the artist is not measured by multitude of instruments, but by the power and beauty of what, under his control, they say to us.

There is another aspect of these forms of Attic tragedy that we must not overlook. Gilbert Murray has made much of their resemblance to the rituals of vegetation spirits, of whom Dionysos was one. He humorously admits that he may perhaps be making too much of a discovery of his own. He notes that tragedy and those rituals have certain elements in common. He finds in the rituals some kind of contest between the spirit and his enemy, followed by some kind of disaster or suffering, that overtakes the spirit, most often death. Often, too, that suffering or death is narrated by a messenger rather than enacted—a very curious point, as he thinks. Then there is a formal lamentation or dirge, and finally there is usually a revival or reappearance of the slain spirit. All this is the ritual history of the annual death and revival of vegetation. And all these elements are curiously paralleled in the elements of tragedy, although for the last point, the epiphany or reappearance of the deity, one has to go mostly to Euripides.

Another English scholar, William Ridgeway, finds a close resemblance between the formal elements of tragedy and the ritual of worship of the spirits of ancestors—the tomb-ritual. He points to the prominence of death in tragedy, and of dirges and of drink-offerings at the tomb, and he finds in these and other resemblances a confirmation of his view that tragedy arose, not from the worship of Dionysos, as Aristotle believed, but from the tomb-ritual of ancestor-worship.

I put these two views side by side, because the juxtaposition at once awakens suspicion—not of the facts, of which there is no doubt, but of the explanation offered. Indeed, Gilbert Murray points out also that these vegetation-rituals are in spirit closely parallel to the Christian Mass, which is also a ritual drama, that of the passion of Christ. But one may ask, in a certain bewilderment, shall we then take one step farther, and find in the Mass a continuation of the old vegetation-ritual? And if not, why not? When we put these parallels and the arguments from them side by side, we recognize that such resemblances, interesting as they are in certain ways, are an insufficient basis for the structures built upon them. The resemblances rest on deep-lying characteristics of the Greek people, or of universal human nature. They manifested themselves in more than one department of Greek life. They contributed, no doubt, to the fixity of the type of tragedy, even while the development of the Greek mind was filling the old form with an expanding spirit that was destined finally to shatter the form. But they offer no basis for rejecting the account, transmitted by Aristotle, of the origin of tragedy.

IV

A little more must be said about the *skēnē*, the "stage-question," and the machinery, as part of the external form of tragedy. First, it is not admissible to do what is continually done, cite existing stage-buildings or any extant commentators or grammarians, without earlier testimony, as evidence about theatrical usage of the fifth century. No one thinks of applying to theatrical usage of 1600 A. D. in London that of 1800 or 1900 A. D. in Paris and New York. An interval of one to three centuries was not less fruitful of change because it came before our era. The great age of Athenian drama was over before a stone of any existing theater—except the scanty remnants from the old orchestra at Athens—was laid; changes were rapid both on the literary and on the material side of the art during the fourth and third centuries, not less rapid than in the like interval after Shakspere's death. It is true that the old tragedies were reproduced, as are "Hamlet" and "Macbeth"; but not in the theater for which they are composed. They were adapted, as old plays are with us, to the contemporary theater, whose arrangements were determined by new conditions. For the time of the great tragedians we must draw our evidence first of all from the text of the plays themselves, and secondly from those authors who stand nearest to them, Plato, the orators, and Aristotle; and the second class of evidence must be used with much caution. The history of the development of comedy from Aristophanes to Terence, of tragedy from Euripides to Seneca, is a subject by itself, complicated by scantiness of evidence—interesting on other grounds, no doubt, but not for any direct bearing on the drama of the fifth century, for it has none.

For a raised stage beside or in the round dancing-plot of the chorus in that century there is no evidence; and modern experiment shows that under the conditions it was not needed. When the background was a palace or a temple, as was more often the case in the latter half of the century, an actor would frequently have occasion to speak from the steps or the stylobate above them. The words of King Oedipus at his opening speech and later would be more effective from that natural position. The rough ground on the shore where the scene of "Philoktetes" is laid offered similar opportunities. No one has claimed that such opportunities for special effect were not used. All agree, however, that there can have been no barrier to prevent the free mingling of chorus and actors, who sometimes enter and go out together and speak in close contact with each other. Fifteen or twenty people on the same level, properly disposed and frequently changing positions, would not, in a circle over sixty-five feet in diameter, hide one another from even the front row of the audience, whose eyes were nearly on a level with the actors' shoulders, while each succeeding row was higher. On our own stages we do not object to an occasional and momentary obscuration of a speaker by other actors.

Plato remarks (Crat. 425 d) that "tragic poets, when they get into a difficulty, have recourse to the machine, suspending gods in the air"; and Aristotle (Poet. 1454b 1), that "the issue of a plot ought to arise out of the plot itself and not, as in the 'Medea,' be forced from a machine." Both criticisms refer to the same point and the "Medea" shows us just what it is. By some machine Medea with the corpses of her children is held suspended above the house in a miraculous conveyance sent by Helios, and is carried off to safety in this car. At the end of several Euripidean plays, and of the "Philoktetes" of Sophokles, a god appears and "from the machine" unties the dramatic knot, usually directing the establishment of some commemorative rite. So "a god from the machine," *deus ex machina,* became proverbial for such an extraneous solution of a difficulty. It is hard to imagine precisely how the contrivance worked—in broad sunshine, be it remembered, not in the modern theater, where any degree of partial obscurity is easily managed. The god, or the miraculous car, is supposed to float or fly down from heaven or from far away; the language of the bystanders or of the god indicates that the spectators are to take it so. But whatever the machine was, it could work no such miracle as that. It was in or back of the *skēnē,* and must visibly have swung the suspended object from a lower level up to the higher from which it might descend.   Aeschylus made heavy demands on this or some like contrivance. In the "Prometheus" the chorus of ocean nymphs are floated in, all twelve seated in a winged car, in which they remain to the end of the *epeisodion,* when at the request of Prometheus they descend to the ground. Okeanos appears, and later goes off again, flying through the air on a huge winged but four-legged bird, which he guides, as he says, "by his will." Before these our imagination is equally at a loss; we may be tempted to join Aristophanes in ridiculing them. Yet there is no question that Aeschylus was a great dramatist and knew his audience.

We learn also from Aristotle that Sophokles introduced *skēnē-painting* (σκηνηγραφία), and we should much like to know just what that was. Scene-painting in the modern sense is hardly possible—landscape or buildings painted in perspective on a flat surface to look like reality. The eye must, in outdoor drama, constantly see such painting and the real landscape and real buildings together. The incongruity, the difference in color scale, would seem to be fatal to the painted scene. The only explanation I can conceive as probable is that, in setting a background, the "properties" that were necessary to suggest the scene of the action, Sophokles made a more extended or more skillful use of painting such "properties"—rocks or other constructions of wood or whatever light material. In any case, where a character gives a full description of a scene, or hails a distant beacon-fire, or mentions the song of birds as indicating dawn, we are to take his words as telling us what we are to imagine, not what we see. When Prometheus, in the final anapests that take the place of the ordinary *exodion,* describes the heaving of the earth, the roar of thunder, the lightning, the clouds of dust raised by opposing winds, he is telling what the spectators are to supply to the picture as the *skēnē* collapses and he and the chorus are plunged below.

I would extend this principle rather far. At least it is better to confess ignorance than to claim a knowledge that no one can have. We may be sure that the Athenians who first saw the "Prometheus" were as ready as Englishmen of Elizabeth's day to supplement a meager setting with the imagination that the great poetry stimulated. In every great period of the drama it is always the spectator who creates, at the call of genius and on the bare suggestion of his material setting, the living vision. Only when drama is become decadent and artificial and needs cherishing is great attention bestowed on perfecting mere accessories. Just how gods and winged cars and four-legged birds and chariots of the sun were suspended in the air we cannot say. For revival before a modern audience, such demands on a machinery so unlike ours are a handicap; we can bring to a "god from the machine" no ghost of the Greek faith to carry imagination beyond what seems to us crude and wooden. But Athenian audiences were ready to ignore what it was necessary to ignore and to see what the poet assumes they are seeing, however inadequate the means of producing what we should call illusion. Nor is it likely, skillful and artistic as the Athenians were, that the mechanical devices with which they were content, if we could reproduce them in the same conditions, would seem to us inadequate. We, too, if with the needful command of the language we could look down with them on the "Prometheus" or the "Medea," should be well content.

VI. STORY AND PLOT

I

"THE first essential, as it were the life and soul of tragedy," says Aristotle,* "is the story or plot; the characters come second." At first blush this doctrine seems to collide with the fact that among people of literary cultivation the interest in character-drawing is keener and more general than the interest in plot. But we have to remember that people of literary cultivation are but a fraction of the public to whom the drama—and drama of the highest type—has always made its appeal, and that a play is not primarily literature. The best plays have always been literature as well, but there have been many excellent plays that were not. But even for those who take more interest in character than in plot the doctrine is true. Some kind of coherent plot is the indispensable framework in which character can be displayed, although it is also true that a poor plot may display an excellent character or two and that a play with an excellent plot may be poor in character-drawing. ⟩Historically, in Greece and in England, plot came first and character-drawing second; and that relation is logical.

But we have to translate Aristotle's one word μῦθος by two, story and plot; and perhaps another metaphor, no less trite than Aristotle's "life and soul of tragedy," is

*"Poetics," 1450 a 38.

119

more accurate in suggestion. Both story and plot, like
μῦθος, mean the combination of incidents; but story is
rather the narrative form, the tale as one would tell it
less elaborately. Plot as a technical term is the story as
reshaped for a drama, adapted to effective presentation
under the conditions of the theater. For a novel or a
romance or a narrative poem the same story would
require a different reshaping adapted to the conditions
and the unlike tone of those types of narrative; each
resulting form might properly be called a plot. Theo-
retically the form adapted to a lyric poem would be yet
another plot constructed on the same story; only we do
not so often, though we may perfectly well, speak of the
plot of a lyric. Then, too, there is the common meaning
of a secret plan or intrigue with some hostile aim, and in
closer conformity with that sense the corresponding
French term connotes more deft interweaving of incidents, more nearly what we mean by intrigue, than plot
as a technical dramatic term connotes in English.

For our phrase "first essential" Aristotle's word is
archē (ἀρχή), a more pregnant word, signifying the
starting-point, the first principle, that out of which the
whole grows. For Greek tragedy at least this is quite
true of the combination of incidents, and is no mere
figure. Even Sophokles, an unsurpassed master in the
portrayal of character, did not, as some modern dramatists and novelists have done, start with a character and
devise a plot to portray him. The myth was first. But
instead of calling the story the life and soul (Aristotle's
word is ψυχή, psȳchē) perhaps we should rather think of
it as the skeleton. It is the firm frame on which grows
the flesh, and within which mysteriously dwells the soul.
The skeleton must be well hidden with living tissue, or

the whole will not be attractive. But there can be no beauty of the human figure without a well-compacted skeleton underneath.

What kind of myths did the tragic poet select for his plots? Why among our surviving tragedies is only one, and that no masterpiece, based on an incident from the Iliad or Odyssey? What was it that made certain stories good material for tragedy, other stories less good, and others not good at all? To put the same question in a modern form, Why can some novels be dramatized into successful plays while others cannot? The difference must be somehow in the nature of the incidents and of their relation to dramatic conditions.

II

It is old doctrine, so old that it may be called traditional—not explicit in Aristotle, but often repeated since Voltaire and Schlegel and Goethe's "Wilhelm Meister"—that the heart of a tragedy is a conflict, a struggle in which one with whom we sympathize fails. The power of tragedy arises from the fact that so much of mature life consists of struggle that fails—or seems to fail, attaining only through great suffering or by death. The tragic poet brings before us a typical conflict of that nature, some form of the unending endeavor, an effort leading not to happiness but to catastrophe—condensed, however, so that in two or three hours the great business of a life, or of several lives intertwined, is concluded. And not only concluded, but clarified, explained, in a manner justified, and related to the order of the world, which we must call a moral order; else his work could not be a

121

re-presentation of life in beauty. A tale of woe powerfully presented, but not so clarified and so related to the
whole, would be merely painful, darkening our vision,
impelling to revolt against life. We have no use for
such a presentation of life; we have great need of that
kind of idealization of life which clarifies and explains
sorrow, which reveals a meaning in failure, leads one
to believe that it is not the wanton infliction of cruelty nor a blow of chance, but is reasonable, and that
in some way suffering restores, or tends to restore,
one's relation to the moral kosmos. That is why a
tragic poet is bound to be in some sense a moralist.
Not in any cheap sense; not an exhorter, but an artist
who sees, and presents, with fidelity to life, the real relations between action and suffering, so that we also see
them. Only so can we go from the spectacle not
disheartened but tranquilized and stronger.

The traditional doctrine of the tragic conflict has been
developed and put in a more penetrating and more com-
prehensive way by Ferdinand Brunetière.* Since the
mainspring of all striving is the will, he rightly takes that
as the basis of the "Law of the Drama." The starting-
point of plays of every kind, tragedies, melodrama, comedies, farces, is the same. "Some one central character
wants something; and this exercise of volition is the
mainspring of the action. . . . In every successful play,
ancient or modern, we shall find this clash of contending
desires, the assertion of the human will against strenuous

*Most readily accessible in F. Brunetière, "The Law of the
Drama," with an introduction by Henry Arthur Jones, N. Y.,
1914; publications of Columbia University Dramatic Museum;
and in Brander Matthews, "A Study of the Drama," Chap. V,
from which I summarize and quote.

opposition of one kind or another. . . . This is what differentiates drama from the novel." Beaumarchais' Figaro has a will of his own, and fights; the hero of Le Sage drifts through life along the line of least resistance. "Figaro acts; Gil Blas is acted upon. The play of Beaumarchais may be made into an acceptable novel; but the novel of Le Sage cannot be made into an acceptable play." By the nature of the opposition, combined with the nature of the hero who wills, we may differentiate the several dramatic species. "If the obstacles against which the will of the hero has to contend are insurmountable . . . then there is tragedy, and the end of the struggle is likely to be death. But if these obstacles are not absolutely insurmountable, being only social conventions and human prejudices, then the hero has a possible chance to attain his desire—and in this case we have the serious drama without an inevitably fatal ending. Change the obstacle a little, equalize the conditions of the struggle, set two human wills in opposition [provided, we must add, the characters be not too serious and too strong] and we have comedy. And if the obstacle be of a still lower order, merely an absurdity of custom, for instance, we find ourselves in farce."

This orthodox view in its most persuasive form is vigorously attacked by Mr. William Archer.* He maintains that, while Brunetière's law "describes the matter of a good many dramas, it does not lay down any true differentia—any characteristic common to all drama, and possessed by no other form of fiction." The last phrase, it may be said at once, implies a demand that is altogether unfair. Conflict of will against obstacles is too pervading an element in life to be excluded from any

* "Play-Making," Chap. III.

branch of letters. Of course such conflicts are the core
of many a novel; among these are the novels that might
be successfully dramatized, as Brunetière says. But the
narrative form and the dramatic are different enough,
though both treat the same story. Mr. Archer has a fling
about "Robinson Crusoe," as a classic tale of struggle
against obstacles, in which no one could see a drama; but
this is probably a bluff. He sees plainly why there is no
drama to be got out of it; the obstacles of Crusoe, shipwrecked alone, cannot be presented through people personating them, and without this personation you can't
have a play, though you can have a classic tale. If
Brunetière's law holds good for all highly successful
plays, particularly for those that keep the stage in successive generations; if it explains the relative ill success
of those plays that do not so hold, even though temporary
influences or the author's cleverness may give them a
sufficient run to remove them from the list of flat failures,
then the law is all that anyone has claimed for it, and
playwrights disregard it at their peril—under peril, at
least, of falling short of high success. The dramatic
form, presenting a story in action through people personating the characters, is in itself attractive and easy to
follow. It has been used effectively by the Church for
moral and religious instruction, chronicles have been
dramatized and the result listened to with pleasure,
M. Eugène Brieux employs it for social propaganda, some
"problem plays" have had fair runs, historical pageants
are a sort of play, and have a legitimate field, though it
differs radically from that of the theater.* Then there
are lyric dramas, poems dramatic in form but never in-

*"Community Drama and Pageantry," by Mary Porter Beegle
and Jack Randall Crawford, pp. 12 f.

tended to be acted—like Shelley's "Prometheus Un-bound" or Moody's "Masque of Judgment"—an entirely legitimate type of poem, not to be judged as plays. In many of these kinds of plays there is no such dominant conflict of will as Brunetière's law postulates. But Brunetière is justified if we find that plays which lack such a dominant trait in the plot are unsuccessful as acting plays, or are distinctly less successful or less lasting. That, I think, is clearly the case. Very recent plays, however, must be left mostly out of the discussion in considering permanent principles, because precisely in these the temporary influences that suffice to secure a fair run, though the play is never revived later, are most in evidence and may easily affect critics as well as public.

But when Mr. Archer goes on to cite the "Agamemnon" as a great tragedy in which "there is no more struggle than there is between the spider and the fly who walks into his net," we must emphatically demur. His own illustration of spider and fly may be turned against him; the spider wills and plots. Klytaimestra determines to kill her husband, the successful general of the Greek army, on the day of his return. This was no easy enterprise; it required a carefully laid plot, well hidden till it has succeeded. The spectators are made aware of it from the beginning; knowing the outcome it is easy for us to interpret hints and forebodings that to people in the play are too vague to put them actively on guard. The watch-man on the roof scents danger in the house and longs to see his master safe at home; the chorus sing of foreboding and give reasons for it which they feel are not enough to explain it; Klytaimestra's excessive protestations of loyalty and love and her wheedling the king to enter the house treading on purple are part of her scheme to put him off his guard, and are ample hints to a Greek audience that she is his bitter enemy and his destruction is at hand; Cassandra's second sight makes all clear, only to the chorus the crime is simply too monstrous for belief; while it was part of Cassandra's fate never to be believed until too late. If this does not point to a powerful will working against obstacles to a fatal success, where shall we find one? That Agamemnon and his natural defenders do not discover the plot in time is due to the very boldness of the plotter, which aids her concealment. Agamemnon is unaware of danger and therefore does not personally struggle; for the cunning plotter the danger was precisely that he might discover and frustrate her scheme.

Mr. Archer's mistake is twofold. First—and this error runs through nearly all of his discussion—he has assumed that Brunetière's law postulates always a human will opposing the hero's will. This is clearly a misreading of Brunetière, who, as Mr. Archer himself quotes him, mentions, under the opposing obstacles against which one struggles, fatality, social laws, even oneself—the ambitions, interests, prejudices, folly, malevolence of those about one. Forgetting part of his own quotation, Mr. Archer leaves out of account the commonest and most serious obstacles against which the human will struggles, such as the force of heredity and the inner moral sense; he narrows the law to a formula which no one—certainly no great critic—has thought of setting up as a law.

He seems also to forget for the moment the well-known principle of method in Greek tragedy, to use directly for the play only the last stage of the action, introducing what precedes by incidental narrative—the method familiar to us in Shakspere's "Tempest." This second mistake

126

is more plainly revealed by his remarks about the "Oedipus." "Oedipus in fact," he says, "does not struggle at all. His struggles, in so far as that word can be applied to his misguided efforts to escape from the toils of fate, are all things of the past; in the actual course of the tragedy he simply writhes under one revelation after another of bygone error and unwitting crime. It would be a mere play upon words to recognize as a dramatic 'struggle' the writhing of a worm on a hook."

It is disheartening that so good a critic as Mr. Archer should so misread the "Oedipus." As we shall return to the play, we will now speak only of the point where he goes wrong. It is true that the action of the play, in the usual Greek manner, covers directly only the final day of revelation that transforms the fatherly king into a blind beggar. But the dramatist so manages that revelation as to bring into it the king's whole life. His suffering under the revelation is one phase of the portrayal of a fine and strong character; it is at once anguish at the pollution and curse which he has brought upon himself, and poignant recognition that the great struggle of his mature life has failed. Not a worm writhing upon a hook; but a noble and affectionate soul passionately willing to avoid doing the deeds which it had been predicted he would do, sacrificing home and a throne to that end, yet through a flaw in his own character doing them—that is the real subject of the tragedy. When the play opens, the deeds are already done. His passionate resistance to the conviction slowly forced upon him that he has committed the crimes foretold is the natural continuation of his long and passionate will to avoid them. He is struggling in vain to escape the consequences of his own acts; that is why so many have thought of him as struggling against fate.

There is indeed no fate more inexorable than one's own past; but between that fate and fate conceived as a malign superhuman power there is all the difference one can imagine. The conviction of his pollution once forced into the soul of Oedipus, there remains only his willful self-blinding, and the suffering that is to endure till his death.

III

It would lead too far from our subject to follow Mr. Archer into the modern plays which he cites in endeavoring to show the inadequacy of Brunetière's law. Much of his discussion of them is invalidated by his erroneous narrowing of the principle. But he sets up in its place a formula which he thinks more adequate. We have still to examine that. "What, then," he says, "is the essence of drama, if conflict be not it? What is the common quality of themes, scenes, incidents, which we recognize as specifically dramatic? Perhaps we shall scarcely come nearer to a helpful definition than if we say that the essence of drama is *crisis*. A play is a more or less rapidly developing crisis in destiny or circumstances, and a dramatic scene is a crisis within a crisis, clearly furthering the ultimate event. The drama may be called the art of crises, as fiction is the art of gradual developments. It is the slowness of its processes which differentiates the typical novel from the typical play."

Here then is the law of the drama as Mr. Archer would state it. I think his formulation describes very well one aspect of the art, which we have found to be very complex. It is true that drama deals preeminently with crises, and Greek tragedy notably so. A trilogy might present three points of culmination, separated by months or years, like three acts divided by the indefinite interval marked by the fall of a curtain; but each single play must be a unit, presenting one major crisis toward which everything converged. The "Oedipus" is a typical example. The presence of the chorus would alone compel such concentration. By the convention of a double standard of time much more than two hours could be included, in the extreme cases of the "Agamemnon" and the "Eumenides" several days. But not often did the dramatic time cover more than one day; and always, even in the "Agamemnon," whose dramatic time is longest of all, we still have but one main event, the murder of the king by his wife on his return.

But if we take Mr. Archer's formula as a definition, the same objections hold that he has brought against Brunetière. "It does not lay down any true differentia—any characteristic common to all drama, and possessed by no other form of fiction." Does not the form we know as the short story, and many a poem as well, deal with a crisis as truly as the drama? What differentiates drama is the combination of suitable story, by whatever formula we describe suitability, with presentation through action, by people personating the characters. Both elements must be included in any tolerable definition, as Aristotle saw. I do not press the objection, however; I only call attention to the weakness of it as pressed by Mr. Archer against Brunetière.

And finally, does not his word crisis come around in the end to pretty nearly the same thing as the old phrase, conflict of will against obstacles? A crisis is a decision, or a time of decision, necessarily a brief time, at the culmination of a course of events. I am not urging an etymology, but trying to arrive at the essence. Many a real crisis, as Mr. Archer admits in his farther discussion, is not dramatic and cannot be made so without an added element that is essential. "Manifestly," he says (p. 38), "it is not every crisis that is dramatic. A serious illness, a law-suit, a bankruptcy, even an ordinary prosaic marriage, may be a crisis in a man's life, without being necessarily, or even probably, material for drama." Here is frank admission of a flaw in his formula. In fact, ten pages later he protests against any attempt to define too closely, as tending to limit art by a code of rules; and he grants that "in a certain type of play—the broad picture of a social phenomenon or environment—it is preferable that no attempt should be made to depict a marked crisis. There should be just enough story to afford a plausible excuse for raising and lowering the curtain."

Perhaps we should not quarrel with one who so freely yields his own position; but what we are trying to do is to find by analysis of drama what kind of stories is best adapted to it, that we may better understand Greek practice. Keeping that end in view, we may follow Mr. Archer a little farther. He goes on to distinguish a dramatic from a non-dramatic crisis by the fact that generally the former "develops, or can be made naturally to develop, through a series of minor crises, involving more or less emotional excitement, and, if possible, the vivid manifestation of character." He proceeds to illustrate by the case of bankruptcy, which is a crisis that is often not dramatic, but sometimes is so. But in enforcing his thesis, development through minor crises, he emphasizes repeatedly the element of personality, without noticing that the point really lies there. To show what I mean, take another type of crisis, say a period of special danger or difficulty in an engineering work, like driving a tunnel. In itself this contains nothing dramatic; to make it so it must be connected with a personality in whom an audience have previously become interested—in fact, with a hero whose will and effort against obstacles toward an end have already won our sympathy. Suppose the hero is a young engineer of genius, whose struggle for fame and fortune and a sweetheart we admire, and his tunnel encounters an unforeseen difficulty that may wreck both it and his fortunes, which the success of the tunnel will secure. Then the crisis becomes dramatic. What makes it so will be the engineer and his efforts against obstacles, not the tunnel itself or the crisis itself. The essence will still be a struggle of will.

In short, what Mr. Archer really wanted to do in urging his theory of crises was to emphasize the rapidity of action, what he calls "the crisp and staccato, as opposed to the smooth and legato, method." That is a point well worth emphasizing. One fixed condition of dramatic art, as we conceive it in the Occident, is the brevity and condensation, as compared with the novel, whose special field is, as he says, the gradual development of action and character. The playwright's opportunity to display development is very limited, even under modern conventions connected with the use of the curtain. The Greek tragedian's opportunity was far more limited. That and other conditions restrict closely the range of stories available for the dramatist; his compensation is the superior vividness and force with which the crises of the struggle of will in many forms can be driven home through the cooperation of eye and ear.

IV

From still another side Gustav Freytag* has given a definition of the dramatic, which we need to combine with the aspects already considered. Although drama presents a story through action, and although struggle against obstacles, especially the crises of such effort, is the appropriate material for dramatic plots, it still is true that action itself, in the primary sense, is not dramatic. A horse-race, a bull-fight, a gladiatorial contest, a battle, is not dramatic; neither is a pantomime, properly speaking. On the other hand, two people seated at table and talking rather quietly with a minimum of gesticulation may constitute a highly dramatic scene. Not action, says Freytag, but *das Werden einer Aktion und ihre Folgen auf das Gemüth*—the origin and growth of an action and its effects on the soul—this is the true dramatic material. The motives that impel to action, human emotions, especially the elemental emotions that stir all of us, and the consequences of action on human souls—this is what interests us all. The story to be dramatized must be one in which those parts can be adequately presented. The dramatic plot must take the mere succession of incidents, as they might be told in a dry chronicle, and must show how the incidents arise naturally from the circumstances and the feelings of men and women, and how men and women we have become interested in are affected by the actions thus arising. That nexus, of motives and consequences, is what makes the play a unit. Whatever has no place in that sort of nexus must be omitted.

*"Technik des Dramas," p. 18.

STORY AND PLOT

This aspect of the dramatic is not inconsistent with the other aspects of it which we have been considering; it supplements them. Recall to mind the composition of a theatrical audience, ancient or modern. A dialogue of Plato, as Mr. Archer remarks, though delivered by the best actors, would interest very few; it is dramatic in form, often paints character admirably, depicts a struggle; but its plot is a combination of intellectual processes, with a minimum of emotion, and that of a quiet kind. A few thoughtful people in every generation for over two thousand years have admired and cherished and learned from Plato's dialogues; but no general audience could endure them. On the other hand a fight, a trial of strength, in its infinite variety of forms, is universally interesting. A dog-fight in the street draws a crowd; two schoolboys settling the question which is the stronger make a delightful spectacle to most of their fellows; it is no wonder that cock-fights are popular where the taste is allowed to develop, as it was in old Athens. Among ourselves, for adults of moderate cultivation, contests of mere physical strength do not attract so much; the painful side of a "prize-fight" prevents most people from enjoying the exhibition of skill in which people of tougher nerve find intense pleasure. But remove repellent features; let the struggle of will against obstacles, the heart of every contest, present itself in a form that we recognize as typical of civilized life, representative of what we are all engaged in; let it be a struggle that can be adequately presented in a succession of crises culminating in a superlative crisis, though it end in failure; let the decisive actions all appear, in accord with life's reality, as growing naturally out of emotions that have their roots in character and circumstances; let every decisive act and the resultant suffering reveal its natural effects on human souls of some magnitude: this will be a theme for serious drama, perhaps for tragedy, which will deeply interest a miscellaneous audience, because it appeals to universal humanity. This is the kind of story that the Greek tragedians drew from their myths, to develop from them the plots of their masterpieces.

V

One other question remains before we take up individual plots and study in detail their relation to the story in its narrative form. It is a question that concerns the nature of the obstacle. It is old doctrine, in recent years growing weaker, that Greek tragedy is distinctively a tragedy of fate; that the obstacle against which the hero most often struggles in vain, defeated from the beginning, is Destiny, a superhuman allotment whereby, from birth, its victim is predestined to ruin. We need not stop to trace the history of the dogma; but will cite some recent allusions to it. Mr. Archer, referring (p. 288) to the "Oedipus" again, speaks of it as "founded on an absolutely astounding series of coincidences"; which nevertheless he excuses by adding, "but here the conception of fate comes in, and we vaguely figure to ourselves some malignant power deliberately pulling the strings which guide its puppets into such abhorrent tangles." Similarly Professor Matthews* finds in "Oedipus" and in Ibsen's "Ghosts" the same massive simplicity, "the Greek showing how fate is inevitable and the Scandinavian seeking to prove that heredity is inexorable." Finally the late Emile Faguet, in an essay devoted to minimizing and explaining away the dogma, still finds it exemplified in the

*"Study of the Drama," p. 7.

"Persians" of Aeschylus. Here are three distinguished critics, American, English, and French two accepting the tradition without demur, and the last-named, while rejecting it elsewhere, still unable to escape the power of fate in one exceptional play. The "Oedipus" is most often taken as an unquestioned example of the dogma. I have already said that I dissent from this view; but we shall have to make a detour and come at the matter from another side.

Start from our own experience; what are our own obstacles? Most of them can be classified readily. The will of other people, who have at one point or another power to resist us or to enforce their wishes; especially the combination of many wills, though it rest on nothing better than ignorance, prejudice, habits, social customs; our own passions or our inner sense of the rights and feelings of others, of the requirements of honor, of obligations intangible but imperative; poverty, which is relative and may constrain a millionaire or a nation no less than a day laborer; luck—the accidents which we thus lump together because finite intelligence cannot calculate or foresee them; the force of heredity and the constitution of the universe, in which our place was determined without consulting us and before we were born; such a rough classification will serve, though none can be exact, no class exclusive, so infinite are the permutations and combinations of life. The determinists affirm that our consciousness of freedom of choice is a delusion—that our choices are all alike reactions to forces outside the soul. Sincerely held and consistently applied, this theory would of course annihilate all distinction between right and wrong, all motives for choice; reducing men to machines it would reduce philosophy to pure fatalism. But the determinists are unphilosophical enough to do just what the rest of us do—choose and struggle instinctively, feeling that the limitation of our power to attain the ends we judge good can be learned only by trial, and that the experiment is worth making. That there are limits we know very well; we make no effort for what we see beforehand is clearly unattainable; we struggle for what we judge may, if we strive hard enough, be within reach. And when we fail, we are prone to lay the blame on something beyond our control rather than on ourselves. Bad luck is an everyday recourse; it sums up vaguely the nonmalevolent forces that have defeated our efforts, usually efforts on which no great consequences depended. Most of us no longer attribute things to the Devil, except humorously. Religious natures may accept adversity or failure as the will of God; the more analytical seek an explanation in the ignorance or the ill will of human opponents. But all who think are forced to recognize in the background, as setting strict bounds that we struggle in vain to pass, the constitution of things. We sometimes call this fate, though the word is not so current as formerly; the Greeks called it *moira* (μοῖρα) or *peprōmenē* (πεπρωμένη) *allotment;* in moments of wise humility we use the old term God or Providence, thereby accepting a religious attitude toward the Power not ourselves.

Now the Greek attitude in this matter was essentially ours, with like variations according to temperament and historical period, but expressed with considerable difference of phraseology, largely growing out of their polytheism and the habit of personifying as divinities forces of nature, and even abstractions. Their word for luck, *Tuchē* (τύχη, Latin, *Fortuna*), meant a divinity, to be entreated; sometimes it approached our idea of Providence; circumstances might point to a particular god, as Apollo or Poseidon, as the cause of ill success; *daimon* (δαίμων) was an old word for divinity with an implication of mystery, of motives for favor or disfavor beyond our ken, of an influence to be propitiated if possible. And back of them all was Fate, Moira, personified, but nowhere strictly defined. The whole universe and all its parts were divine; a phrase like our "constitution of things" is the product of modern analysis, and had no place in popular Greek thought.

Herodotus was rather inclined to explain personal catastrophe by the phrase, "it was fated (ἔδει)" that the person should do so and so; Thucydides has none of this; only once—as if to emphasize his superiority to superstition—he mentions a popular belief, based on old oracles, that a certain event was fated. No doubt such popular beliefs were widely held, but there is surprisingly little of them in tragedy. The chorus of the "Persians" declare that divine allotment (θεόθεν μοῖρα) gave their race power on land, but they have impiously transcended those limits and ventured upon the sea; hence the present anxiety and foreboding. Can God's punishment of pride and arrogance be called an action of malign fate? There is no other in the play. In "Seven against Thebes" the messenger attributes to Apollo, "accomplishing the unhappy counsels of Laïos," the chance that brought the two brothers to the fatal encounter at the same gate; Elektra exclaims that when gods give evils none can escape; and that her father's curses are fulfilment-bringing. But the dramatist makes it quite clear that the young king's own choice is what really fulfils the curse. So Oedipus, when the blow has fallen, exclaims upon the unnamed *daimon* and Apollo as accomplishing his ruin,

137

at the very moment when he is admitting that his own hand blinded him. It was not fate or a vague malignant power, but his own lack of self-control under great provocation that fulfilled the old prediction. The "Oedipus" does, however, lend more color to the dogma than any other tragedy, because, as was said, all is in fact done before the play opens. For years no escape has been possible, though it was possible once. In "Oedipus at Kolonos" Antigone plainly points out to Polyneikes that he can defeat his father's curse, but that against warning he is choosing the course that will lead surely to its accomplishment. In "Antigone" again a messenger makes the commonplace observation that "Fortune exalts and Fortune brings low." Kreon recognizes that God hath smitten him, the chorus affirms that for mortals there is no escape from the event that is fated. Meantime the course of the play has shown that human passion, folly, and obstinate disregard of religious law are what have brought on ruin, not Fate and Fortune or any mysterious *daimon*.

We need not go through Euripides in search of tragic catastrophes brought on by Fate. There are gods beneficent and friendly and gods vindictive, whose influence on events is part of the plot; there are references of the familiar kind to Fate and to a hostile *daimon*, as in the older tragedians. The choice of the particular phrase indicates the mood of the sufferer, who inclines, like ourselves, to place blame elsewhere than on himself. But of the Fate that has held a conspicuous place in dramatic criticism—or rather in modern explanation of differences between modern and ancient tragedy—there is no more to be found than in "Othello" or "Macbeth." I wish this particular ghost might be finally laid.

VII. STORIES AND PLOTS

I

IF our study of the relation between story and plot has been somewhat abstract, perhaps principles will be rendered plainer by concrete examples. As we have seen, suitable stories were chosen out of old myths, for one extant tragedy out of recent history. The difference between myth and history, which we make much of, was hardly felt in the first half of the fifth century; were not gods and demigods and heroes as real as Athenian kings? Were there not living descendants from both, familiar figures in Athens? The story had to be one to which a chorus could be fitted, and for fullest success one at the heart of which lay a struggle of some magnitude, a story typical of a serious side of life if not actually ending in catastrophe and death. Such a story must be recast from any previous epic or lyric form, both of which many available stories had already received, and must be adapted to the conditions of dramatic art, within the limits of the Athenian type of tragedy, limits flexible yet not fluid, conforming to tradition and to a popular expectation which had a core of conservative religious feeling.

And perhaps this is the place to answer the question before raised, why the stories were not taken, or were so rarely taken, from the Iliad and Odyssey, but rather from the less known epics—less known to us because they have perished, and less admired in antiquity. Probably—for only a probable answer can be given—because the two great epics were so well told and so universally admired. The tragic poet needed a good deal of freedom in the details; fitting to dramatic form with a chorus involved not a few changes. The characters themselves could be transferred without difficulty and with a certain advantage; they were familiar to everyone. An Odysseus, however the setting might vary, could be still a man of many wiles, Agamemnon a king with royal virtues and failings, and so with the rest. Tragedy portrayed several varieties of the general type of the epic Odysseus. But if a story was told in detail in the Iliad or Odyssey, it was perilous to set up a new version that must inevitably enter into rivalry with that of a master hand—with a version well known and almost consecrated. The tragic poet would subject himself to a competition too dangerous. In a lesser degree there is a like risk, not quite prohibitory, in making a play from a favorite novel of Thackeray. In like manner, too, after Aeschylus had exhibited his "Agamemnon" it was perilous to offer another "Agamemnon"; if anyone did so, the piece died very soon. The second play of the Aeschylean trilogy was less great; Sophokles could, from another angle entirely, make an "Elektra" that retold the same story—made essentially different, however, by the new angle of approach; and his "Elektra" is better than the "Libation-pourers." So Shakspere could remake an old play into a far better one; but no one would attempt a better "Macbeth" than his. And when Euripides tried another "Elektra" he was ill advised. His new angle of approach was not different enough; his "Elektra" has merits, if the rivalry with the greater play were not so severe. A Greek tragedian found it more promising to get plots from sources that permitted greater freedom and offered a better hope of surpassing the original.

II

To take first our one exception to the rule as to the source of plots, how does Aeschylus make from a Greek victory the plot for a tragedy? The historical facts are familiar. Xerxes gathered a vast army and fleet to subjugate Greece. He was defeated at Salamis, and the next year at Plataea. Henceforth Greece was free from the Persian danger. In these events the Athenians took a prominent part, and had good reason to be proud of it ever after. Herodotus made this war the climax of his great history; there is in it much of the epic quality. Single incidents inspired many poems or passages in longer poems, some of which have come down to us. But how shall such a story be compressed into a play? Above all, how can a great national triumph be made the subject of a tragedy? Aeschylus had fought at Salamis, as had many among his audience; when the play was brought out, Plataea was but seven years past. How could the poet not only himself take the true perspective of such an event, but so idealize it in the sense before defined, and so compress and develop it into a tragic plot, as to make this the one great tragedy of the world on a recent historical occurrence? Adorning, setting forth in orderly beauty, a most excellent deed (κοσμήσας ἔργον ἄριστον)—this is the phrase by which Aristophanes in the "Frogs" makes Aeschylus himself describe his work.

First, he transfers the scene to the Persian court, following in this Phrynichos, who had already exhibited a tragedy on the same subject—a play that was successful but was overshadowed by this. All the characters are Persians; the chorus are the faithful counselors (πιστοί) appointed by Xerxes before his departure. These are wholly the invention of the poet. This device not only meets in a natural way the requirement of a chorus; still more, it sets their points of view in the foreground. For them the event was tragic; and success in the drama requires first of all that the audience be brought into sympathy with the characters. If we cannot take, for the time being, the point of view of the men and women who act and suffer before us, we are bored and withdraw. If many do that, the play is a failure. At the outset, or very soon, we find ourselves in sympathy with *these* Persians, whose anxiety for their king and his army soon turns to sorrow at a national disaster, though it may be triumph for us as Athenians.

For, secondly, while the chorus are nominally Persians, the poet makes them Aeschylean Persians—a folk that never was on sea or land. In their persons, and in the other characters whom he calls Persians, he puts underneath the whole story an Aeschylean religious basis. That basis is, to be sure, at bottom identical with a large element in all highly developed religions, including Christianity; yet it is clothed in peculiarly Aeschylean terms. These people are Persian enough to feel Salamis as a national disaster; they are not Persian enough to prevent their winning the dramatic sympathy of Athenians. The entering song of the chorus begins the play; there is no preceding *prologos*. Their song, after the entering recitative, paints their anxiety about the absent king and army, though they cling to the belief that the army is invincible. Very soon comes the explanation of their anxiety: "From

God was the allotment established of old that on the Persians enjoined the waging of wars on land alone; yet they have dared to attempt the sea, transgressing divinely appointed bounds; what mortal (they sing) shall escape the wily deceit of God?" This assumed ordinance of heaven—which is really not in conflict with history—was of course one likely to gratify Athenian pride and not likely to stir hostility toward men who acknowledged so flattering a doctrine. There is nothing here that can properly be called fate. The doctrine of bounds not to be transgressed was embedded deep in Greek morality, and this application of it, while it moved their pride, moved also a religious feeling that warned against arrogance and reminded them that God, not their own might, had given them the victory. The struggle is made not simply one between Persians and Greeks, but still more one between Persians and God, in whose hand the Greeks had been but instruments.

Finally, Atossa and the ghost of Darius, the chief characters, are as characters wholly ideal; their names are historical and they were the father and mother of Xerxes, but the real persons were not what the poet makes them. The account of the battle of Salamis apparently is accurate; the poet was an eyewitness of it, and there was no dramatic reason for departing from the facts, which were highly dramatic in themselves and were fresh in the memory of the Athenians. The battle of Plataea also, which Darius predicts, and in a general way the disasters of the retreat, were historical; the rest is the poet's invention. All speak Greek of course and utter Aeschylean ideas of Greek gods and Greek religion. For the tragedy, the story is like this.

An ideal folk, of Oriental type and called by the Persian name, yet so Greek that an Athenian audience can understand and to a certain extent sympathize with them, proudly attempting to overstep the limits prescribed by divine ordinance, have set out by sea as well as by land under the lead of their king to subjugate the Greeks. The wise and faithful at court feel their exultant sense of Persian power shaken by religious fear of the outcome. The revered queen-mother Atossa, moved by foreboding dreams, meets with the council of the realm that they may advise her. While they are conferring upon the fearful signs, a messenger from the army comes, who reports in stirring narrative the catastrophe of Salamis. They now recognize the sin and error into which Xerxes has led the nation. To obtain help in their need they call up from his tomb the shade of the great Darius, father of Xerxes. He enforces the moral lesson, foretells farther disaster, and returns to the realm of the dead. Xerxes then appears, in deep despair, leading a few survivors, and he and the chorus lament together, with Oriental extrava-gance, yet not too far beyond the style that is customary in Greek tragedy.

Here is a version that makes a true tragedy, of uni-versal import, yet with an undertone of satisfaction to a Greek audience that gives it a unique cast. To meet the conditions of the theater the location, as we saw, is some-what floating. It is somewhere at the unnamed Persian capital, not rigidly fixed nor yet definitely shifted, yet somehow assumed to be now before, rather than in, a council chamber, now at the tomb of Darius, and now at such a place that the returning king meets them before anyone else. The time is the day of Xerxes' return; the coincidence of the coming of a messenger just before his arrival, combined with narration of the past, partly lyric narration, and supernatural prediction of the future, enables the dramatist to condense a long train of events into a two-hour play.

Those who object that this tragedy contains no action forget what dramatic action is. It is not bodily movement, as we have seen. It is to be found rather in just what constitutes the substance of the "Persians," the emotions and mental attitudes out of which the expedition grew and the changes of emotion and mental attitude produced by events. Of course this would be no sufficient plot for a French tragedy, which demands more of intrigue in the Gallic sense, more complex concatenation of emotions and events, with total omission, or at least a very different expression, of all the lyric part. The Elizabethan type, again, would have required several acts with lapse of time between them. But the plot of the "Persians" is typically Aeschylean. Simple as it is, two subordinate crises precede the final one. The suspense of the chorus is heightened by Atossa's dream, though they flatter her with soothing words; the appeal to Darius for relief brings increase of sorrow. The emotional climax begins with the entrance of Xerxes, his clothing rent and few attendants left from the great army with which he had set out.

III

Another class of plots are those which aim to explain historically a rite or a popular custom. Euripides rather favored such etiological myths, and we will take one of his plots as an example. The "Iphigeneia among the Taurians" includes the mythical explanation of several such rites. At Halai in eastern Attica was a temple of Artemis Tauropolos ($\tau\alpha\nu\rho\sigma\pi\delta\lambda\sigma$), at whose festival a man was taken as a victim. But he was not sacrificed. The knife was put to his neck and blood was drawn; that was enough; the goddess was satisfied, the victim was released. The rite was taken to indicate that in ruder days a human victim was really slain there. The form must be preserved, though the reality was too savage to maintain. At Brauron also not far away was another temple, of a goddess Artemis-Iphigeneia. Now Iphigeneia, signifying mighty in birth, was an appropriate epithet of the moon-goddess, who was also goddess of birth. Then there was Iphigeneia, a daughter of Agamemnon, sacrificed at Aulis that Artemis might be appeased and allow the ships to sail against Troy. The epithet Tauropolos, whose meaning had once been transparent, had become obscure. Perhaps it meant simply that she had to do with the herds of cattle. Again, *tauros* (ταῦρος), *bull*, was a sacred ancient name for Dionysos, as god of fertility. Euripides in the "Bacchants" makes much of this, in passages wherein some modern readers find a deep spiritual meaning—purely fanciful, in my judgment. Also, there was a savage people to the north of the Black Sea, in the modern Crimea, who were said formerly to have sacrificed strangers, shipwrecked on their shores, to a goddess whom the Greeks identified with Artemis. These savages were known as Taurians (ταῦροι). Here are coincidences and resemblances enough to set people guessing, and guesses became myths. The line between plausibility and general belief is always easy to cross. So we have, out of these elements, the following story.

Iphigeneia, when sacrificed at Aulis, was by miracle snatched away by Artemis and borne to the Taurian land, there to become priestess of the temple where strangers were sacrificed, as she had been. Her family supposed her dead. Orestes, her brother, having slain his guilty mother and her paramour for killing Agamemnon and usurping the throne, was tried and acquitted at Athens, as Aeschylus related in the "Eumenides." But some of the Furies who had pursued him for slaying his mother did not acquiesce, but continued the pursuit. Apollo directed him to go to the Taurian land, and bring *his sister* to Greece. So he should be finally freed from persecution, and should return home to a peaceful rule in his own kingdom. I have deliberately introduced the ambiguity of *his sister,* which Goethe makes the turning point of his "Iphigenie." In Euripides it is the ancient image of Artemis, worshiped by the Taurians, that is to be brought. So Orestes goes, is caught, and is about to be sacrificed by his own sister. The relationship is revealed in a very natural way. Brother and sister then devise means of stealing the sacred image and escaping with it. There is an exciting scene of doubt, they are caught in the moment of escape. Then when all is lost, Athena, the special goddess of Athens, appears. This is one of the cases where the epiphany of a god is introduced, though not the vegetation god that perished. She is the *deus ex machina,* coming to untie the knot which has been tied too fast for the dramatist to untie by the natural action of the characters in the play itself. She directs the Taurians to let the strangers go, taking the sacred image with them. She then gives explicit directions whither he is to take the image, what rites he is to institute—namely, the rites existing in the poet's time that need explanation. Iphigeneia, too, receives directions to go to Brauron, and live there as a priestess of Artemis Tauropolos, where also in later times her grave shall be shown. To such clear directions from an evident goddess in person no one can refuse assent.

To us this is no tragedy, because it does not end in death or even in failure, but in success and reconciliation. Yet it is no comedy—except in the medieval sense that led Dante to call his great poem the *"Divina Commedia,"* because it ends in Paradise. It falls under the Greek conception of tragedy, because its action is serious; failure and the death that would follow are imminent, until the god from the machine comes to the rescue. Athena's interest in Athens and in the sufferer whom her support before the Areopagus had not quite freed is apparently the reason why she rather than another is selected by the dramatist for that purpose. The main struggle is that of Orestes to escape the Furies; to this is joined the longing of Iphigeneia to return home.

The welding of the two struggles is effected in one of those scenes of recognition (ἀναγνωρισμός, ἀναγνώρισις) which are so effective. Learning that the stranger she is to sacrifice comes from Argos (which in this play includes Mycenae, destroyed a generation earlier), Iphigeneia prepares to save either him or his companion (for Pylades has loyally shared his dangerous enterprise), if the one who is released will carry to her brother a letter informing him that she lives and begging him to come and take her home. To guard against the possible loss of the letter, as by shipwreck, she recites the contents of it. That reveals to Orestes who she is. He soon proves who he is by recalling things in their home life which no one out of the family could know. For a moment they give play to the surprise and joy of the recognition; then they plan together how to escape. Aristotle notes this scene as one of the best of its kind; the modern reader finds a special

148

charm in its naturalness and simplicity. Euripides is here in one of his happiest moods.

IV

The plot of "Oedipus King" is the most elaborate of all we have from Greek tragedy. Perhaps the very difficulties of the problem stimulated Sophokles to work out every minutest detail. The germ in the myth is simple enough. Laïos, king of Thebes, was warned by the Delphic oracle to have no children by his wife Iokaste; else his son should kill Laïos and wed his own mother. A son was born, was exposed to die, was saved, and fulfilled the prediction. Whatever the origin of this primitive tale the first narrators took no thought of the high improbability of it as a bit of real life. In what possible circumstances could a stranger, ignorant of his parentage, marry a queen without such inquiries on both sides as would reveal the relationship, or at least reveal that the late king had been killed by this stranger? The tale of the Sphinx and her riddle, solved by Oedipus, met part of the difficulty; of course we must accept, as the Greeks did, such marvels as the Sphinx. But it did not meet the most serious part of the problem, which was insoluble if clearly recognized. That was inherent; the myth assumed as occurring something that could never have occurred at the Greek stage of civilization. Sophokles therefore ignored it, as the myth did, that a great tragedy might exist, and we are ready to do the same.

In its earliest version the myth assumed that Oedipus acted in ignorance. He does not discover his parentage until all is completed. To meet the requirements of Greek tragic form, the play must open just before the discovery of what he has done. It presents the discovery itself and the effects of the discovery on others and on himself. The condensation that ensues is of itself an augmentation of power. In the play, and in the mind of Oedipus, one bit of truth is revealed after another in an order chosen for dramatic effect, not corresponding to the chronological order of occurrences. That cannot confuse any listener, for the story is already familiar in outline. The interest of the audience is in watching the play of motives, the progress of the revelation, and its effects. In narrating the plot chronologically, however, we are perhaps following its natural development in the poet's mind. The construction of the play on this development is a second problem. So in telling any anecdote one may for a variety of reasons follow another order than the chronological. In short, we have two distinct senses of the word plot, even after we have reduced it to our definition of dramatic plot.

Following his usual method of asking, "What manner of people were they who would naturally so act and suffer as the myth tells us that they did?" Sophokles makes the character of Oedipus the foundation. He was an unusually attractive child even in his earliest days. His parents dared not rear him for fear of the prediction. Following ancient feeling they did not kill him, but inflicted an injury that would hasten his death by exposure, piercing his feet near the ankles, and gave him to a specially trusted shepherd, a slave, to leave on the mountain to die. The shepherd was loth to make way with so winning an infant. A shepherd from Corinth, a free man, had come with his flocks to the same region of Kithairon two years in succession, a discreet man, who knew that Polybos, king of Corinth, and his wife Merope, being childless, would be grateful for a foundling, if it were so brought to them that it could be adopted and passed off on their subjects as their son. This babe was but three days old, was unusually strong, else it could not have survived; it was autumn, and the Corinthian was just about to return home with his flocks. The two men agreed that he should take it and make the attempt. The next spring, when the Corinthian shepherd and Theban slave again met, the Corinthian told the other of his success. The child grew up as prince of Corinth. He was affectionate and lovable by nature; the tie between him and his foster-parents was very close. When therefore a companion over their wine declared that he was a <u>supposititious</u> child, and the young man next morning questioned Polybos and Merope, they declared the story false. Adoption was common enough, and was readily accepted in lieu of blood-descent. From their standpoint there was no good reason for their insisting on the falsehood, except the closeness of their affection. For the plot this was necessary. The rest could not otherwise have followed; Sophokles furnishes an adequate and touching motive—in perfect harmony with all else in Oedipus. Though satisfied at the time with the reply of his foster-parents, the suggestion of another parentage, once made, kept troubling the young man. Without their knowledge he went to Delphi to settle it. To his question about his parentage the oracle gave no answer, but told him he was <u>destined to kill his fa</u>ther and marry his mother. In horror he determined never to return to the only parents he knew. There is but one road through Delphi on its narrow mountain shelf. Oedipus had come from the west; he strode forth eastward, a lonely exile, with one purpose only, never to see his father and mother. It was the road to Thebes. At a lonely place where a road from the north joined that from Delphi and that from Thebes, a carriage met him. It carried a man a little past middle life and a driver. These were accompanied by a herald and two other attendants. The driver attempted rudely to thrust the lone foot-passenger out of the narrow road; Oedipus resisted; the personage in the carriage struck him a vicious blow on the head with his driving goad. Oedipus struck back with the long staff of a traveler. He struck a fatal place; he was a vigorous and angry man. In the affray that followed he killed the whole insolent party, as he supposed, and strode on, more concerned with his own thoughts than with the fate of his assailants. It proved afterward that one man had escaped—who was in fact the faithful shepherd that had exposed, and saved, the infant Oedipus. On his return to Thebes what account should this man give of the affair? That one "lone-girded wayfarer" had, on provocation from the king himself, killed four, while he alone had escaped to tell the tale? The truth would have been incredible; it would also entail his own condemnation as a weakling and coward. He must tell something more plausible and safer. What he reported was that a band of robbers had done it. This departure from the truth, which at the time seemed necessary, made the rest possible and delayed discovery many years. But the leader of the slain party was Laïos, killed by his own son—who was a far finer character than his father, but had inherited his father's quickness of temper. Had Oedipus been a man of unusual self-control, or if, remembering the prediction, he had recognized that possibly after all Polybos was not his father, and he must above all things never strike any man who was older than himself, he would have said at the moment of provocation, "This insolent man is gray-haired; let him have the road." So he would have made the prediction vain. But he was a prince, accustomed to deference, giving up home and position for exile. The only father he knew was Polybos, who had not long ago assured him that the disquieting rumor was baseless. The provocation was wanton and extreme. The lack of exceptional self-control was his undoing. He was guilty of nothing else. His father, not he, was the guilty one.

After the affray, following the most direct road, which led to Thebes, he found the city in terror of the Sphinx, taking her continuing tribute of Theban lives till someone should answer her riddle. And their king, who had gone to Delphi to ask help of Apollo's oracle, had been killed by a band of robbers. Oedipus solved the riddle, whereat the monster dashed herself down a cliff to death. The queen was of the royal line by her own descent; their benefactor was found to be a Corinthian prince, who for some reason was unwilling to return home. And apparently he was a favorite of heaven. The Thebans offered him the hand of the queen, *who was childless,* and an equal share in the royal dignity. He accepted them—fulfilling the rest of the prediction.

The shepherd of Laïos, as soon as it was known that their saviour and new king was the son of Polybos, knew all. That meeting with the Corinthian shepherd in the third summer had told him. Thenceforward his constant terror was lest the truth, and his part in it, should be brought to light. For many years he had held a favored position in the royal household, in personal attendance on the king. That position, due to his own character, explained his presence at the fatal affray. He now besought the queen to send him back to his old occupation with the flocks. To the queen this appeared as a confirmation of their old confidence in his loyal attachment; he could not bear to see another in the place of his former lord. And the shepherd hoped, being constantly away from the palace, much of the time far away, at least to have no part in the discovery, if that should come.

Things went on peacefully and prosperously some years, till two sons and two daughters were born of Oedipus and Iokaste. Then came a blight and plague from Apollo on land and cattle and people, in consequence of the pollution—to Greek popular feeling always the obvious explanation of a pestilence.* At this point the play begins. Bit by bit all that precedes is revealed, and I have scrupulously refrained from introducing in my summary any circumstance that is not distinctly mentioned or of necessity implied in the play itself. What Mr. Archer calls "an absolutely astounding series of coincidences," and would explain by the conception of fate as "some malignant power deliberately pulling the strings which guide its puppets into such abhorrent tangles"—all these coincidences are provided with a natural explanation, mostly growing out of personal character. Only those improbabilities that could not be eliminated from the tale are accepted silently, with no attempt at explanation, that no one may reflect upon them. It was highly improbable that private talk between husband and wife should not have raised suspicions early, but this is left "outside the play" (ἔξω δράματος). And even this we may think of as not unnatural, considering the nature of the

---

*In contrast with this the attitude of the educated and the Greek physicians, essentially like our own, is well illustrated in Thucydides' account of the plague at Athens in 429 B. C.

dreaded prediction and the universal belief at Thebes that the infant was dead. That Laïos was coming to Delphi to seek help against the Sphinx just when Oedipus was leaving Delphi by the one road that led away from Corinth is indeed pure coincidence, but no improbable one. Each man had reason enough for being where he was, and the coincidence would have done no harm had Laïos been a man of dignity suitable to his station, or had Oedipus recollected his danger, and refrained from striking back. It was not fate, in the ordinary meaning, but the personal character of the two men, father and son, that struck out the fatal spark.

As the opening scene of the play, the people come to the king in solemn supplication that he who rescued them from the tribute to the "hard songstress" will find some way out of the woe that is now upon them. He has already sent to Delphi for guidance, and is expecting momently the return of his messenger, his brother-in-law, Kreon, who presently arrives. The god has answered that they must find and put to death, or at least exile, the slayer of Laïos, since that unpurified pollution is the cause of the pestilence, and that the slayer is now in Thebes. The earnestness of the king has caused this announcement to be made in public; the investigation and ultimate revelation must therefore be altogether public. Since urgent inquiry brings out no clue to the murderer, the king calls together his council—the chorus—who represent the entire people, and makes proclamation, adjuring anyone who has knowledge of the matter to speak out, declaring that the guilty man may content the state with the milder penalty of exile, and pronouncing a solemn curse on the guilty person if he does not reveal himself, and on anyone, were it Oedipus himself, who aids in concealing him. It is suggested farther that the blind old seer Teiresias be summoned. He has been already summoned, and now appears, with the utmost reluctance. Having no heart to tell what by his art he knows, he refuses to speak. To the king this is disloyalty to his people, a refusal to help in time of need. Little by little Teiresias hints that Oedipus is the man. Circumstances make it seem to the king not improbable that Kreon, the next heir to the throne, has concerted with Teiresias this scheme to get Oedipus out of the way. Indignant at the seer's attitude, Oedipus becomes more and more angry, and by accusations and taunts angers Teiresias, who speaks more and more plainly. To the king such charges are the height of absurdity, and merely prove the seer's own guilt. Kreon is indignant at the king's accusation. The council try to allay the quarrel; at their request the king recalls his threat against Kreon. Iokaste, to assure the king that he need not be troubled at any prophet's charge, tells Oedipus of the old oracle about Laïos and his child, which has proved false in every particular. But in her story, which includes an account of how the child was exposed, she mentions the trivial circumstance that the scene of the attack on Laïos by a band of robbers was a place where three roads meet. That recalls to his memory that in such a place he had slain a man. Questions bring out coincidences that confirm his fears. His one hope now is that the shepherd— the attendant who has escaped—will assure them that it really was a band of robbers who committed the deed, not one man alone. While one goes to fetch the shepherd a messenger from Corinth comes to report that Polybos is dead and the Corinthians will make Oedipus their king. The talk about this new situation leads to mention of the reason why Oedipus fears to return to Corinth—lest he fulfill the other half of the prediction by marrying his mother. But the Corinthian was no official messenger. He had come of his own accord, because, being the free herdsman who had taken the infant to Polybos and Merope, he had a special interest in the good fortune of the foundling. In smug satisfaction at being able to relieve Oedipus of that fear, he tells all he knows about the foundling's origin. He never had known—the shepherd of Laïos had concealed the fact—that the child was the son of Laïos and Iokaste. But what the Corinthian tells is enough for Iokaste. Her effort to stay the investigation is vain; she knows the whole when Oedipus himself knows but half. She rushes into the palace to take her own life, while he awaits the shepherd, who reluctantly, under threats, and as slowly as possible, yields the information that completes the horror. When the last possibility of doubt is gone, Oedipus goes to the room where Iokaste has hung herself, and in self-punishment for his blindness seizes a brooch from Iokaste's robe and with it strikes out his eyes. Finally the playwright shows him again, that we may see the changes, not merely physical, wrought by his awful experience. First the pathetic change of his physical blindness; then the deeper change within. Recognition of his injustice to Teiresias and to Kreon was complete, when he realized that he was indeed the curse of his country. He is completely humbled. And finally is brought out a trait most significant of his nature. Like many a modern father, his love for his little girls has been peculiarly tender. The boys can make their own way, if need be; the helplessness and undeserved disgrace of his innocent daughters fill him with poignant foreboding. This is the virtual close of the play; he is guided into the palace to suffer and endure.

V

This plot, which demands and is worth so much time for even concise summary, illustrates well the "reversal" or "peripety" (περιπέτεια) on which Aristotle lays emphasis. This is the change from prosperity to adversity or the converse. As an example of this Aristotle takes the Corinthian messenger, who expects to free Oedipus from fear about his mother by revealing that she is not Merope, but produces the opposite effect. Such a reversal is most effective when it results, as it does in this case, from a "recognition"—from learning facts before unknown that completely change the situation. Indeed, this entire plot is for Oedipus and Iokaste a reversal produced by recognition of facts before unknown. Such a condensed form of crisis must always be striking.

And the "Oedipus" raises also the old question of "tragic guilt," of which German critics have made a good deal. Perhaps the wider meaning of the word *Schuld* is what explains the prominence of *tragische Schuld* in German discussion. With the English word in view no one could seriously maintain that the tragic suffering is always due to the victim's guilt. One needs only to think of Hamlet, Cordelia, Lear, Desdemona, Antigone. Guilt implies conscious and intentional violation of law; we recognize criminal negligence, it is true, but that concept has no application here. In human life, as we know very well, the suffering that most moves our pity and fear is not that which results from one's own guilt, but that which flows from ordinary human imperfections, such as

158

we recognize in ourselves—the lack of wisdom and fore-sight in the tangle of life. Nature is as merciless to igno-rance as to wickedness, and human life no less, with one important difference; rectitude of will wards off the keenest pangs of remorse, and may transmute all other suffering to inward tranquillity and even to inward tri-umph. For tragedy Aristotle ("Poet." 1453 a) puts the matter quite accurately. "Pity is occasioned by unde-served misfortune, and fear by that of one like our-selves. . . . The good plot therefore must be single rather than double, and the change must be from happiness to adversity, and that not from the hero's depravity, but from a great mistake on his part, the man being either such as we have described or better rather than worse." In evidence he cites Oedipus and Orestes as among the most successful tragic characters. Oedipus is not pun-ished for any guilt on his part. In his human weakness, eager though he was to avoid the acts foretold, he failed to school himself never to strike an older man, even in self-defense; he accepted as his wife an older woman, not dreaming of the possibility that Iokaste could be his mother, because he was misled by the solemn asseveration of Polybos and Merope that they were his parents. Fatal blindness was the error for which he could not forgive himself, and for which physical blindness appeared to him, in his passion of grief, the just penalty to in-flict upon himself.

VIII.   INTERNAL FORM

I

INSTEAD of our division into acts, which are separated by a fall of the curtain and a complete break in the play, we have seen that a Greek tragedy is continuous, dialogue and choral song alternating without pause. These are striking differences, but they are matters of outward form, which grow out of local and temporary conditions and vary with period and place. On the other hand, in the fundamentals of structure, in what we may call the internal form, tragic plots of all ages and all types of tragedy agree. This internal form was clearly understood by Aeschylus and skillfully embodied by him in the external form that seemed natural to him and his contemporaries. Shakspere embodied the same essentials of structure in the external form that suited his theater and his time. Racine, Schiller, and Ibsen did the same for their several theaters and times. Departure from these permanent essentials of internal structure means risk of failure; at best it means falling short of the highest dramatic success. We shall see that Euripides could so depart and still make a great play; but he made greater plays when he observed the law. No playwright ever had a sounder instinct in these matters or a surer hand than Sophokles. In fact this is one of the regions in which the Greeks reached finality. And on the whole, nobody has described this internal form better than Aristotle. Freytag, starting from Aristotle, attempted a better description; his formulas have been widely adopted in classrooms, but not much elsewhere. They are less descriptive and less illuminating, resting in part on a metaphor that is misleading. We will go back to Aristotle.

As we saw, Aristotle does not distinctly adopt the conflict theory of drama, but he almost seems to take it for granted. He could not overlook the contest in Old Comedy, the whole tragic exhibition was a contest for a prize, and his terms for the successive phases of the internal form are perfectly consonant with that conception of a dramatic plot. At the same time his terms are wider and more inclusive than that conception—as a plot, though a story of conflict, is really much more than that. It may be that he consciously refused to confine himself to that single aspect of a tragic plot, important as it is. The conflict is indeed only the central thread on which the whole is strung, the unifying force that makes a mimic section of life present itself as an organic whole. The greater the play the richer and fuller the elements of life that are strung upon that central thread of a conflict. And here we meet a real difficulty, a sufficient reason for the fact that Aristotle's terms for the successive phases of the action are not more current; the English translations of them are inadequate, and for one no acceptable equivalent is at hand.

When he says that a dramatic action must have a beginning, a middle, and an end, we may think he is putting it in a rather commonplace way. But the Greek words which must here be rendered beginning and end mean much more than beginning and end. The former is *archē* (ἀρχή), a word which we have considered before.

In other contexts it means rule, in the widest sense, and hence, among other special applications, office, magistrate, and empire. That whole side of its meaning has no application here. In this context it is not only beginning; it is also origin, starting-point, and first principle. It is that out of which all the rest grows. All these are common applications of the word, which the Romans covered, not quite so clearly, by their *principium*. And *telos* (τέλος) is not only end in contrast with beginning; it is also an end at which one aims, employing appropriate means for bringing it to pass, a goal toward which one strives. It implies completion and consummation as well as finality. Used of the final stage of a play it implies that the action is arriving at a natural close, a close which has grown, like a plant from a seed or bulb, out of the source, in characters and situation, which was presented to us in the opening scenes. We shall soon return to the application of these pregnant terms to the initial and final stages of a plot, after taking a look at Aristotle's analysis of the middle, or what lies between *archē* and *telos*.

The stage next after the *archē* he calls *desis* (δέσις), the tying, as of a knot. It is what we have in mind when we say, "the plot thickens." Opposing wills or forces are coming to a grapple, approaching the moment of decision, which is not yet. Complication is our usual word, based on a different figure, but equally descriptive. Aristotle's *metabasis* (μετάβασις) is simply transition, the going over from the stage of growing complication to the stage of clarification, which he calls the *lusis* (λύσις) or untying. Perhaps our best rendering for this would be solution, unless the more literal untying will do. *Dénoûment* is not quite suitable. Not only is it French instead of

English, but it has been appropriated more especially to the end of the untying, the final result of it. What Aristotle meant was the continuing process, the opposite of complication—what goes on from the moment we see which side will probably win to the moment of final decision. This is likely to be shorter than the complication; it may be very short. But it is not to be confounded with the catastrophe itself, the final blow. And this word catastrophe, though a good Greek word, is not used at all by Aristotle in this sense.

These five stages, then, a good dramatic plot must have, whatever the external form in which they are embodied. A good modern comedy will have them no less than a good tragedy. Perhaps we should say four stages instead of five, not counting the *metabasis* or transition, which is only the turning-point from complication to solution, too brief to be placed quite on a level with more extended phases of the action. This is indeed the most important transition in the play, and that no doubt is why Aristotle includes it. But there is another turning-point that requires notice. I mean the definite statement of that central conflict—what in the more striking cases we might call the challenge, or the declaration of war. Freytag calls it *das erregende Moment*, the exciting force—not a happy term. That Aristotle makes no mention of it is easily explained; to recognize it is to accept the conflict theory, which he nowhere does explicitly, and after all it is merely one item, an outstanding point, in his *archē*, for which our accepted term is exposition. That is obviously no translation of the Greek word. It describes that section of the plot from another point of view, but is a fair equivalent. The playwright must at the outset of the play, and as early as possible, make clear to us, by their action and speech and by the setting, who the leading characters are, what their relation is to each other, and what they are trying to do. As a part of this exposition, if there is a struggle on or in prospect, this must be brought out with due dramatic emphasis. When the audience are by this exposition enabled to understand the moves, then complication, the deploying of forces for the struggle, can begin. At the transition it becomes clear who is winning, who is losing. The *lusis* or solution is the presentation in detail of that winning and losing—a longer or shorter stage according to circumstances, often a very short stage. And the *telos* or final stage, for which I know of no good English term, presents the result of it all—the final situation and relations of characters, to which the struggle and the changes wrought by its issue have brought the people most concerned. Modern plays tend to abbreviate this final stage. Modern audiences—perhaps because it is late in the evening—get impatient to leave after the struggle is decided; they are less interested in seeing results fully set forth. The Athenians, on the other hand, liked a longer and fuller *telos*. That of the "Persians" is an extended Oriental dirge; that of "Oedipus King" is of considerable length, showing the changes in Oedipus by the awful revelation and including the pathetic scene with his young daughters. After Agamemnon's death we have Klytaimestra's bold avowal and defense of her crime, the lament of the chorus, and the entire scene with Aigisthos; the *telos* of the "Eumenides" shows us the Furies fully reconciled, and closes with the processional pageant that escorts them, now the "Kindly Ones," to their new shrine.

It must be noted that these successive stages of the action are not sharply separated, a new stage beginning where the preceding ends. On the contrary they are likely to overlap or dovetail into one another. Especially do the first and second often overlap. The forward movement, the deploying of forces, may begin before exposition is completed, whenever exposition has gone far enough so that we can see the bearing of what is going on. The less the time required for pure exposition and che sooner complication can begin without confusion, the sooner the audience will be thoroughly interested. Exposition can be completed while the complication is progressing. A typical example of skill in this point is the opening of "Antigone." Two girls come out from the royal dwelling which is the *skēnē*. In forty-six lines of passionate conversation we get a complete outline of the situation and a clear conception of the contrasted characters of the two sisters. It is the morning after the Thebans have repulsed the Argive army; the dead king Eteokles has been buried with honor, Kreon is king and has forbidden the burial of Polyneikes. Antigone and Ismene, offspring of unwitting incest, have lost in dreadful ways father, mother, and both brothers; Antigone is driven both by affection and by religion to bury her brother, in defiance of the edict. The major part of the exposition is completed, the heroine is in conflict with the king, and is alone in her struggle. The second stage might begin. At line 99, after entreaty and expostulation between the sisters have deepened our understanding of their respective personalities, Antigone goes out to commit her righteous crime. The chorus, Kreon's councilors, enter, celebrating the victory. Kreon comes out from the palace to meet them, and in a formal "speech from the throne" proclaims his principles of government and his edict forbidding burial of Polyneikes—which the council receive with formal assent, but coolly. Not till line 223 does the guard come to report the surreptitious burial, which we saw Antigone go to effect. Complication is now in full course, but when did it begin? Certainly by line 99, the departure of Antigone, if not at line 47. Yet all the while exposition has been also in full course, and the more prominent. The first forty-six lines gave a full outline of it, which Antigone, Ismene, chorus, and Kreon have been filling with color and life. The transition from one stage to the next is likely to be of this general sort, interlocking. A play resembles a living organism, not a structure of squared blocks. To dissect it too closely, according to any scheme of plot-division, would be to overlook its vitality—would be treating it too much like a cadaver. The parts are clearly discernible; but it is no less important to discern the continuity. Its movement is that of group-life, of which it is a representation.

II

Accordingly an abstract and schematic view of a plot is not what interests either audience or reader of a play. What we care for is men and women, the people who are living the story before our eyes. A group of people in whom we have become interested enlist our sympathy and stir our feelings. In the opening scenes the first task of the playwright is to make us acquainted with them. Who are they? what sort of people are they? what ties and relations connect them? what are they driving at? Such are the questions floating more or less consciously in our minds. The playwright's answers to these questions, answers given in dramatic form, by the people themselves, as they live their intensified life in apparent unconsciousness of onlookers, is the *archē* or starting-point, the exposition. As soon as the characters and their mutual relations are clearly before us, and we know what they want, we see that their clashing aims will produce conflict and trouble, perhaps disaster. We begin to take sides. The men and women are so brought before us that we understand and in some degree sympathize with aims and points of view that are opposed; yet we recognize that one person's aim, that of the hero or heroine, is higher or more reasonable than the opposing aim—or at the worst is well grounded and is the will of a stronger character, toward whom on that account we are drawn by our involuntary admiration for strength. As the conflict develops, what we called by the cooler name of complication we feel as a personal struggle, appealing to our sympathy more and more as our acquaintance with the characters deepens. There is included also the interest of team-play. It isn't a fencing match between two; on either side there is interplay of several persons in various relations to the action.

The transition to the solution becomes the turn to victory and defeat of our friends. In a pronounced tragedy with tragic ending we now see, in most cases, defeat approaching for the person with whom, on the whole, we sympathize most. Yet the matter is not quite so simple. In the first place, it is only in melodrama that the hero is quite perfect, his opponent altogether black; in tragedy, as in life, there is right and wrong on both sides, strength and weakness in every character. Nothing is simple. Does Medea win or lose? She gains her revenge and is rescued by a favoring miracle, but she acknowledges herself a most unhappy woman. Antigone is defeated and goes to death; but her cause triumphs and her destroyer suffers more than she.

The solution, then, is the winning and losing of people who on both sides and in manifold ways hold our interest, and hold it more as the end approaches. When we no longer can doubt the issue, we still follow the struggle with anticipatory questions about details. Particularly, when one of the contending parties must acknowledge defeat, we wish to know how he will be affected by the change. Here, in the latter part of the play especially, our interest and our keenest artistic pleasure center more in the inner experience of the characters instead of the externals of fortune. The attraction of the final stage, after all curiosity about the outcome of the action as a series of external events is satisfied, is precisely, even at the first hearing of the play, in the effects of those events on the persons whose fortunes we have been following. Here, even more than in the rest of the play, we may apply Mr. Archer's dictum, that "dramatic interest is entirely distinct from mere curiosity, and survives when curiosity is dead." There is no descent of interest, but rather a rise till very near the end. Especially if the play draws us to repeated hearing, curiosity about the external event melts into sympathy with the inner experience induced by it.

The reason for this lies in the accumulation of memories as the play proceeds, in the growth of our acquaintance with the persons of the story. They came before us at first as strangers; in a Greek tragedy they came before the audience on first presentation as legendary figures, as Homer or somebody else had painted them, but little better in this play than strangers, because now newly studied or shown in a new light. The dramatist makes them reveal themselves to us in a way that leads us to desire closer acquaintance, which we gain by seeing them act and speak and suffer in serious vicissitudes of life, such as bring depths of character to the surface. If the play attracts us repeatedly, knowing the main course of it we have mental leisure to look deeper—to discern lights and shades of character that did not appear at first, motives and suggestions that before escaped us. We find that a Macbeth or a Medea is not a vulgar criminal, but a great nature warped by the stress of life. Ambition, passion, injustice, may have led astray, but the crime is intelligible; the criminal wins pity and awakens fear as we discern kinship with our own weaknesses. Condemnation of the criminal act does not destroy sympathy with the person, the sympathy that springs from full knowledge of circumstances and motives. This knowledge is what the dramatist gradually builds up in us as the play unfolds. Condemnation tempered by such knowledge is what awakens the tragic fear and effects the purification. The elemental stresses of life on men and women like ourselves are the real subject of tragedy. We see these stresses through the inner eye of the sufferer from them; pity and recognition of kinship are closely interwoven with the recognition of error. As the whole miniature world of the play is disclosed, it becomes for the time being our world, in which we live more intimately—that is, with fuller knowledge—than is possible in any but the smallest part of our real world. This our real world consists of people whose motives, thoughts, and aims we have largely to guess at, and we are painfully prone to guess wrong. Not so with the little dramatic world, which author and actor make so much more fully known, removing from it most of that incalculable part that plays

so large a rôle outside the theater. It is this accumulated knowledge and sympathy, I say, that we bring to
each new scene. Every crisis met and passed augments
them; in the *telos* they have reached their height, and
render this, not indeed the most exciting, but the climax
of interest. No doubt some plays that are on the whole
great are not wholly successful in this final stage; entire
success here is difficult. So far as there is a modern tendency to slight the full development of this final stage, that
is artistic recession, not advance. "Agamemnon," "Oedipus King," and "Herakles" are fine examples of such full
development.

III

A concrete example may make part of our analysis
plainer. The "Medea" of Euripides is a famous study of
passion and revenge, emphatically a plot of conflict. If
it lacks ethical qualities that characterize other Greek
tragedies, perhaps it is the more instructive in certain
ways.

The *skēnē* is the house of Medea in Corinth, the orchestra is the open space before it. The old nurse of Medea
comes out from the house to be alone—the usual convention that we have described—and to "tell to earth and
sky" the unhappy situation of her mistress, whose devotion to her husband has been repaid with desertion. By
her cunning and sorcery combined she had enabled him
to overcome the dangers in his way and win the golden
fleece. She had fled with him, destroyed his enemy,
become a second time an exile; he has taken to wife the
daughter of the Corinthian king and left Medea in
despair. She listens to no consolation, even hates her

children, and the nurse fears the outcome, knowing the passionate nature of her mistress, and that she is a dangerous opponent. This typical Euripidean prologue—we should call it a soliloquy—has possessed us of the outlines of the initial situation, and is now supplemented by dramatic conversation. The two children come home, with their old slave attendant or *paidagōgos*, who imparts to his fellow-servant, with real or pretended reluctance, a new cause of fear. He has overheard one say amid the gossiping in the square at the fountain of Peirene, that the king has determined to banish the children together with their mother. Still more alarmed at this news, the nurse, bidding the boys go into the house, adds expressions intended to quiet their childish fears, while she urges the attendant to keep them out of sight of their mother, so fierce and ominous is the look the nurse has seen their mother bend upon them. At this point Medea herself, still within the house, is heard, in the anapestic measures that suggest the approach of the chorus, crying out upon her fate and longing for death. Yet more urgently the nurse bids the children go in, but avoid their mother's presence; another outburst from Medea, including an imprecation of death upon her children and their father as well as herself, adds to the nurse's excitement. And now the chorus, Corinthian women who have heard the lamentations of Medea, come to offer sympathy. On farther outcries from Medea they beg the nurse to call her out to them—again the convention that requires even private interviews of condolence to occur before the house and not within it. So at the close of the *parodos* Medea comes out; after apologies for her conduct and bitter reflections on the unhappy estate of women—reflections in substance very modern—she entreats them to aid her by silence if she finds a way to make her husband suffer for his base treatment of her. Here then, after two hundred and sixty lines, the nurse's forebodings are confirmed in a clear intimation from Medea that her passion is hardening to a resolution. It is a declaration that she is at war with Jason. It marks the close of the exposition and the beginning of the complication.

We have compared the complication to the deployment of forces, each hostile power seeking the most favorable position. Our sympathy goes with Medea in so far that her faithless husband richly deserves punishment, and we grant that a woman of her nature must inevitably do her utmost to compass it. The question of moral approval is hardly raised; but popular Greek morality, like natural morality today—the old Adam, if you will—approved the general principle of returning evil for such evil, and returning it in good measure. The king, who is of necessity Jason's strongest ally, now comes in person to proclaim her banishment and harshly declares that he will remain till his command is obeyed. Medea's first move is to ask humbly his reason for banishing her; to which he frankly replies, Fear: she is cunning and has threatened not only her husband but his new bride and himself, the bride's father. To blunt this fear Medea points to her weakness, lamenting the harm so often done by an undeserved reputation for subtlety; besides, while acknowledging hatred for her husband, she has no ground for hostility to the king; she entreats him at least to allow a single day's respite, for her innocent children's sake, that she may have a few hours to form plans for their future. Reluctantly the king grants her this much, and withdraws. Whereupon to the chorus Medea freely displays her feeling of triumph at the success of her feigned

humility, and meditates aloud before them on the per-
plexities before her, particularly on her need of some
secure refuge after effecting the revenge which now still
more openly she declares she will accomplish upon all
three of her enemies.

Between this and the next *epeisodion* intervenes a
choral ode of lyric reflections, first on the repute brought
by Medea's skill to the sex which the poets, as men, have
maligned, and then on her unhappy present lot. Jason
himself now appears, proffers money for her exile, laments
the harm which her excessive emotion is bringing on herself, and explains how his entire course has been dictated
by interest in Medea's welfare and that of their children,
if she would only look at matters calmly. This line of
argument lays him open to scathing replies; sophistry is
met with the directness of righteous wrath—a magnificent opportunity for a great actor. To a Greek audience
verbal contests like this were very attractive—before the
jury courts, longer and more coolly argumentative, condensed and well spiced with passion in the theater. The
dramatic object here is threefold: it completes the exposition, bringing the opposing pair before us together, it
exasperates Medea and sharpens her resolution, and it
makes a most effective scene in itself. The chorus now
sing of the baleful results of excessive passion, the charms
of quiet love, the unhappiness of a lonely exile like
Medea's.

Then follows an *epeisodion* rather detached from the
main story and of no great interest in itself; its dramatic
value is that it provides the needed refuge for Medea
after she shall have secured her vengeance. Aigeus, king
of Athens, is passing through Corinth on his return from
Delphi, whither he had gone to seek from the oracle some

means of relief from childlessness. The god has returned no satisfactory or even intelligible response. When Aigeus has thus explained his presence here, he notes and inquires the reason for Medea's evident dejection. She explains, and begs him to receive and defend her when she leaves Corinth, promising that she will procure him that relief which the oracle has not definitely provided. This Aigeus grants, only stipulating that he shall not actively aid her departure from Corinth, that he may be blameless in the eyes of his Corinthian ally. Thus is removed the one obstacle to action on her part. One may ask how a king of Athens could call at Medea's house in Corinth without seeing his ally the king of Corinth. The question would be out of place, confusing tragedy with real life. It is part of the necessary condensation of action that in the play itself any such question is ignored. Why waste time on a triviality that does not bear on the plot? An explanation could easily have been devised, had it been worth while. Another dramatic end is attained, however, by this episode; the crisis, the decisive moment, is delayed, and its effect heightened by a scene which definitely prepares for the crisis, while itself contrasted with it by being emotionally so quiet.

On the departure of Aigeus Medea reveals to the chorus her plan. She will send to Jason and beg him to come once more to her house; to him she will pretend submission, pretend to have acceded to his view, acknowledging her own error, and will entreat that her children be excepted from the sentence of banishment. To this end she will send the children themselves to the bride to ask that they be spared, and bearing as a gift from Medea to win the bride's heart a fine robe and a golden wreath. These ornaments Medea will so prepare with magic drugs

174

that when the bride puts them on they will destroy her and whosoever tries to save her. Finally Medea will kill the children, that Jason may be left without issue and without hope of issue—to Greek feeling the most terrible of disasters. Here is evidently the transition to the untying, the winning and losing. We may now anticipate the catastrophe with probability, but not with sufficient definiteness to exclude questions or dull our interest. The dramatic suspense with which we look forward to the progress of the solution is still keen at every step.

In the following *stasimon* Euripides avails himself, as he is fond of doing, of the opportunity to sing the praise of Athens, which took pride, as America has done in the past, in offering refuge to the oppressed. To their praise of Athens is added expostulation with Medea for her murderous purpose toward her children. In both these notes of their song the chorus are expressing reflections that are natural in the situation. The one thing they omit which in real life could not fail is vigorous disapproval of Medea's purpose to kill their own king and his sole heiress. To a Corinthian audience this might be intolerable; but the play was meant for Athenians, who could more readily forgive it. The dramatist prudently makes no allusion to the matter; that would call attention to it; as it is, few in any audience—unless at Corinth—would think of it. A sound principle of play-making is that difficulties in the plot that are inherent and insoluble must be silently ignored, and may safely be ignored provided they are not too serious, so that the play is on the whole a good one.

Jason comes, Medea skillfully deceives and wheedles him, playing cunningly on his deep-seated vanity, and sends the children and their attendant with the fatal gift.

The interval before their return, a half hour or more, is filled by a five-minute song, which anticipates the success of the device and commiserates the murderous mother. At its close the *paidagōgos* reports that the gift and the children's petition have been accepted; and Medea, dismissing him into the house, retains the children while she awaits farther news from the palace. Then follows the famous scene, in spirit a soliloquy, though spoken nominally to the children and the sympathetic chorus, in which Medea reveals the whole inner struggle between her love as mother and her hatred as a deserted wife; in form she bewails the separation due to their remaining at Corinth while she will be at Athens, while to us and the chorus she is wrestling with her purpose to kill them. It is a scene that aims to blunt our condemnation and to deepen our sympathy, while exhibiting the sharpest contrasts of emotion.

Presently a messenger, one of Jason's servants, comes in haste, narrates the death of the bride and of her father, and urges Medea to escape. Again she expresses her will to fulfil her purpose and kill the children, though knowing well the misery of it for herself. She enters the house; we hear the children call for help; a moment's quiet, and we know that all is over. The murder has taken place within; the appeals of the children and the helpless response of the chorus make a strophe of lyric dialogue. A single antistrophe from the chorus, recalling the myth of Ino, who also slew her children, must have had for the Greek audience a peculiar effect in softening the horror, by connecting Medea's deed with a similar deed of sacred story. Then Jason hastens in, demanding Medea; he affirms the certainty of her punishment for such a crime upon the royal family, but seeks above all to obtain his children. Informed that they are dead, he demands admission to the house that he may punish the murderer. Whereupon Medea appears in the air above the house, with the corpses of her children, in the miraculous car sent by Helios, the Sun, her father's father. This is the solution "from the machine" which Aristotle condemns and which Euripides too often employed.

From her place of security Medea conducts the *telos*—to us, in this case, a peculiar mingling of dramatic and non-dramatic elements. Jason's distress at his utter bereavement, Medea's taunts and her acknowledgment of her own misery, are a natural dramatic fulfilment. Her institution of expiatory rites—the rites existing at Corinth in the poet's time—and her elevation to a semi-divine plane by the miraculous intervention in her behalf, are wholly undramatic, but were no doubt interesting to the Greek audience for whom the play was composed.

As we have seen before, the half-conscious questions in which dramatic suspense is embodied and made definite change their character after the play has become familiar. Those which concern mere curiosity about externals of the plot die out, or fade into a shadowy reminiscence of themselves, as Mr. Archer describes. In their place arise questions of a more penetrating kind; motives, traits of character, relations to our own experiences, technical skill of dramatist or actor, poetic beauty—these and the like attract more of our attention, if the play be one that contains these qualities in sufficient wealth. We note that Medea, for example, as the heroine of the play, succeeds fully in her plan of vengeance; Jason deserves his reward, the king little less; the innocent bride is not shown to us and is so faintly realized that she commands no great sympathy; the children we pity, as the death or

177

suffering of children always moves our pity, but we realize that their pain is brief. No theory of guilt can justify dramatically any of these deaths; they are merely incidental to the quarrel between Jason and Medea, in which they were by circumstances arrayed on the defeated side. And Medea, who commits these murders with impunity, not only has divine favor at the end, but has our own sympathy. The conjunction is a strange one. But Medea is, in fact, one of the few well-drawn and consistent characters in Euripides as we have him. She succeeds in carrying out to the full her heart's desire for vengeance, but is herself, perhaps, the keenest sufferer.

IV

We return to the chorus for a moment to note a bit of the Greek external form that bears a peculiar relation to exposition and complication. I mean the entering song of the chorus. This cannot be, like a *stasimon*, simply an emotional meditation on the situation thus far developed. It must first of all unite the chorus with the action and explain their relation to it. In so far it may always be considered part of the exposition; for the presence of a chorus is an essential element of the situation from which the rest of the play develops. And according to the nature of their relation to the action, of course the substance of their entering song, or that part of the substance, must vary. In form also the variety is greater than in *stasima;* but that for our present purpose is secondary.

When the chorus opens the play, in the Aeschylean "Suppliants" and "Persians," the entire exposition, in-

cluding the statement of the conflict, is of course assigned
to them. The suppliant Danaïds set all this forth with
sufficient fullness within the thirty-nine lines of their
opening anapests. The Persian elders make a longer
story of it. Sixty-five lines of recited anapests and three
short strophes and antistrophes are given to narrating the
situation; with pride and apparent confidence they count
up the contingents of the great host that has gone out to
conquer. Not till we reach line 108 is the real nature
of the conflict mentioned—Persian pride in their invincible might struggling against the ordinance of Heaven.*
And complication does not begin till line 176, with
Atossa's account of her dream.

The *parodos* of "Medea," as regards substance, is of a
simple and frequently recurring type. The sympathetic
Corinthian women have heard Medea's cries and come
to inquire and condole. It is dramatic in form, a conversation with the nurse, merging into conversation with
Medea. We have seen (p. 171) that it belongs wholly
to exposition, as the statement of the conflict is not
clearly made till much later.

The followers of Neoptolemos offer another simple
type of *parodos,* one which does little more than define
the relation of the chorus to a leading character. They
are the loyal subjects of their prince. Their later songs
have a dramatic function, in drawing out Philoktetes by
their sympathy and in supporting their leader; but their
entering song is merely a request for orders and an expression of pity for Philoktetes before he appears. These
are indeed the two notes of their entire part in the play,
but the immediate effect of this first introduction of these
notes is very slight. Except that a chorus is necessary,

*Compare pp. 141 ff.

exposition is completed, and the nature of the conflict indicated, before the *parodos*. But a chorus is necessary; their *parodos* does add a little to exposition.

The chorus in "Antigone" is far more significant. They are leading citizens and represent the people. Their entering song, celebrating the victory, presents them as natural supporters of the new king, sure to be unsympathetic with rebellion, and isolates Antigone still farther. This *parodos* is a distinct addition to the exposition, while at the same time it suggests an aspect of the complication. We are shown that Antigone may have to face not only Kreon, but the united force of the whole state in the first flush of triumph.

The *parodos* of the "Eumenides" is notable in that it belongs quite as much to complication as to exposition; its form is also remarkable. The Pythia has discovered the Furies already in the temple, snoring in their chairs around their victim.* Their first words, after some inarticulate muttering, are a huntsman's call to seize the prey—whether from one or several of the still sleeping Furies, we are left to guess. More urgent reproaches by Klytaimestra's ghost are answered by them in three trimeters, which are apparently divided unevenly between several Furies, awakening one another. Then follow three short and agitated pairs of antistrophic stanzas, of self-reproach and complaint. I conceive these stanzas as sung while the chorus are moving out from the temple to the orchestra, and in the orchestra. It is true that Apollo's command to leave his dwelling follows instead of preceding. But we can hardly conceive them as sung and danced within the temple. And after that command of Apollo the chorus still remain for some

*Compare p. 84.

fifty trimeters of acrimonious dispute with Apollo. Evidently we have here an entrance of a chorus from the *skēnē* instead of the usual entrance from outside. After those fifty lines of dispute the chorus go out by one or the other parodos in pursuit, leaving the place vacant for a moment, and the scene is changed, as described above (at page 84 f). The conflict has been fully stated before, and the initial situation is simple. The *parodos* develops the character of the avenging *daimons* and suggests the nature of the coming struggle.

The "Agamemnon" exhibits a most elaborate intertwining of exposition and challenge, with suggestions of the complication. The struggle is vaguely hinted in the watchman's opening soliloquy: There is trouble in the house; the queen is feared; the king's arrival, it is hoped, will set things right. In the course of their march-anapests the chorus address the queen, and quietly accept her rebuff. This first glimpse of the queen bodes no good! Turning to song while awaiting her royal pleasure, they recall, in dactylic measures that suggest the epic tone, the omens that ten years ago, when the army was setting out, portended a long war, final success, and some trouble to follow. Thus a significant bit of the background of the play is given; foreboding is the burden of their thrice-repeated refrain. The rhythm now changes to one befitting the thought in which they take refuge— rest in the Lord, confidence in the ruler of the world, who, in chastising, by pain brings wisdom. In a slightly different rhythm they sing now of the contrary winds at Aulis, and the king's sacrifice of his daughter. They dwell on the reluctance and final submission of Agamemnon, the vain entreaties of Iphigeneia; they recur to the thought of just punishment and of wisdom thus hardly won—and glide over to ceremonial compliments to the queen, who now appears.

The basis of the song is lyric narrative of events that occurred ten years before, but are part of the initial situation and relations. So far it is exposition. In lyric reflection upon these events the note of foreboding is touched repeatedly, and we are made familiar with that which is to be Klytaimestra's excuse for hostility to her husband. And we are left in no doubt that the chorus, when they connect the thought of justice, suffering, and the gaining of moral wisdom thereby, with the story of human sacrifice, are thinking of punishment for Agamemnon—to whom none the less they are wholly loyal. Which does this train of thought belong to? In form, to the exposition; in spirit, to the complication. The plot is such that explicit statement of the conflict is impossible until after the struggle is decided. If any person in the play were informed of the queen's plan, it would be frustrated. The art of the lyric poet puts the audience in possession of elements which the poet as dramatist could not bring out in dialogue.

IX. AESCHYLUS AND CHARACTER-DRAWING

I

WE make much of character-drawing, and we incline to draw it in painting and elsewhere with heavy strokes or with a palette knife. Especially on the stage we rather look, in that feature of the art particularly, for the exaggeration which is necessary in other ways for producing on an audience the desired effect of naturalness. But that recognized necessity concerns the contributory art of acting rather than the art of the playwright, who must allow the actor freedom to meet the conditions of the stage, but need not put his own picture out of drawing, making it false to life. The Elizabethans, including Shakspere, did habitually present character with bold strokes and heavy contrasts; and most of their plays are relegated to the shelf and the scholar's laboratory. In their best plays, however, both comedies and tragedies, strength is mingled with delicacy. But in Attic drama, as in other branches of Greek art, heavy strokes and Rembrandtesque light and shadow would be out of harmony. In sculpture certainly, in painting as far as we can judge, realistic portraiture, faces deeply marked by age or passion, had no place during the fifth century, the great period of tragedy. In the preceding century, apparently, the inclination toward what we call realism was developing. It was checked, or rather took a happier direction toward an ampler region. Polygnotos and Pheidias, along with Aeschylus and Sophokles, did not fall short of something which Euripides and Apelles and Roman portraiture, in different fields and at different stages, attained. Rather, they of the fifth century valued, sought, and attained a kind of portraiture, a manner of exhibiting life, which was more profound, broader, more inclusive, and which could not have existed along with that narrower and less penetrating style. The later age could not maintain the level, and declined to a plane more congenial with our own. The character-drawing of the two elder tragedians, and of Euripides in his happier hours, was of that larger type, by no means lacking in individuality, but presenting clear-cut figures, gods or idealized men and women, comparable, in that earlier period, to the pediment figures of the Parthenon.

In one particular possibilities of character-drawing were indeed limited. Since the formal conditions of Attic tragedy required that only the last stages of the tragic action be presented, development of character, the growth which had preceded the climax, had to be largely taken for granted. Changes produced by life's progress, by contact with other natures or by clash with other wills, could be presented only as these changes came quickly. In life these changes are commonly not quick but gradual. Here is indeed the special opportunity of the novelist. A drama which employs no curtain must mostly forego that side of life. It can at most be narrated, hinted, or taken for granted.

But such changes are sometimes rapid; these the drama can use. Even in the curtain drama, where successive scenes are separated by the fall of a curtain, which means an indefinite lapse of time, a lapse defined only by visible outward change and by clear reference to it, it is true that change itself is not often presented; it is only implied by presenting the same people at different stages. But that is enough for the art; it makes these changes part of the plot. Such changes are too valuable material for drama to give up. And to make a wider variety of change available, it becomes a dramatic convention that changes are far more rapid than they are. People do, rarely, fall in love at first sight; in Shakspere they always do. An ambitious soldier and his wife may, within a few days after receiving a prediction of royal station, nerve themselves to murder in their own house the present king and then all who stand in their way. Confident love might conceivably be in brief period transformed by a villain's machinations to insane jealousy, leading to murder of the innocent without investigation. That he may present the passions involved, Shakspere takes these transformations as normal; his great tragedy leads us to accept his postulate, wildly improbable though it be.

Still it is true that great crises of life effect great changes in brief space. Especially a sudden disaster, overwhelming loss or reversal of fortune, the kind of crisis that offers the stuff of tragedy, quickly stirs the depths. In every great war thousands learn this, both at home and in the field. Latent passions are let loose, unknown resources are tapped, unsuspected weaknesses revealed. Changes thus effected are quite within the range of Attic tragedy, and have a large place there in the Sophoklean type. Euripides, too, is fond of bringing out in a powerful scene some inner transformation, either caused by an outward reversal or coming suddenly to light from silent reflection on a situation. We shall look at some instances later.

Character-drawing in tragedy began, however, with something else—with the portrayal of characters as established and static rather than in growth or transition. Given the myth, a group of people doing and saying certain striking things, the aim was to present in dramatic form the gods and men concerned doing and saying those things. Thespis may have gone in the direction of characterization little beyond the names, with indication of sex and age and fundamental relationships. This mere foundation of character-drawing would in the beginning furnish novelty and interest enough. As the infant art grew, types would be more distinctly differentiated. In Aeschylus as we have him, in all but the last trilogy—in the adult but not yet fully matured art—the leading characters are typical figures, broadly drawn, all minor traits suppressed that contribute nothing to the action. There is a peculiar dignity and strength and largeness about them. They are truly individual, not mere embodiments of classes; they are Aeschylean, not such as any other dramatist has presented, beings as of a larger breed, suitable to an antique age when gods and men could mingle. Gradation according to importance in the plot is also distinct; no lesser personage is allowed to withdraw attention from the more important. On that ground Aeschylus is perfectly sure of his footing.

The chorus of fifty Danaïds, though not in the least differentiated among themselves, one multiple person, as a chorus ordinarily is, stands out in spite of the unhappy mutilation of text as like no other suppliant band—strong, passionate, insistent, ready to die rather than fall into the hands of their hated cousins. They accept meekly, as Greek maidens, their father's admonitions touching modesty of behavior before strange men, but they lead him not less than he leads them. They are young women fully capable of murdering their bridegrooms on the wedding night. Their father Danaos, though taking the nominal lead in action, is yet subordinated to them. They not only sing at length their prayers and fears and the fortunes of their ancestress Io, Danaos taking no part, but they conduct the entire discussion with the Argive king. It is Danaos who goes to negotiate for them with the popular assembly and brings back report of the people's decision to accept and defend them; his part in the plot is saved from weakness, but the daughters are the dominant character. And the king is the anxious ruler, fearing the impiety of rejecting a suppliant, but unwilling to bring war upon his country without his people's consent. We may say that the characters are all such as the story demands; and contrasting their massive simplicity with later subtlety one may fail to see how great an achievement it was to draw so firmly, at that stage of dramatic art, just the characters that the incidents of the myth presupposed, and yet make them individual, and at the same time draw them so well grouped and related.

Likewise in the "Persians" the chorus are the real center of the picture, if not of the plot, rather than Xerxes or the queen-mother. They represent the Persian people—Aeschylean Persians, as we saw, not the historical Persians. They comprehend and state the grounds for dread of disaster, which Darius later reinforces with like reasoning. And Atossa is the proud queen-mother, more anxious for her son's person than for his kingdom—Oriental queen, but woman first. Beside her and Darius, the sainted hero, Xerxes is merely the Oriental despot, despairing and effeminate in defeat as he had been unwise in leadership, recognized without question as foremost in station, yet least worthy of that station. No 'prentice hand could draw these figures so surely.

The chorus of the "Prometheus" are distinctly subsidiary—sympathetic, maidenly, admiring, apprehensive, but loyal to the end. In so much bolder relief stands out the Titan as central figure, defying, for love of man, the conqueror of the Titan race and ruler of heaven. Has any other image of righteous rebellion so taken the imagination of the world? The picture of a god suffering the utmost for men could not but strike the early Christians as the nearest pagan approach, in spite of all difference, to the passion of Christ. The reluctant Hephaistos and the ruthless minister, Strength, who nail Prometheus to the cliff; officious and shallow Okeanos, quickly sketched as additional foil; the patient Io, as another victim of Zeus' injustice—from the point of view of Prometheus, which the dramatist does not quite convince us is mistaken—well adapted to excite still further the indignation and defiance of the Titan; these make again a little group of distinct characters, each helping to define Prometheus more fully.

The story of the "Seven against Thebes" offered a different problem. The young warrior-king and the chorus are alone really characterized, both on pretty general lines. The most personal trait of the former is the spirit in which he accepts the turn of fortune that has placed him as the antagonist of his brother. A mingling of hatred and of royal pride and courage impels him to reject the entreaties and well-grounded advice of the chorus and put fate to the test. Except in this episode the chorus are typical frightened women, who know well how women fare in a captured town. The scouts merely report the situation in resounding verse.

The thing to be noted is that in all these cases characterization just meets the need. Not merely the action or plot in the narrower sense exhibits a protagonist, with other people variously subsidiary and contributory, the character-drawing does the same. It is always broad, never minute, suited to the conditions of a large auditorium and an outdoor theater, but it is enough. Whoever really knows the plays will agree that no dramatic characters stand out in memory more distinctly, within the limitations which are prescribed by dramatic conditions.

II

But then it must be granted farther that much the same style and degree of characterization are habitual in Homer. In the leisurely epic as well as the terse and emotional tragedy the same kind of restraint appears, the same adequacy of characterization with economy of means and absence of exaggeration. There is a deeper reason for the agreement. As to the fact in Homer there can be no doubt. Are not Achilles and Menelaos and Agamemnon and Hector as distinct as any figures in literature? But so are others who appear less often; not only Odysseus and Penelope and Telemachos, but the swineherd Eumaios and the maiden Nausikaa, and so on. Also, if Nestor and Thersites and the Cyclops are pretty strongly marked by physical and other unmistakable traits, the most are not so, but are drawn by delicate touches, few or many according to the needs of the story, in many

189

cases largely by fitting use of stock epic phrases. If standing epithets, even, appear at first reading to be conventional, convenient verse-fillers, every little while one suddenly realizes that they lend themselves nevertheless to very delicate applications, and are not applied haphazard. Professor John A. Scott has brought out much evidence that the poems were composed with clear conceptions of many different personalities, carried consistently from beginning to end, one touch added here to receive a fuller meaning by another touch perhaps in another book, the entire personality being so built up slowly, as in life. And with few exceptions, this is done quietly, without exaggeration, and in easy gradation, so that minor personages in the story are no more individual than their place in it requires. The Poet Laureate, in connection with his experiments in "quantitative" hexameters, has lately pointed out the reticence and delicacy with which Priam, on his way to the camp of Achilles, lets the disguised Hermes know that the latter is recognized, without openly recognizing him, and Hermes with equal delicacy accepts the mutual understanding. This perfection of courtesy between king and god is closely akin to Homeric methods of characterization—of which indeed the entire episode is a masterly illustration.

The truth is, in essentials no literary art known to man is more mature than that of the Iliad and Odyssey. If they constitute for Hellas and for us the starting-point of European letters, they were themselves the final flower of a long development. I never could make much out of current definitions that place those two poems in a class of "popular" epics, over against "literary" epics like "Paradise Lost" and the "Aeneid." As commonly given those definitions imply that the former are somehow more primitive, composed with less conscious literary skill. Nothing could be less true of Homer. His old material was home-grown, from the life of his own people, not gathered out of a foreign tongue from the legends of another race, legends laboriously learned in school and familiar only to the educated, as was that of Vergil. But there never was a more conscious literary artist, the product of a long poetic past. And to return to character-drawing: As early as Homer the Greek race had artists in words who knew how to paint personalities adequately. The art of doing so was traditional; at least it was traditional after Homer. Aeschylus is master of it in the earliest plays we have.

III

Yet in the "Agamemnon," when the poet was past sixty-five, he went a step farther. Here, in a play extraordinarily rich in dramatic material of every kind, is a group of characters portrayed with a vigor and directness never surpassed, exhibiting a fullness of individuality that the greatest actors would find inexhaustible. The dramatic form nowhere departs from the antique canon. Externally the figures are antique—mid-fifth-century conceptions of Homeric personages adapted to dramatic use. In substance they are no less modern than antique, and the methods of portrayal as congenial to Shakspere at his best as to Aeschylus.

The chorus, old men useless for war even ten years ago, are highly deferential to the queen, though aware of her adultery, and apprehensive. Loyal to the king, they are yet unable to acquit him of bloodguiltiness, and frankly remind him, while they rejoice in his success, that they had thought his expedition unwise. Their sympathy with Cassandra is so kindly that it leads her to pour out her heart to them. After the murder they roundly denounce the murderess and defy her despised paramour, but yield to force of arms. They would be too individual for a chorus in any play where the other characters were less strong than in this.

Before she appears, the watchman on the roof has alluded to Klytaimestra's masculine will and to her disordered rule. Since the chorus directly address her, shortly after their arrival, it would seem that she shows herself for a moment, giving orders about sacrifices, but deigns no answer to their respectful greeting. They accept the rebuff and turn to a long choral song, awaiting her pleasure, and then humbly repeat their modest request for information; which goes to characterize both. In her way of announcing that Troy is taken, in the splendor of her account of the beacon-message, and in the vivid pictures evoked of scenes in the captured city, there is a haughty tone, perhaps not unsuited to a queen-regent; but a sinister light is thrown back upon the whole by the allusion to dangers that the victors may still encounter in returning home. (We have been introduced to a strong, daring, passionate woman, capable of desperate plotting, which those about her evidently fear.) When the herald appears she does not come out at once to receive him. As delivered to the chorus alone his message is freer in its personal emotion; the queen comes only to send to the king by him a message of welcome and assurance of fidelity—a message not unsuitable to the situation,) though the chorus-leader, on her withdrawal, vaguely hints at another aspect of it. She reappears at the entrance of Agamemnon. This is the ceremonial meeting of king and queen in the presence of court and council and representatives of the army. Before dismounting from his chariot the king offers formal thanks to the gods, and then, responding to the council's "dutiful and loyal address," he refers to known disorders to be publicly righted—plain suggestion of a day of reckoning. With direct reference to this, Klytaimestra from the palace steps begins by informing the council that she will feel no shame in speaking before them—whose knowledge of her falsity was her nearest danger—of her wifely devotion: "Fear dies out at last." (This bold defiance, with the double meaning of the final words, is part of her plan for securing the few minutes more that she needs to bring her plot to a head. It is the proem to that astonishing picture of her nights and days of loving anxiety, that voluble protestation of joy at her lord's return—the whole address an expansion of the message she had sent by the herald. "Methinks the lady doth protest too much." The council know and Agamemnon would suspect it to be untrue; but her boldness displays her skill. (It puzzles the council and tends to lame with doubt whatever suspicion of pressing danger might suggest itself to the king.) Then the huge flattery of spreading his path with purple, that the monarch may reenter his palace in Oriental splendor after his Eastern triumph, shows that she has gauged his royal weakness. No Greek could fail to scent the danger in such public exultation in success. But his protests are half-hearted, soon overcome by a little wheedling; and when she has carried her point, she endeavors to quiet his last scruple by lauding the unlimited wealth of his kingly house. Commanding kindly treatment for the captive Cassandra, he walks on purple to a bloody death, while Klytaimestra completes her venom-

ous welcome with an ambiguous prayer to Zeus the Ful-
filler. After a foreboding song from the chorus she
returns for a moment, to hasten, with feigned gentleness,
the entrance of Cassandra, the second victim of her hate.
Baffled by the latter's unresponsiveness, she goes back to
her main enterprise. She is next seen standing over the
corpses of her husband and Cassandra, displaying the
weapon, boasting of her deed, exulting in the falsehood
and cunning that had brought success, rejoicing in the
splash of her husband's blood upon her as growing corn
rejoices in the fresh rain. When the chorus predict popular execration and punishment, she answers with a personal threat and with an appeal to divine justice, affirm-
ing that no thought of fear treads her hall so long
as Aigisthos lives. Having thus openly acknowledged
her adultery she now vents her contempt on the corpse of
Cassandra, her husband's concubine, whose death, she
says, adds relish to her marriage bed. Another phase of
the high tension of her emotion hints, but only hints, at
a breaking down. As the chorus continue their dirge and
even long for death, she joins in an expression of horror
at the successive woes of the Pelopid race, and conceives
herself as the latest incarnation of the old demon of the
house; gladly would she now make truce with him that
the present woe shall be the last. But as Aigisthos now
finally ventures to show himself, with a bodyguard, Klytaimestra intervenes to allay the altercation between him
and the chorus. She is the wiser ruler as well as
the stronger criminal.

One thinks at once of Lady Macbeth as a kindred
spirit. But Lady Macbeth was not intended to dominate
the whole play as Klytaimestra was. Ambition is a
larger factor in Lady Macbeth's motives than could be

the case with one who was already queen. She loves and is ambitious for her husband, while Klytaimestra's prime motive is adulterous passion, which she glosses and supports, to herself as to others, with pleas of just vengeance. Both nerve themselves to murder, both are stronger for the bloody deed than their mates. But in conformity with the whole dramatic intent for the respective plays Lady Macbeth is broken physically by brooding on her guilt, while Klytaimestra remains unbowed. She is tormented for years by fear of the avenger, but her ghost in the "Eumenides" is still unbroken.

If Klytaimestra is the "star," her support would demand a strong company—Agamemnon, the watchman, the herald, and Cassandra, all vigorously drawn. Though his fate is the center of the plot, Agamemnon's active part in the play is brief, less than a hundred lines in all. He is much the same man as in the Iliad, only portrayed in a different medium, condensed drama instead of epic. His qualities are not so much those of personal endowment, as those that go with his station and are developed by it—easy dignity, social superiority, the habit of making great decisions for a people, and of having his decisions accepted. The chorus have described him as not strong enough to resist nor able to devise a solvent for the pressure of circumstances that drove him to sacrifice his daughter; for which they distinctly blame him without themselves suggesting a better course. We are made to see the tragedy of that position for him, as well as for others. Even more distinctly than Klytaimestra the chorus speak of the dangerous burden that rests on him who is responsible for the waste of life in war; we are made to feel that Agamemnon carries upon him that burden, inseparable from his office. The herald an-

nounces him as vindicator of justice on Troy, most
worthy of living men to be honored as destroyer of the
city and people of Paris. This is of course the achievement that is foremost in the mind of Agamemnon himself; he offers thanks that the gods who have brought
him safe home have aided him to punish with destruction
the guilty city. But this honor which is freely accorded
him as king he is inclined to accept as due to personal
merit; he allows himself to disparage all his helpers except Odysseus. While deprecating excess, bidding the
queen honor him as man, not as god, at heart he thinks
the proposed honor of spreading his path with purple not
unfitting to his fame. He is kind to his captive, has the
royal virtues as well as the royal faults, wins the personal
devotion of high and low; but he has laid good foundations for the secondary pretexts for assassination.

The watching domestic, who opens the play by thinking aloud, may be conceived as already on the roof when
the audience begin to gather. He traverses in his thirty-
nine lines the emotional range both of his months of
waiting and of the moment of release. The weariness
of his lonely nights and enforced study of the stars, fear
of his stern mistress that prevents an instant of sleep,
thoughts of the sad plight of the house, moving him to
tears when he would sing or whistle to while away the
discomforts of the night, his longing for the signal—this
complex is dissipated by sight of the beacon. His
thoughts then are of the joy for Argos; he dances a little
prelude of his own at the lucky throw for himself as well
as for his masters. He anticipates the delight of touching
his lord's dear hand, whereupon the vision of that arrival
forces his mind back to the evils which the king alone can
put right, which the servant must not reveal. The comic

touch in this masterly exposition we might call Shaksperian, except for its brevity and restraint. It enhances by contrast the double reference to the latent tragedy of the situation; and the man, doubtless a slave, amply recognizes a coming storm.

In the herald what one notes first is his wealth of poetic expression and the depth of his feeling. The soil of his native land, in which he had lost hope of burial,— hope dear to every Greek,—the home aspect of the sun, then the gods of home, Zeus and Apollo, Hermes the herald's patron, the native heroes that sent them forth, the palace of his kings—to all these he offers joyful greeting and the prayer that they will receive with favor Agamemnon, who has now returned, great instrument of Zeus in the punishment of Troy. The present happiness and the very image of Apollo, who had scourged them with pestilence, recall the sufferings on sea and land, in the snows of winter and the heat of summer, now past and gone— recall the comrades also who shall never return. But in spite of all, victory with its trophies, and gratitude to Zeus who has given them, are the final and all-pervading notes. To the formal message of Klytaimestra no response is needed; the questions of the chorus about the storm and the delay of Menelaos he answers with reluctance at recalling dangers and loss, but hopefully for the event. No other herald is at all like him, in Homer or elsewhere. Incidentally, in him more than in any other character we may assure ourselves that Aeschylus felt the beauty and sublimity of the sea in storm, as well as the drowsy charm of its calm midday sleep in the heat of summer.

If one simply accepts the mythical basis, Cassandra is one of the most pathetic figures in dramatic literature.

That mythical basis, which represents Apollo as wooing a mortal woman and punishing her for rejecting him after promising compliance, is quite out of harmony with the poet's higher conception of divine nature. But as in Pindar—or in the ancient Hebrews—old concepts from a primitive age could coexist, in Aeschylus the dramatist, along with the purified concept that was in the end to annihilate the old. For his dramatic purpose that part of the myth, a popular datum wholly outside of the play itself, was an antecedent essential to the specific character. He therefore accepts it without remark, that he may present powerfully a bit of life that in essence is true in every age. .It puts no great strain on the imagination for us to do the same.

Cassandra comes in Agamemnon's train with other spoils, but conspicuous by costume and a separate conveyance. There has been no allusion to her until Agamemnon, in his last words before dismounting to walk to the palace door, commands a kind reception for her as his choicest prize. She is first named by Klytaimestra, trying in vain to induce her to enter the palace. We must suppose that her action during this scene showed that she was absorbed in her prophetic vision, beside which the words of Klytaimestra and the chorus-leader were unheard or sounded far away. This is one of the cases for which the poet was famous, where persistent silence is made more significant than speech could be. Left alone with the friendly chorus, overmastered by the vision, in wild words and in rhythm and music that paint her horror, she cries out on Apollo, who has endowed her with prophecy with the addition that she shall never be understood nor believed—the frequent penalty of clearer insight. Slowly the elements of the vision become more distinct—the old murders the house has known, infants bewailing the cannibal feast on their own flesh, the new murder planned by wife against her husband. Still the chorus do not comprehend, but growing pity for her and growing dread now finally draw them, too, out of calm spoken trimeters into agitated song. Fifty-five lines more the lyric interchange continues; she sings of the fatal robe, foresees her own murder, couples the rivers of the dead with Skamander's banks that she knew in childhood. Then, more fully mistress of herself, turning from song to speech in trimeters, she tries to explain more clearly. She alludes to more details of the dreadful history of the family; in answer to questions she tells how she acquired her fatal gift, describes more fully the designs of Klytaimestra, but in language so emotional that the chorus still fail to grasp it. At last her plain words, "I say ye shall behold Agamemnon's death," are received as mere words of ill omen, not to be spoken or listened to—the old fatal disbelief. She knows that her struggle to convince is vain; she sees Apollo himself stripping off her prophetic robe, dashes on the ground her mantic wand and the chaplet about her neck, sees her own death blow, prays that it be instantly fatal, and foretells the future vengeance of Orestes. She has no wish to postpone her fate, surviving longer all her royal line; yet she pauses in horror at the smell of blood as she nears the threshold, and still delays for still more pathetic utterance. A moment after the princess disappears within the king's death cry is heard. We acknowledge that even such a death is for her a blessed release.

It may be said with some truth that all these portraits are still broadly drawn, all minor traits suppressed that do not contribute to the action, as in Homer. That indeed would be true of all the best Greek art. But the difference is that the people are far more complex; more traits contribute something to the action, life is fuller. The dramatist has learned to draw into his plot more of life, and so vividly that we are moved by aspects of life hitherto little employed in art. And in fullness of individuality of its characters this play stands quite alone, for us, until the "Aias" and "Antigone" of Sophokles, something like sixteen years later. One is tempted to say that Sophokles learned character-drawing from this play; only we must remember the paucity of our materials for judging.

The two other plays of the trilogy are nothing like so rich in this regard—more on the level of his earlier plays. It is as if the unusual length of the "Agamemnon" left him too little room for corresponding elaboration in the others. More probably the poet and his contemporaries estimated more highly than we do the other elements, which are more remote from our thoughts, and so they did not miss the richer personalities. In the "Libation-pourers" the chorus, though of slave women, are nevertheless stronger characters than Elektra, who asks and follows their advice. Orestes is the youthful prince, returning by divine command to fulfill his stern duty. He is the rightful king, the rightful source of legal justice, come to resume the throne. The dreadful fact that one of the usurping criminals is his mother does not deter him, though he feels the horror of it, and to him and Elektra alike the ghostly help of Agamemnon was naturally to be sought with the most elaborate adjurations, in the *kommos* that fills so large a section. He faces the consequences, pursuit by the Furies of his mother, with hope in the promise of Apollo. Klytai-

mestra, confronted with what she has feared, calls for a
weapon and is ready to fight; she appeals to her child,
when fight is impossible, to respect the breast that
suckled him, and pleads with rapid argument, but never
weakens. The old nurse is another case of a comic touch
judiciously employed, more marked than in the watchman of the preceding play. She recalls her troubles in
caring for the baby, of whose death word has just been
brought; and at the request of the chorus-leader she aids
in the outcome by taking to Aigisthos a message contrary to the one with which Klytaimestra had sent her.

In the "Eumenides" Orestes is quite subordinate as a
personality, though his trial and acquittal are the main
action. Even Apollo, his advocate, and Athena herself,
president of the court that acquits him, are dramatically
subordinate to the Furies. In this his last play, when
Sophokles was already gaining on him, Aeschylus again
makes a chorus the protagonist, as in the "Suppliants."
The Furies are indeed hardly to be classed as human
characters. They are a dramatic embodiment of elemental moral law in primitive form, mysterious *daimons*
that punish the matricide. The playwright is explaining
dramatically a local cult, of highly salutary influence;
to his audience these black-robed incarnations of the
dread beings, who required ever-renewed propitiation
that they might remain to their worshipers the Kindly
Ones, must have been most impressive. As was said
above, local beliefs that we do not share, pride in their
ancient court, reverence for the goddess, in whom cen-
tered both patriotism and religion, and the splendid
pageantry of the final scene, were elements in the play
that the modern reader must supply in imagination—a
thrilling combination for an Athenian festival.

X. SOPHOKLES AND THE DRAMA OF CHARACTER

I

LATER tradition said that Euripides was born at Salamis on the day of the great battle in 480, Aeschylus fought in it at the age of forty-five, and Sophokles, as a beautiful boy of fifteen, danced in the festival in celebration of the victory. The round numbers have awakened suspicion; legend may have rounded out the facts, but connecting all in this way with one great event is for us as well as for the ancients a mnemonic convenience, and it is accurate enough for our purpose. A thirty years' interval separated the two elder poets. Aeschylus' home, Eleusis, with its mysteries of Demeter, and the battle of Marathon, in which he fought at thirty-five, may well have strongly influenced his nature. He was serious, reflective, deeply religious, accepting fully the view that a poet should be also a teacher of the people. Homer makes about every god of Olympus ridiculous upon occasion, Zeus as much as any; is there any exception but Athena? It is as if the way were preparing for Ionian philosophy. Aeschylus, Pindar, and Sophokles have not a trace of that genial mockery; to them Zeus is the unquestioned ruler of the universe, a wise and righteous ruler, in spite of some accepted myths not easy to reconcile. Instead of accepting and helping forward the incipient decay of the old faith, Aeschylus consciously tries to purify it, developing profounder views out of elements connected with the old names, and maintaining the old connection, the old names. Sokrates and Plato continue the Aeschylean line of development rather than the Homeric. But Aeschylean religion goes much deeper than names and attributes of deities. Underneath all differences of expression its spirit is akin to that of the Hebrew prophets. Its best expressions one can appropriate in as universal a sense as those of the Psalms. Righteousness, judgment to come, punishment for transgression, under the governance of Zeus, and rest in the Lord—such are the doctrines that his tragic plots and his choral songs enforce continually—doctrines the more vigorously enforced by the massive simplicity of his tragic form. And yet it must be admitted that they are nowhere more effectively enforced than in the "Agamemnon," the most complex of all in structure. "To the wrongdoer, suffering!" and "By suffering, knowledge!" is a recurrent theme. The beneficence of punishment, whereby one learns moral wisdom, is a doctrine that Plato, two to three generations later, so powerfully develops in the "Gorgias."

II

Sophokles is reported to have distinguished three periods in his dramatic life. At first he imitated the pomp and elevation of Aeschylus; then he aimed at a somewhat harsh incisiveness and even artificiality of style; only after these two periods did he attain his own proper manner. The saying as reported by Plutarch is very brief, was perhaps half humorous, and seems to refer rather to language than to dramatic technic. But the special point for us is that the seven extant tragedies all belong to his third period, after his distinctive manner was fully mature. All were composed after he was fifty, the earliest twenty-five years or more after his first victory in 468, and the last shortly before his death in 405. This is an extraordinary fact in his career, to which no other great dramatist offers a parallel—that his best work was done between the ages of fifty and ninety, the latest, "Oedipus at Kolonos," showing no trace of waning vigor. Think how many dramatists have ended their work and died before reaching the age at which Sophokles, for us, began. Shakspere, for example—and Marlowe, and Beaumont and Fletcher; Lessing, too, and Schiller, and Molière. Is it perhaps something more than accident that the three great tragic poets of Athens all lived to a ripe old age, writing great plays to the very end? But Sophokles surpassed the others in this by many years. Mellow maturity, complete mastery of his art, and that quality which Matthew Arnold put in the oft-quoted line,

"Who saw life steadily and saw it whole"—

these characterize all the seven. Doubtless we should have a different conception of his genius, a fuller and truer one, if we had several tragedies from the earlier periods. Some of his experiments would be most interesting. But there is little likelihood that we should place him higher; we should merely be able to trace his growth better. And no doubt there would be among them some fine plays for which we should be grateful. As Egypt has lately restored to us half or more of one of his satyr-plays of earlier date, and small fragments of tragedies, there is still a possibility of recovering entire plays.

SOPHOKLES AND DRAMA OF CHARACTER

What differences in form are most noticeable between the Sophoklean type of tragedy and that of his predecessor? First of all, no chorus of the seven is the protagonist, which we saw was the case in the earliest and the latest that we have of Aeschylus, while it is nearly so in the "Persians." Of course one of the later plays may have followed this earlier type; but so far as our evidence goes, Sophokles in his third period did not return to it, and this is a natural negative result of his most characteristic enlargement of dramatic art. His choruses are well attached to the action—perhaps least well in the "Women of Trachis," who are merely sympathetic maidens, not capable of the fullest sympathy and having really no part in the *exodos*—but stronger characters always take the lead. Accordingly the chorus never enters first, as in the "Suppliants" and the "Persians." There is always a *prologos;* the chorus comes to a situation already well defined, to an exposition well under way.

Accordingly, also, no choral songs are so long as in most of the Aeschylean plays. Of these the "Prometheus," one of the earlier, and in some respects very antique in form, in that single particular might belong to a far later period. In Sophokles no choral song has more than three strophic pairs with an epode; though the *parodos* of the "Elektra" varies this by dividing each unit between Elektra and the chorus, thus introducing greater complexity. The usual type is of two pairs, and a single pair often suffices. He has no such invocation as that in the "Persians" to the ghost of Darius, or that in the "Libation-pourers" to the spirit of Agamemnon, the latter invocation peculiarly complicated in the interlacing of responsions, though in each of these cases the stanzas are short. Not that there is any loss of flexibility in adapting lyric forms to the varying emotion and new situations; all three tragedians—and Aristophanes no less—are complete masters of the lyric as one aspect of their trade as tragic poets. More subtle adaptations of rhythm to sentiment than in Sophokles cannot be found. At the same time it must be granted that his range of meters is not so wide as that of either of his rivals. But we need not dwell on this, as no trace of it can appear in translation.

No change of scene is even implied after the "Aias," as was remarked before; this is one of the two earliest among our seven, dated not later than about 440, and is the most Aeschylean in spirit. The tendency toward placing the scene always before a house or temple seems to be growing more general; and yet freedom is retained, for in the two latest, the "Philoktetes" and the second "Oedipus," no building is near. The scene of the former is on a rocky shore, of the latter on the edge of the sacred grove of the Eumenides.

We have no Sophoklean tragedy in which, as in the "Prometheus" and the "Eumenides," the characters are immortals. In the *prologos* of the "Aias" Athena appears, and in talk with Odysseus and with Aias explains her part in the action; at the close of the "Philoktetes" the deified Herakles, as a "god from the machine," commands the only solution which was possible without derogation from the character of the two chief personages, and which at the same time would preserve the outcome prescribed in the myth, that Troy should be taken with the aid of Herakles' bow in the hands of Philoktetes. In Sophokles as we have him this is the only "god from the machine," and the poet makes no other call upon theatrical machinery for bringing in strange creatures, such calls as Aeschylus made so freely.

Every play of the series requires three actors for one or more scenes in which two characters besides the chorus display differing reactions to a third. Simple as it may look, this device of a third speaker was the distinctive advance of Sophokles, and though Aeschylus adopted it, he seems to have made slight use of it. Only one of the great scenes of the "Agamemnon" requires it, that where Klytaimestra receives the king; and in this Cassandra does not utter a word. Her presence and her minimum of action are highly effective, and her part must be taken by an able actor, because she remains, and is the great figure of the next scene. The third speaking actor could not be dispensed with here, and no one can say he could be put to more impressive use; but he is not used in Sophokles' way. In the "Libation-pourers" Orestes, at his mother's appeal that he will respect the breast which he had sucked, turns in momentary hesitation to ask the advice of Pylades, who replies in three lines; but this is slight enough. The trial scene of the "Eumenides" is nearer to Sophokles; Orestes, Apollo, and Athena all have speaking parts. But the aim here is rather impressive spectacle than character-drawing.

Put beside these the *prologos* of the "Aias." Though Odysseus stands aside and is invisible to Aias, he remains and himself sees and listens while Athena exhibits Aias in his delusion. This ocular demonstration gives dramatic force to the moral lesson which Athena reads her favorite, and determines the attitude of Odysseus, which determines the issue in the final scene. Again, in that final scene the presence of Teukros, as the representative of Aias, during the interview between Odysseus and Aga-

memnon, is what makes natural and lasting the reconciliation of the rivals, and completes the restoration of
the honor of Aias. Again, Antigone and Ismene are
questioned by Kreon together; in no other way could
the subtle relation between the sisters be so well shown.
It may be remarked, however, that unless the reader can
in imagination see and hear the scene, the text loses most
of its meaning; it calls for skillful acting. The contrast
between Neoptolemos and Odysseus—the Odysseus of
the "Philoktetes"—is brought to a climax, as it could not
be otherwise, in the two scenes where both appear with
Philoktetes, and most dramatically at the moment when
Neoptolemos hands back the bow and then restrains
Philoktetes till Odysseus can escape. The three characters of Elektra, Orestes, and the *paidagōgos* are all
lighted up by the contrasts between them in the scene
after the recognition, when the old slave comes out and
finds the other two delaying dangerously. He at once
takes charge, scolds his master and Elektra roundly,
responds coldly to Elektra's outburst of affectionate gratitude, and brings Orestes back to the business in hand.
Such were the scenes for which Sophokles wanted a third
speaking actor. Aeschylus had lifted dramatic art to a
wonderful height without one, but the addition opened
new possibilities, which have been ever since a matter of
course in the playwright's resources.

III

It was no doubt his interest in character and the presentation of it that led Sophokles to this addition. We
have seen that that interest and great skill in portrayal
were nothing new; Sophokles merely gave such portrayal

new depth and a more inclusive range. He was no preacher of righteousness like Aeschylus. He took the traditional religion and traditional morality as given, betraying no inclination either to propagate or distinctly to purify, and still less to criticize or oppose; he simply presented the better aspects of them as normal. He was a man of the world, in the best sense of those words, as well as poet. Like other Athenian gentlemen he was active in public affairs, an associate of Perikles, was elected to the board of ten "Generals" who were at the head of the civil and military administration under the lead of Perikles. He may not have contributed much to the administration, though his courtesy and wit probably had some diplomatic value; he served as treasurer of the empire. His election to such offices showed at least that his fellow-citizens thought he would not be out of place there. With such an endowment, enjoying the universal esteem of his countrymen and mingling on equal terms with all classes, he looked out upon life, in the city where life was then fuller than anywhere else in the world, during more years than were granted to Shakspere and the other dramatists named, before his dramatic production, for us, begins. The spectacle of life, the interplay of motive, the elemental emotions that give rise to action, the effects of experience on the soul—these were what interested him. Yet it is remarkable how little trace the distinctive features of contemporary life made upon his plays.* Mingling actively in it, as poet and playwright he rose to a serene level above it. Democracy, social disintegration, the manifold confusion of the time, the growth of philosophy,

*Croiset, "Histoire de la littérature grecque," III, p. 270.

which left such marks on the work of Euripides, deepened the elder poet's knowledge of human hearts, but disturbed neither his personal calm nor his ideal of tragedy.

Given an old myth to be dramatized, his primary question was, Just what sort of people were they, must they have been, who naturally did and suffered what the tale says they did and suffered? That was his method of analysis. How could Oedipus unawares kill his father and marry his mother? Why was he, when exposed by his parents, rescued and reared? In what circumstances could he grow up, to be accepted later as king of Thebes? And so with all other details; the answers to these questions gave him the features of his plot, as we have before analyzed it. We have seen how he found the answers mostly in the characters of the people concerned. The newborn baby was unusually strong and winning, so that the slave desired to save him, at some risk to himself. The incident of the Corinthian shepherd was invented to make this possible; a childless Polybos and Merope, the affectionate nature of the supposititious prince and his foster-parents, the impetuosity of Oedipus, his quick temper inherited from his father, the character of the slave of Laïos—in a word, the human traits of the people concerned were the source in which he found, as we find in life, the most significant fortunes of men. As with Oedipus, it is in part, sometimes chiefly, the characters of others that are determining; it may be inheritance, the character of parents. Where the myth involved occurrences not explainable by character, there accident or coincidence—again as in life—was accepted without explanation, but only in minor degree, as part of the background. And largely, in Sophokles, it is the finer and better traits of character that are the source of action. There is ignorance, human error, lack of foresight, human passion, but no tragic villain in Sophokles as we have him. There is no Iago, no Richard III. Klytaimestra in the "Elektra" is the nearest to one; she is an unrepentant criminal who deserves her fate; but her crime was one of passion rather than of cool villainy, and it preceded the play; within the play it is fear of vengeance that makes her harsh to Elektra. Sophokles must have met and recognized villains enough. They apparently did not attract him for dramatic study; and he did not find in them and their motives a natural explanation of the myths which attracted him for dramatic rendering. One cannot but infer something in regard to his own nature.

The Sophoklean method of analysis and plot-construction is of course frequent in modern use; it is the natural method for serious drama when one takes the outline of a story from another, or from history. But we hear of quite other methods. Dramatizing a novel would seem to be in general a problem of selecting and simplifying— of eliminating what in a novel cannot be used in drama and adding in dramatic form any necessary elements that the novelist gave in a non-dramatic form. We are told that some playwrights begin at the other end, with an interesting character or group of characters, for whom incidents are then supplied to exhibit them. Many an acceptable comedy has been built in this way, perhaps a few tragedies. That is how plays are written to fit an individual actor or actress, or a given company. One may even begin with an abstract problem, and then embody that in characters and so end with plot. But Shakspere's method was nearer that of Sophokles, and

I doubt if great tragedies have been constructed otherwise.

So far as was possible in the limits of ancient dramatic form Sophokles portrays also development of character, its change under the stress of life. There is none of this in any Aeschylean single play; only the trilogy made it possible for him. And in the one trilogy we possess very little use is made of the possibility. Klytaimestra in the "Libation-pourers" is in constant fear, but is otherwise unchanged, and she is there a minor character—the object of vengeance from major characters, but not requiring to be fully drawn. In the "Eumenides" again Orestes is minor and nearly passive. The object of the trilogy was not to follow a personality in changing circumstances, but to present three separate plots more or less connected; succession in time was not the only kind of connection employed. In the "Prometheus," however long the ideal or dramatic time between the beginning and end, the Titan is the same defiant rebel at the end as at the beginning. In the lost "Prometheus Unbound" no doubt his spirit was softened by ages of suffering; but it was compromise, not defeat, that he accepted, and we cannot be sure just how the poet painted his attitude. Within the "Agamemnon" Klytaimestra, successful in her plot, is unchanged; she is openly triumphant, with a suggestion that she begins to realize the horror of her act; that is all. So with every Aeschylean character. But for Oedipus the hours of revelation have been a fire of transformation. From a proud and fatherly king is become a blind beggar, humbled by the knowledge of what he has unwittingly done, confessing his injustice to Kreon and Teiresias, conscious that he has been the curse of his country, of father and mother and children. Again in the second "Oedipus" the approach of his supernatural end effects a second transformation. The wayworn beggar, in exile, broken by years of suffering of body and spirit, assumes a new sort of kingly dignity. The powers most dreaded by mankind are receiving him with favor; he is to confer a royal gift, a worthy return for the hospitality of Athens. Physical blindness yields to an inward light. He who entered helpless, led by a girl, and conspicuously needed her hand to guide him in moving a few yards at the command of the chorus, now rises without aid and goes out, leading the way, to meet the death which he welcomes. In every Sophoklean play at least one character exhibits a like change, the result of the action.

A striking case is that of Neoptolemos. The play is named from Philoktetes because the action centers in him; the aim of the expedition is to bring him to Troy. And his character is admirably portrayed, but in the static manner. He is a mature man, deeply wronged, embittered by the treatment he has undergone. Naturally frank and trusting, he responds with open heart to the sympathy that meets him in the son of his friend Achilles, and is correspondingly cast down by unexpected deceit from the same quarter. But to the end, until the deified Herakles appears, he remains of the same mind, determined to accept no reconciliation, holding the youth to his promise to take him home, hating those who have wronged him, Odysseus above all. To the divine command to go to Troy he assents; we are left to suppose that he loyally cooperates thereafter with Odysseus and the rest; but there is no dramatic evidence of it. Odysseus also is in middle life, a man of the world in the more ordinary sense—wary, accustomed to indirection and skillful in it, a shrewd judge of character, possessing no illusions, but patriotic, devoting all his powers loyally to the Greek cause. But for him this enterprise is merely one of many in his active years; it makes no change in him.

The great interest of the play is in the contact of these two characters with Neoptolemos, their influence on him, and the effect of the whole experience in developing his nature. He is young, has just entered the war, is ambitious to emulate his great father; Odysseus has taken him as a partner and tool precisely because he is young and Philoktetes does not know him. After identifying the lonely cave by the shore in which Philoktetes lives, Odysseus unfolds his plan, appealing to the young man's sense of honor and loyalty to accept guidance in circumstances new to him. He appeals also to his ambition; the bow of Philoktetes, a gift from Herakles, must be obtained, or he can never take Troy. It can be obtained only by deceiving its owner; and Odysseus explains the tale of mingled truth and falsehood which the youth must employ to win the confidence of his victim. Such a scheme is wholly hateful to the son of Achilles; it requires a sympathetic and cautious explanation of the necessity to gain his acquiescence. Assent once yielded, however, Neoptolemos, with some embarrassment at the outset, proceeds to execute the plan with great skill, and by his Odyssean tale gains the full confidence of Philoktetes. He pretends to be retiring from the army in disgust at the chicanery of Odysseus and the rest; on the moving entreaties of Philoktetes he promises to take the sufferer home. As they are preparing to start, a sudden access of his dreadful disease makes Philoktetes shriek with pain, and before falling in a sleep of exhaustion he hands over the bow to his new friend for safekeeping. The ruse has succeeded.

But the utter trust of the man he is cheating has been slowly working in his soul; the renewed manifestation of that trust when the sick man awakes is too much for him to endure. Acknowledging the truth, he accepts as deserved the storm of reproaches from Philoktetes, but is unable to accept as yet the full consequence of repentance by handing back the bow. Odysseus reappears, to renew the opposite influence. To obtain a few minutes for reflection, escaping both the appeals of Philoktetes and the masterful spirit of Odysseus, Neoptolemos withdraws, on the pretext of overseeing the preparations of the sailors—and for prayers—leaving the chorus with Philoktetes. The decision is thus left in suspense while a long *kommos* between Philoktetes and the chorus paints in lyric verse and in music the pathos of the situation. At its close Neoptolemos and Odysseus are seen returning in haste; the decision is taken. An appeal to come willingly to Troy is rejected; the bow is restored. The intervention of Odysseus draws the attention of Philoktetes, who aims an arrow at him. His precipitate flight, while Neoptolemos prevents the shot, is a gratifying symbol of his defeat.

Now again on the new basis Neoptolemos presents his plea. He points out that the noisome wound by the serpent's bite was the providential means of delaying to the predestined time the fall of Troy; going with them now he will be cured and gain glory; and there is no other cure. To it all the final reply is, in brief, "Let me suffer to the end; I cannot aid those who have wronged me; keep your promise to take me home." And Neoptolemos makes the complete surrender. He gives up all ambition, is ready to go back to his island home and renounce all hope of fame, that he may keep his honor clean. The crisis, of hardly two hours' duration, has brought him face to face with the fundamental questions of life, changing him from a boy to a man. He and Philoktetes have both been tested to the utmost, and a god is the only agency that can untie the knot and preserve the fated issue—to his audience the historical issue. Herakles, whose bow has been held before our minds from the opening of the play, appears and reveals the will of heaven.

It is remarkable that this study of a young man's nature was made by a man of about eighty-five. There is a *stasimon* in "Oedipus at Kolonos" in which a pessimistic theme on the unhappiness of long life, a theme already ancient, is applied with dramatic fitness to the old age of Oedipus and the chorus. Some have fancied that Sophokles wrote it, being then about ninety, with a side reference to himself. That seems to me incredible of one who retained so lively a sympathy with the finest qualities of generous youth.

In the "Antigone" it is not so much the heroine as Kreon who is changed. His obstinate spirit is broken by successive waves of calamity, and he confesses his folly; but no special access of grace wins our personal sympathy. That goes, with our admiration, to his victim, Antigone, who is indeed the heroine of the play.

IV

Of other leading characters perhaps Aias shows the least change during the action. This is one of several ways in which this play is more suggestive of Aeschylus and an early date. We have already discussed one other mark of that sort, the shift of scene. But there is a farther ground for giving special attention to the "Aias," in the light it throws on the poet's religious attitude. The story is this. After the death of Achilles his wonderful armor, made by Hephaistos, was offered as a prize to him who had done most for the Greek cause before Troy. It should have gone to Aias as the greatest warrior after Achilles, but was awarded by the chiefs to Odysseus. Angry and humiliated at the slight, Aias went out by night to kill the chiefs, was driven mad by Athena, and killed some captured sheep and other animals instead. Coming to himself, he committed suicide. Now Salaminian Aias was the eponymous hero of the Aiantid tribe, which was one of the ten divisions of the people. He was taken by the Athenians as their great representative in the Trojan war. The subject of the play, then, is the restoration of the hero's honor, misprized by the chiefs, then fatally compromised by his own act.

In the first *scène* of the *prologos* Odysseus is examining some footprints that have led him to the cabin of Aias on the edge of the Grecian camp. The Greeks have found the havoc among the flocks and someone had seen Aias alone with a bloody sword not far off; Odysseus had therefore undertaken to investigate whether he was the guilty one. Athena hails him, unseen by Odysseus, though visible to the audience, draws this explanation from him, and in turn informs him that their surmise is correct. She explains in what spirit Aias had acted, and how she by confusing his wits had saved the chiefs, including Odysseus. To her proposal to call Aias out, that Odysseus may enjoy the discomfiture of his enemy,

Odysseus demurs. Fear of a madman is mingled with distress at the fall of a great hero. But Athena assures him that he will not be seen, and Aias comes at her call. He fancies that the victims he is still torturing in his dwelling are the Greek commanders, thanks Athena for her help, while she in mockery cheers him on. He goes back to his work of vengeance, and Odysseus takes the lesson to himself: "I pity him, unhappy man, although my enemy, looking not more to his case than to my own; I see that all we who live are naught but shadows." This, as was said above, is henceforth his attitude, the spirit in which at the end he secures for Aias dead the honor which he deserved.

We will not retrace the play in detail. The chorus are the Salaminian sailors and subjects of Aias, who come to learn if the rumor of his mad deed can be true. His slave-wife, Tekmessa, tells the events of the night as she knew them; their accounts confirm and explain one another. Aias comes to himself, realizes his disgrace, knows that death is inevitable, and feels it more honorable to inflict it with his own hand. His half-brother Teukros is absent on a raid; Aias calls for his little son, displays in his last wishes for him almost the only traces of tenderness—toward the child and his mother—that the stern warrior permits himself, commends him with confidence to his brother and the chorus in common, and gives commands about his own burial. After choral reflections, of longing for Salamis and sorrow for their chief, Aias again comes out, pretending to have been dissuaded from his purpose by the entreaties of his wife. He now prepares to go to the shore outside the camp for rites of purification and to bury his sword, a gift from Hector, which had brought him only evil. This provides

for the change of scene, as we saw. And here is introduced one of the distinctive bits of technic of Sophokles—a choral song of joyful anticipation just before the
catastrophe. Aias has led them to believe that all
thought of suicide is abandoned—that reconciliation and
happiness are sure. There is a similar moment of hope
at the corresponding point in the first "Oedipus," in the
"Antigone," and in the "Women of Trachis," while on
the other hand Elektra is brought to the lowest depth
of despair just before the joyful moment when Orestes
reveals himself. The contrast is the same in all these
cases, in five plays out of seven.

In the new scene, after burying the *hilt* of the sword
that he may fall upon the point, in a soliloquy of subtle
characterizing power which would demand a great actor
to bring out, Aias makes his final prayer and then falls
upon the sword. His own struggle to retrieve his honor
is ended. His first method was by killing his enemies
who had slighted his good right. That had failed and
had increased his disgrace. The play makes no suggestion that self-murder had in itself lightened the disgrace. But Sophokles saw life as it is. For one like
Aias suicide was the only possible issue. Then, too, when
justice was fully satisfied by the criminal's own act, when
all occasion and opportunity for punishment were removed, and every disturbing influence had disappeared,
men were free to discern once more his great past, his
heroic worth. Death is often a great clarifier of human
vision, restoring perspective where passion had confused
it. Teukros, who is really the continuation of Aias, can
now fight for him with hope of success; even meaner
natures, like the Menelaos and Agamemnon of this play,
cannot now hold out against the plea of Odysseus, suc-

cessful rival of Aias, when he solemnly affirms that the dead warrior was the best man of all the Greeks at Troy except Achilles. His great fault has not been veiled or softened, but the honors accorded him in Athens are justified. And his self-inflicted death is a necessary step in the dramatic process of demonstrating this. So far from breaking the plot in two, as some have maintained, it clears the way for its consummation.

We have still to take up the poet's religious attitude, which readers are apt to miss, because it is rather implied in plot and character-drawing than explicitly stated. As described by the seer Kalchas the offense of Aias is pride and self-confidence, which lead him to insult Athena; his punishment is due to her anger. That is the natural explanation in terms of Greek theology, of which Kalchas is an official exegete. No one in the play doubts or takes exception to it or feels any need of interpreting it. When Aias was setting out from home his father had said to him, "My son, desire to prevail in fight, but ever with God's help." To which he haughtily replied, "Father, with gods to help, even a weakling would gain the victory; I shall win that fame without them." Our feeling about such an attitude would be much the same as the Greek, however different our way of expressing it. Again, when Athena was cheering him on in battle, he said to her, "Goddess, go stand by the other chiefs; where I am the fight shall never break through." It was for this, the seer declared, the wrath of Athena would pursue him for this one day; if he could survive the day, they might with God's help save him.

But the goddess herself in the *prologos* puts the matter in another light. It is true that in pointing the moral to Odysseus she says, "Therefore never thyself utter words of pride before the gods nor puff thyself up, if thou in prowess or in wealth surpassest, since a day brings low and again exalts all that belongs to man; and the gods hate the wicked and love the good." This is not at bottom inconsistent with the view of Kalchas; the moral is familiar enough to us, and is inculcated by every religion. But there is nothing here about personal wrath at Aias, and nothing about a brief term, after which her wrath will be appeased.

And how, in fact, has she punished him? Her account agrees with that of Aias himself, that he started out, while quite sane, with the deliberate purpose of murdering Agamemnon and all the rest. He had almost succeeded when Athena "cast upon his eyes the sick fancies of insane joy," and so turned him against sheep instead, which he supposed were the victims he sought. By so doing she saved him from the intended crime and saved the army from a great catastrophe. There is no vengeance in that, and no vindictiveness, but only kindness. This was her only act of punishment. It is true that the insanity was made to take a form that was humiliating to him, in that the great warrior visited his vengeance on harmless animals. In so far the punishment was well suited by the divine wisdom to his pride. In making Kalchas announce that Athena's wrath would pursue him only that day, it is as if the poet meant to put in theological language the fact that we should put in psychological terms; if he could digest for one day the disgrace he had brought upon himself, reflection might refine his sense of humiliation to humility. That would be his moral and physical salvation.

In fact, as Sophokles presents it, the case of Aias can be readily stated in rationalistic and modern terms.

Paranoia, though a good Greek word, had not received its modern definition; but Sophokles had observed men closely and knew the dangers of a temperament like that of Aias. Such an enlarged sense of his own greatness borders on disease; it finds a slight where none was meant, and magnifies a real slight to an intolerable wrong. And though a grave fault, it is not incompatible with real greatness. Brooding over the withholding of due honor, Aias crossed the line into paranoia; in that state he felt that the proper way to right the wrong was to kill the wrongdoers. This he started to do, taking needed precautions to insure success. The excitement of executing such a plan disturbed his brain-action still farther, producing a degree of insanity that frustrated his plan. Slowly, after he supposed he had succeeded, the excitement subsided; he came to himself and realized how he had failed and how deeply he had disgraced himself. His condition was still that of paranoia; he did not in the least repent of the attempt, but only regretted its failure. Repentance and humility would have been recovery from his paranoia, which alienists tell us is almost or quite impossible. Sophokles saw that for Aias it was psychologically impossible. No thought of for-giveness occurs to him, no lessening of his sense of wrong, not a shadow of repentance. In his last soliloquy he curses the sons of Atreus and the whole army. As I said, Sophokles portrays the attitude and the action of Aias without cloaking in the least the darker side of it; such Aias must have been, just that he must have done, if the accepted story was true. Only, along with that the poet shows the other side—the great traits that justify the honor his fellows had felt for him, the honor accorded him in Athens. The whole is a masterly portrait.

And the remarkable thing is that he presents the case with such completeness and such permanent truth that all three modes of statement harmonize, when properly understood. To us the traditional religious formulas employed by Kalchas are as inadequate and unsatisfying as are the similar formulas of the Old Testament; they imply a lower conception of deity and moral government. But they would satisfy most of the Athenian audience, who would not care to go deeper. So, too, the corresponding Hebraic formulas would have satisfied our Puritan ancestors. The second mode of statement, which is clearly that of the dramatist himself, embodied in his plot, is on a higher plane of religion, and implies nothing contrary to the modern and more scientific third formulation, which we may prefer. But Sophokles was writing a play, for which purpose Athena and her words are better suited. His view of divine agency in the case is not less modern and rational than ours, though he employs the current mythological terms instead of those current in the Christian world.

V

Among Sophoklean characters his women form an interesting group. Ismene and Chrysothemis are alike in that each is the foil to a stronger sister; both are affectionate and well-meaning, both submit unwillingly to a rule which the other sister is ready from a sense of duty to defy, and each declines to join in the hazardous plan of disobedience to which the stronger invites her. But Chrysothemis on her first entrance begins to chide Elektra for her folly; to persist so openly in provoking their mother and Aigisthos merely makes trouble for Elektra.

223

Chrysothemis, for herself, while she recognizes that loyalty to their father and refusal to come to terms with his murderers is the nobler part, which she would gladly adopt if it were safe, thinks it better to preserve her freedom by submitting; personal freedom and bodily comfort are worth more to her than a clear conscience and freedom of soul. Yet she is ready to accept advice, and make her prayer, with the offerings of Klytaimestra at Agamemnon's grave, in Elektra's sense. Finding at the grave the offerings of Orestes, she interprets them correctly and returns in joyful haste to report that deliverance is near. But again the weaker yields to the stronger. Elektra, under the influence of the false report of Orestes' death, convinces her that they have nothing to hope from him. But her ardent urging of Chrysothemis to join her in attempting to kill the usurpers with their own hands Chrysothemis meets with cold reasoning, and has the better of it as mere argument. So they part—finally so far as the play goes—in sharp disagreement, with Elektra rather in the wrong. Yet our sympathy is not with Chrysothemis; her first speech and her last in the play are far from winning.

Ismene is much more attractive. Not sufficiently heroic to join Antigone in burying their brother, since defiance of Kreon's edict could effect nothing but their own destruction, she is tenderly affectionate toward Antigone. Her expostulations express love, admiration, solicitude for one who is dear, but no faultfinding spirit. She is confident the dead will pardon her, as acting under compulsion; she entreats her sister not to add another shameful death to the list in their family. Her final word, closing the scene of dispute, is one of sisterly affection. And later, when accused by Kreon of sharing in the crime, she assents, entreating Antigone, in the only way that is under the circumstances possible, to accept her as an accomplice, which she had been in spirit and by connivance. She has no wish to outlive her entire family. Antigone's refusal to accept the sacrifice, a refusal which is only just and right, but made in a somewhat irritating way, Ismene receives with patience, and makes one last appeal to Kreon that he will not put to death the betrothed bride of his one surviving son. She is much more than a mere foil to Antigone—a consistent and carefully studied character. The Ismene of the second "Oedipus," which was composed some thirty-five years later, is more slightly sketched, but is quite natural as a picture of the same girl at an earlier stage. The absence of a quixotic heroism does not make a woman less lovable.

Tekmessa is a captive in war, the slave of Aias, treated as his legal wife. We no longer approve that form of marriage, but those who know Turkish life well inform us that marriage by purchase is often in Turkey a happy one for both parties. Much depends on the personality of the wife. We see Tekmessa only under the stress of the catastrophe to her husband. She has perceived that her only hope of happiness lay in accepting her lot and building upon the fine qualities of her husband. She has therefore learned to be submissive and loyal, devoted to him and their son, finding under his rough and stern exterior a loyalty and affection that compensate for much. One of her greatest anxieties in her husband's madness was the safety of the child. After the body of Aias is found, we recognize that she is a princess by birth and by nature. She can but anticipate slavery; but while his Salaminian soldiers give way to an agitated dirge, her calm trimeters, in meter and words alike, express dignity, strength, and self-control.

Deianeira is more fully drawn, and is akin to Ismene and Tekmessa, as Herakles her husband has some traits in common with Aias. Narrating how she was wooed by the river-god Acheloös, she recalls her dread "lest her beauty should bring her pain." From that fear Herakles had 'rescued her; life with him has been happy, though lonely in his long absences. Now by old prediction she knows that after fifteen months of absence a crisis is near; either a peaceful life hereafter will be his, or death is at hand. Learning that a year of slavery is past and that he has succeeded in destroying Oichalia, and seeing the train of captives which Lichas brings, her anxiety is dissolved. She is struck with pity for these women, lately free, perhaps of noble blood, now homeless orphans and slaves. She prays heaven that such a lot may not befall her children. One girl especially attracts her pity, and she asks her name and parentage. Lichas professes not to know. Deianeira soon learns that she is Iole, daughter of the king of Oichalia, and that it was to obtain her as a concubine that Herakles had sacked the city. This, then, is her trial; how shall she meet it? She has known and patiently endured Herakles' weakness for women; but—this beautiful girl in her own home? For Iole herself Deianeira has no word of reproach; for her it is pain enough that "her beauty has destroyed her life." Nor will she reproach her husband, who is still her great hero. She decides to try to win him back by a love-charm. She anoints a rich garment with blood from the wound of the centaur Nessos, whom Herakles had shot with his poisoned arrow. Nessos had assured her that this would be an unfailing charm, if used as he directed. Though she feels doubts about it, the need is great, and she decides to send the garment to be worn first at a festal sacrifice. Only after the bearer is gone does she get ocular evidence that the charm is dangerous. Then too late she recognizes that the dying Nessos could desire no good to the enemy that had caused his death. She awaits in fear the report of the effect of her gift, determined not to live, if harm results to her husband. Accordingly when word comes that he is in fearful torture and near death, without a word of defense or explanation she goes to her bedroom and stabs herself. Nothing can be finer in its way than the delicacy, the mingled gentleness and dignity and the resolution with which she combats her human weakness. Such women, however old-fashioned, will never lose their charm; they will always command love, admiration, and honor.

Klytaimestra in the "Elektra" is one who has lived for years in fear, and has come to look on her son as the dreaded avenger, and to hate Elektra as the implacable reminder of her danger. Yet for a moment, under the influence of the vivid narrative of Orestes' death, the natural mother revives in her. There is a fine bit of psychological study in the few lines in which she gives utterance to this feeling—perhaps conscious that, though genuine, it was also a good pose—and then, as if she were herself the one wronged by his absence and alienation, gradually returns to what has become her normal mood, that of hatred for both son and daughter.

Iokaste is a more complex character, yet not easy to define, because her part in the play is more passive, and has little determining effect on the course of events. It is as if the exposure of her first-born had left a scar upon her nature; their supposed success in defeating the oracle

certainly had done so. The overwhelming horror of the
revelation leaves but one course open—to take her life.
It is indeed curious that Sophokles in our seven plays
offers no less than six suicides—including Antigone, who
does not wait for starvation that she believes to be the
alternative. I do not see any safe conclusion to be drawn
from this.

Antigone is of a stronger type, ready to sacrifice everything rather than duty and loyalty to her brother. She
is the true daughter of her father Oedipus—passionate,
quick to resent Ismene's inability to share her unyielding
will. She has grown up under the shadow of her inces-
tuous birth, her mother's suicide; though nothing in this
play implies the events of the "Oedipus at Kolonos," her
father's self-inflicted blindness and his death are mentioned. And her brothers have just fallen in battle, each
at the other's hands, and while one has been buried with
due honor as the late king of Thebes, burial of the
other is forbidden under penalty of death. To leave
enemies unburied was an extreme severity, never quite
approved; a truce for the recovery and burial of the dead
was usual after battle, the side that asked for the truce
thereby admitting defeat. But to Antigone Polyneikes
was no enemy. He was no less her brother than Eteokles; of her sacred duty to perform the last rites for him
there was no question. Her soul is swelling with anger
at the indignity as she leads Ismene out; she is astonished
that the "new general"—she will not call him king—
should so little know her as to suppose that she would
submit to such a decree. She is burning with the resolve
not to dishonor her brother; the crime of disobedience
is a holy deed, death for that an honor. But if she is
angry and unjust to Ismene, her response to Kreon's curt

questioning, after the guard has caught her in the act, is one of great dignity, as she vindicates the higher claims of the unwritten divine laws over decrees of a mortal king. To Kreon indeed her tone of exaltation, the tone of a superior rather than a subject, is an aggravation of her offense; and the chorus of his councilors note in it her father's temper and unbending will, which Kreon fancies he can break. Yet under the submissive words of the chorus, perhaps in their manner, Antigone sees, and boldly declares to the king, that they are at heart more in sympathy with her than with him. Her final answer to his argument is the verse, which loses in translation much of its beautiful simplicity, "I cannot join in hatred, but in love." The scene with Ismene which follows we have considered. On Antigone's side there are subtle transitions of feeling. She will not accept the offered sacrifice; possibly her manner of rejection is influenced by desire to save her sister, for the old affection is also plainly still there. As I said, good acting is needed for the full interpretation of the scene, and Kreon is quite unable to understand the spirit of either.

Antigone's dirge illustrates the facility with which the Greek dramatic form admits a delay in the action—action in the narrower sense—for fuller expression, in music and in lyric verse, of the emotional content of a situation. She is allowed to delay, though setting out under guard for her living grave, while she laments her untimely end along with the half-sympathizing chorus, who are the council of state. Impossible in real life, of course,—as are all the other conventions of drama,—but justified as the others are. To the ardent enthusiasm that inspired her act and sustained her till sentence was pronounced succeeds the inevitable reaction. She makes no mention of her affianced bridegroom, whose manly defense of her she has not heard, nor of any expectations as future queen. It is the common lot of humanity from which she is cut off—marriage, children, the light of life—cut off as a criminal for an act of simple piety. Do gods care for justice? May no worse fate come upon her enemies than they have visited on her! In her final words, deserted as she feels herself, even Ismene is forgotten; she speaks of herself as the last of the royal line. And once immured in the ancient tomb, unconscious that powerful agencies are working for her rescue, she hangs herself with her girdle, thus making futile the love of Haimon and the late reversal of judgment by the king. Sophokles had no thought of lifting any of his heroines out of humanity by making them perfect. Her final act was quite in character. Yet her personal defeat, even her rash suicide, are essential steps in the complete victory of her cause. The poet never loses the long view of life, the true perspective.

Everyone sees a likeness between Antigone and Elektra, but circumstances, aims, and foundations of character are unlike, as the dramatic issue is unlike. Elektra has also a sinister background, but much of it farther removed, in her ancestors. Her father's murder by her adulterous mother and the necessity of living on with the two paramours and in subjection to them have been the great formative influences. Sophokles can re-dramatize the story of the "Libation-pourers" by taking it from the new point of view, that of Elektra. Ever mourning her father, refusing to be reconciled with the murderers, accepting rather, in honor of him, their constant maltreatment, ever awaiting the return of Orestes, and hoping to assist in righteous vengeance—that is her life. She catches at Klytaimestra's dream as a gleam of hope and gains a modicum of cooperation from her less faithful sister. Then comes the news of Orestes' death, so circumstantially told that no one can doubt it. In despair she is ready to attempt the deed of blood herself, if Chrysothemis will help; her refusal cuts off the last hope. The lament over the urn which she believes to contain her brother's ashes is the climax of her suffering, and leads directly to the recognition of Orestes, who has brought it as part of his disguise.

Then appears the other side of her nature. Years of resistance, suffering, and waiting, her thoughts bent always on mourning and on vengeance, have developed qualities that are abnormal and in themselves repellent, however we may admire her constancy. Now, with the great burden lifted from her, she gives way to simple affection, sure that her brother will soon make everything right. The formal *kommos* becomes a duet of rejoicing, in which Orestes nevertheless remains calm, while Elektra forgets all danger in unrestrained expression of emotion. The natural woman, so long repressed and thwarted, has full course. Recalled by the *paidagōgos* to the need of action, she carries out her assigned part in the scheme, glad to follow and not lead. Only at one point, when her mother's first cry is heard, the harsher side returns in the exclamation, "Strike, if thou canst, a double blow." This has been much criticized by those who forget what Klytaimestra is—how to her public crimes of adultery, murder, and usurpation have been added years of hatred and persecution of her daughter, and this very day the intention of starving her daughter to death in prison. Elektra is perhaps even less of a saint than Antigone; but Sophokles has none of that mawkish sentimentalism which could fancy that a daughter should retain a sense of a tie which the unnatural mother has rooted out from herself.

It is remarkable, an illustration of the poet's practical skill as a dramatist, how the "Elektra" comes to its own in the theater. Autopsy clarifies, as the author intended, both situation and characters. This is not merely the writer's personal impression; in translation this play, like "Oedipus King," has in recent years had a lasting success in Paris, steadily drawing full houses. The heroine is seen more truly—her loyalty, the agony of her situation, the cruelty she endures. Motives which the mere reader finds remote, part of a creed outworn, are seen to be simply human. In the recognition scene—but hardly less in the lament over the urn, and indeed from beginning to end—the winning feminine nature, although so long outwardly starved, is felt deep-seated within the heroine, sustaining, pervading, and outliving the temporary shell of implacable resistance. The reader who has not seen the piece fairly acted should hold any adverse judgment lightly.

No doubt that would apply to other plays, as the "Women of Trachis," of which the entire *exodos,* the Herakles scene, has been disparaged. Sophokles was repeatedly judged second, but never third, in the dramatic contest. The probable explanation of so striking a fact is precisely his technical skill in meeting theatrical conditions—that side of his art which is least evident in a poetic text.

XI. EURIPIDES AND NEW AIMS

I

UNDER Euripides' name have come down to us nineteen plays, including our only complete satyr-play and the "Rhesos," of uncertain authorship; the "Alkestis" is neither tragedy nor satyr-play, but a romantic drama with happy ending. Whether this larger number surviving is due to accident, which played no small part in the preservation of Greek literature, or to the greater admiration for Euripides in the later period, or simply to the fact that his language was more modern, more readily understood in the Byzantine age, we cannot say. No doubt all three factors cooperated. That matter of his language would naturally go far. Anyhow it is good fortune in itself, and it affords a wider basis for estimating him. Although but a fraction of his work—the fecundity of all three was prodigious—it is not a narrowly selected fraction. It is indeed probable that one manuscript, containing eighteen plays, formed part of a complete edition of Euripides—an entire section, therefore, and not a selection at all. That must be borne in mind, to avoid doing him an injustice by comparing the general run of his work with small selections from his predecessors. Yet the collection is large enough to enable us to say that its character as a whole is in a way typical of his best plays. These also—certainly all but one or two—exhibit striking defects coupled with striking merits. A selection com-

233

parable with that from Sophokles would show him as a great dramatist, but with notable lapses. And if we put aside the question of merits and defects, his conception of tragedy differed from that of his predecessors; his tragic form was different, his aim and his vision of life were not the same. These elements cannot be altogether separated from one another, the outer form being a manifestation of the inner spirit. They blend continually, but we will begin with externals.

As with Sophokles, the chorus is never the protagonist, and never opens the play. Unless, we must add, the "Rhesos" be his, and there we may not have the original opening. Not only does every play have a *prologos*, but every play as it has come to us—there is question about the original opening of "Iphigeneia in Aulis"—begins with a speech that approaches what we call a prologue. The speaker of it may be one of the characters of the play proper, who at the close of his prologue addresses another, from which point the play goes on in the ordinary way. Or he may be a god or a ghost, who after the prologue has no further part, except as an unseen influence. In such a case the prologue may be an effective way of informing the audience of an important influence which without it would be obscure. The opening speech, if given to a mortal, may in form suggest a prayer, addressed to a god or to some personification of nature, while in substance it is addressed frankly to the audience, telling them things which will help them to understand the plot. Medea's nurse offers a good illustration. Usually no plausible reason is provided for a soliloquy, as there is for the watchman who opens the "Agamemnon." It is a straightforward, undramatic statement, such as we might print on the program.

EURIPIDES AND NEW AIMS

To get a fresh plot or a new setting any playwright might alter something in a well-known myth or take a less known variation of it. In such cases it may save confusion if a deity gives the clue at the outset. So Aphrodite opens the "Hippolytos" by explaining that she desires to compass the destruction of Hippolytos because he neglects her and worships Artemis; therefore she has inspired his stepmother Phaidra with insane passion for him, and intends thereby to lead his father Theseus himself to destroy his own son with the aid of Poseidon, who was bound by a rash promise to fulfill any three curses that Theseus might choose. So the "Ion" is opened by the god Hermes, who tells us that his brother Apollo lay by force with the Athenian princess Creüsa; and when the child was born, his mother exposed him in the cave where she had been forced; whereupon Hermes, at his brother's request, brought the infant in his wicker cradle from Athens to Delphi to the door of Apollo's temple, where a Pythian priestess, a mouthpiece of the oracle, found him. Reared by her, the youth is now a temple-ministrant, knowing nothing of his parentage; and Apollo plans to give him to Xuthos, the husband of Creüsa, in such wise that the god's fault shall be hidden and the youth receive a suitable position. With this foreknowledge of relations and the issue, the audience can enjoy the complications that to the characters in the play seem to threaten ruin. The "Bacchants," again, opens with a prologue by Dionysos, who tells something of his previous history and for what purpose he has come to Thebes. In the prologue of the "Hecuba" the ghost of Polydorus, son of Priam and Hecuba, informs us how Thracian Polymestor has murdered him for the treasures that had been sent with him to Polymestor's court for safekeeping, and that in the course of the play Polyxene is to be sacrificed at the tomb of Achilles, and he himself is to reveal his fate to his mother. For the "Trojan Women" we have in the *prologos* not only a prologue by Poseidon, which elucidates the present situation, but in addition a forecast of suffering beyond the play itself, having really nothing to do with the captive women of Troy. After Poseidon's prologue Athena comes and concerts with him trouble for the victorious Greeks in returning to their homes.

If these and similar openings are undramatic, evidently they are sometimes effective, and they have certain advantages. But they become monotonous. One wishes the poet had not followed that method alone; Aristophanes in the "Frogs" ridicules them unmercifully. Euripides did not lack ability to construct dramatic openings. He sometimes adds to the prologue a dramatic scene which with little change would have been quite adequate without the prologue. For instance, the monologue of Medea's nurse merges in a conversation with her fellow-slave, the children's attendant; this conversation might easily have included all the exposition required. For "Iphigeneia in Aulis" it is plausibly maintained that we have two distinct openings, written at different times. A prologue by Agamemnon is followed in our text by a highly dramatic scene between Agamemnon and an old attendant; either scene might have stood as the entire *prologos*. But Euripides simply preferred the method of opening with a narrative. This was indeed to disregard one plain fact, that he was thereby giving to the speaker of the prologue a double function. That speaker is at once the direct mouthpiece of the poet and also more or less a personage in the story. Beyond question this is

236

an artistic confusion, and in that regard is in fact characteristic of Euripides.

So, too, he rather prefers a "god from the machine" as the way of ending a play, and the author of the "Rhesos" follows him in this. We have seen the form of that device adopted in the "Medea," and have seen the same method adopted by Sophokles in his "Philoktetes." In the latter case there is dramatic justification for the intervention of Herakles. A dramatic excuse, if one looks for it, can always be found when Euripides does it. If a deity is not strictly necessary for untying the knot, some information or instruction is desirable that a god only can supply. In the "Hippolytos" Aphrodite in her prologue had revealed her scheme for ruining the young man. After the scheme had succeeded there was no human agency that could reveal to Aphrodite's victims the whole truth. The false charge, it is true, might have been cleared up by the nurse; but to put forward a slave in that way was contrary to all precedent. Such anticipation of New Comedy was too much to expect, even of Euripides. And her revelation could be but partial. Artemis therefore properly comes to clear her favorite's name, showing that Hippolytos was not only innocent but exceptionally faithful to honor and right, and that back of Phaidra's charge was the malice of Aphrodite, with whom Artemis promises to get even by destroying in like manner some favorite of Aphrodite. To disentangle the complications of the "Ion," Athena, as goddess of Athens, Ion's future realm, comes at the request of Apollo, who is reluctant to expose himself to reproach for his original fault. She imparts the needed information and instructions and foretells the great future of Ion's race. For "Iphigeneia among the Taurians" we feel that the complications might have been solved without Athena's direct command. But only a deity, with knowledge of the future, could introduce into the play the cultus usages which the play was supposed to explain. To us these usages are mere antiquarian lore; but the Athenian audience, and therefore the dramatist, cared a good deal for them and for the story of their origin. A certain degree of dramatic unfitness was abundantly compensated by this interest of another kind. As with the prologue, this way of closing the play was a matter of dramatic theory and purpose, in which Euripides broke with previous practice and purely artistic principles.

Certain minor differences of form may be grouped together. To begin with the smallest, purely metrical ones that disappear in translation, his trimeter, the usual dialogue verse, admits many more resolutions of long syllables. The effect is like that of trisyllabic feet in our blank verse. This is a nearer approach to daily speech, one of the ways in which the old tragic dignity is brought nearer to common life. One little mannerism is a fondness for thus resolving the third down-beat, by putting a word of two short syllables—like spirit or city—just before the exact middle of the line, especially if a longer or shorter pause in sense occurs there. One may illustrate the effect by a line like this:

The deeds are wrought by many, the glory goes to one.

Such lines are found, rarely, in Aeschylus and Sophokles, but often enough in Euripides to be a distinct mark of style which any attentive ear will note.

One other bit of metrical structure may with some difficulty be retained in translation. Robert Browning retains it, with obvious effort, in his version of "Herakles" in "Aristophanes' Apology." This is what is known as stichomuthia, or line-dialogue, an extended conversation progressing by single entire lines for each of the alternating speakers.* This, too, in moderate extent, occurs in every extant play of his predecessors. But Euripides makes a specialty of it. Fifteen of his plays contain one or more such passages apiece, of thirty or more lines each. Seven have passages of sixty lines or more, four have passages of seventy or more lines; in "Ion" is one of ninety-one lines and another of a hundred and four. This "thrust and parry in bright monostich," as Browning calls it, conveys a peculiar impression of rapidity and excitement held steadily in restraint. Closely akin, but allowing a little more freedom, is dialogue in trochaic tetrameter (the meter of "Locksley Hall," but of course without rime), where each line is divided between two speakers. In the "Ion," besides the two longest passages in iambic stichomuthia, is one in tetrameters, thus divided, of thirty-four lines. In "Iphigeneia among the Taurians" a stichomuthia of forty-one lines runs into a group of nineteen divided tetrameters; in "Orestes" forty tetrameters in stichomuthia are continued in twenty-three divided tetrameters. Clearly we have to do with a technical facility in which Euripides took special pleasure.

In lyric meters Euripides has much greater variety than Sophokles. It has often been remarked that in this respect he is nearer to Aeschylus. Not that he copies Aeschylus; no dramatist and no writer of choral lyrics would allow himself to repeat exactly the metrical combinations of a strophe employed by another. But like Aeschylus he makes free use of ionic, dactylic, and tro-

*Matthew Arnold in "Merope" has some good examples of it, one a passage of twenty-two lines.

chaic meters, which Sophokles employs but sparingly. From our scanty material we cannot say with certainty how far he is influenced by Aeschylus, but it looks rather as if he were consciously reviving Aeschylean types, while making them vehicles of quite another spirit. For dialogue as well he makes much use of trochaic tetrameter, which Aristotle tells us belonged to the oldest type of tragedy, and which we find still used, though less, by Aeschylus and Sophokles. Putting these metrical facts with some others we may think of Euripides as to some extent a conscious archaizer in certain externals, while in other externals he parted company with his elders. In spirit he has little sympathy with antiquity; at heart he is an innovator, preparing the future.

In another way his technical facility in versification appears. His lyrics are famed for a certain verbal sweetness, of a sort that occasionally reminds one of Swinburne. Even when the content is unimportant, dilute in imagination and in thought, and especially when it is pathetic, the grace and music of the words charm the ear. Where the rhythms are perspicuous, not too unlike our familiar rhythms in English verse, the lines are already half song, even to our ears; they call up for us a distant echo of the ancient voices and a suggestion of the Attic dance. His lyrics contained other innovations, most of which, being in the musical composition, we lose; but one is very plain. Frequently, especially in monodies, antistrophic responsion is abandoned. The rhythm flows on with no attempt at a return to pattern. Milton, in "Samson Agonistes," wrote all the lyric parts in this fashion. So familiar are we with this in modern music that we may easily fail to appreciate how great the innovation was.

II

Again, in Euripides alone—so far, that is, as we can judge from the plays now extant—we find plots that do not exemplify the principle on which we insisted in opposition to Mr. Archer. The "Trojan Women" especially is not unified by any dominant struggle of will. It is constructed rather on the principle of the chronicle-play—a succession of pathetic episodes. One character, Hecuba, stands out above the other captive women, because she is their queen and the most conspicuous sufferer. There is one chorus and one locality. There is no other unifying bond, and these alone, as Aristotle saw, do not make unity of action. In the *prologos* Poseidon agrees with Athena to send storm and disaster on the Greeks in their homeward voyage, presently to begin. Their sufferings, as was said before, do not otherwise come into the play. They are merely brought before the mind as a future reversal, to balance present success and the present sufferings of the Trojans. Then, after Hecuba and the chorus have lamented their unhappy situation, Talthybios announces the approaching fates of Cassandra, of Polyxene, of Andromache, and of Hecuba. Next is the powerful scene of Cassandra, whose prophetic visions extend far beyond this play. Then Andromache becomes the central sufferer. Then the episode of Helen and Menelaos is followed by the funeral of the child Astyanax; finally Troy burns as the captives are departing. Successive waves of woe beat upon one after another; the victims cannot struggle, they can only suffer. It is a powerful presentation, in dramatic form, of some of the horrors of defeat in war; as such it holds a modern audience, and is a moving plea—

especially to those who need no such plea—against aggressive war. Mr. Archer might cite it as overthrowing Brunetière's law. It undoubtedly testifies to the poet's genius. But no thoughtful spectator can fail to note its grave defect. The absence of a dominant struggle withdraws from the scenes of painful and unrelieved pathos just the element that would lift them to the true tragic level. The real tragic heroine, even though a criminal, commands at least a kind of admiration. These women, however, are but helpless victims whom we can only pity. The ravings of Cassandra, because they offer a certain semblance of moral resistance and moral victory, bring her nearest to the level which the play as a whole fails to attain. In spite of a measurable success, the plot goes to confirm the soundness of the law, as formulated by Brunetière.

The "Phoenician Women" is another play whose plot approaches the chronicle type. There are resistances, fragments of several plots, not fused into one plot by a dominant struggle, but tied together by a single chorus, by unity of place and time, and by being successive episodes of one war. The chorus is provided by a singular device. Some Phoenician women on their way to Delphi, to serve there as temple attendants—a purely mythical incident—are stopped at Thebes by the war with Argos; thus they become witnesses of what happens there at the crisis of the Argive attack. They are thus really bystanders, interested but not vital parts of the action; their songs are correspondingly detached, though not irrelevant nor unsympathetic. All the incidents belong to the last day of the attack; it is the story of the "Seven against Thebes," which could be unified in any one of several ways. But in this play groups of incidents stand apart. Iokaste and the rival brothers make one group. Kreon, Teiresias, and the youth Menoikeus are a separate group. The banishment of Oedipus is tacked on at the end. Besides, Kreon the suffering father and Kreon the king are two different men; Antigone, in the *prologos* a timid girl, is at the end a strong and resolute woman, with no explanation of the change.

The "Hecuba," again, falls into two parts and Hecuba herself is two persons. The story of Polyxene is one section; her shrinking from death and the change to heroic acceptance make a pathetic piece in the true Euripidean manner. The second section is Hecuba's fierce vengeance on the treacherous Polymestor with the help of her fellow-captives and the connivance of Agamemnon. In both parts Hecuba is the suffering mother. But in the former she is passive, the spiritual victory of Polyxene furnishing the element of tragic struggle and making her the heroine; in the second part the controlling principle is the queen's determined will. Externally the two sections are bound together by the prologue, in which the ghost of Polydorus informs us of his murder, which calls for vengeance, and then also by the slave woman, who finds his corpse when she is fetching water for the funeral rites of Polyxene. Decharme* finds also a bond between the two moods of Hecuba. He maintains that her inability to avenge the former bereavement makes all the keener her determination to avenge the second. I would not deny that an actor might so conceive the rôle, and perhaps might so render it as to convey that thought to the audience. But I find no suggestion of that conception in the text, and I find a simpler and more probable explanation of the contrast in an

*"Euripide et l'Esprit de son Théâtre," pp. 325 f.

inclination of Euripides which we shall consider later. I mean what we may call his habit of presenting sharply contrasted moods in the same person—a tendency of which Polyxene herself is another example. In any case a considerable defect in unity remains.

In the "Andromache," likewise, the first part presents the imminent danger and the triumphant rescue of Andromache and her child. The extravagant despair of the foiled Hermione is the transition to the second part, in which Orestes comes to claim Hermione as his wife, and the death of Neoptolemos at Delphi sets Hermione free, and incidentally Andromache, too, for their respective new unions.

Some scholars, with defective dramatic insight, have placed the "Herakles" also in this list of divided plays. Is it not in fact simply the final struggle of Herakles with his lifelong enemy Hera? In the earlier scenes we are shown the hero returning victorious from his journey to Hades, rescuing his family, killing the tyrant. It is this human, self-reliant, jovial, beneficent hero on whom Hera makes one more assault. From this contest also he comes off victor, with the aid of a strong and loyal friend, in a moral victory, powerfully portrayed, such as any human sufferer may win over the blows of adversity, if he can but summon up the needed moral force from within his own soul. The substratum of old myth is left dominant in the earlier scenes. But it is made to yield a plot in which criticism and purification of old mythology are animated by a fine humanity that reveals Euripides at his best.

Yet even those plays that lack unity of action contain, each of them, single scenes of great beauty, of much pathos, and of great dramatic effectiveness in themselves.

EURIPIDES AND NEW AIMS

If these plays illustrate a weakness of Euripides, and are not his best, they illustrate also some of his peculiar merits, which made the plays effective in the ancient theater. A dramatist who could now make scenes as good would be no less acclaimed on the modern stage.

III

We have seen gods appearing pretty freely in *prologos* and *exodos,* in ways characteristic of Euripides and nearly confined to him. In general they appear there as the superhuman cause of human fortunes, especially of human misfortunes, and as powers that, under limitations, can solve the difficulties into which humanity is brought by passion, by ignorance, or by hostile super-human agency. They can also foretell the future and command action with direct reference to rites and cere-monies of the poet's time, which is conceived as ages later than the events of the play.

In two plays, however, deities are active characters in the body of the tragedy. One is the "Bacchants," in which Dionysos is a prominent figure, the other is the "Herakles." In the latter Iris, as Hera's messenger, comes to introduce Frenzy, a *daimon* sent by Hera to work harm upon Herakles. Superficially that is like Aeschylus in the "Prometheus" and "Eumenides," but how different the spirit and the aim! "One man," says Iris, appearing above the house, "is the object of our joint attack, who they say is son of Zeus and Alkmene. Before he ended his bitter labors fate ever saved him, nor did his father allow either me or Hera to do him evil; but since he has completed those labors of Eurystheus, Hera wills, and I with her, to fasten on him new blood-

shed in killing his children. Come, with pitiless heart,
daughter of black Night, thou unwedded maid, send upon
this man madness, even to slaying his own children,
that he may learn what Hera's wrath against him is, and
mine; else gods are nowhere and mortals are great,—
unless he pay the penalty." Whereupon Frenzy, warning Iris and Hera that they will regret their mistake,
and protesting that she obeys unwillingly, because she
must, since the victim is not only innocent but a great
benefactor, does what she was told to do; and Herakles
in madness kills his wife and children. The messenger,
who soon comes out from the house to narrate what has
there befallen, tells how the hero's violence was ended by
Pallas Athena, who hurled a stone at the breast of Herakles, felling him to the ground. Here is an exciting and
tragic incident, partly seen and heard, partly narrated,
in which gods are the agents.

In the opening lines of the "Bacchants" Dionysos has
explained that he has come from Asia to his native
Thebes to establish his worship there first in Greece.
Since Pentheus, king of Thebes, opposes with ridicule
the acceptance of the new worship, although his aged
grandfather Kadmos, his mother Agaue, and the wise
Teiresias accept it, Dionysos has driven the women of
Thebes, including Agaue, out into the mountains, where
in bacchic enthusiasm they are celebrating his rites. He
intends to display his power, convincing all that he is
verily a god, son of Zeus no less than of Semele, a Theban
mortal. With this purpose he now goes out to join the
Theban women, leaving here before the palace the chorus,
his attendants who have followed him hither from Asia.
Pentheus is led to go out also and spy upon these women
of Thebes who are acting so strangely. They detect him,

set upon him under the lead of Agaue herself, who under the power of the god fails to recognize her son, and tears him to pieces. Agaue brings his head, fixed on her thyrsus, in triumph to the city, supposing it to be a lion's head, and praising Dionysos as her fellow-huntsman, who has given her glorious victory over the mountain beast. Gradually she is wakened from her bacchic madness and recognizes that it is her son she has killed, his head that she holds. Such is the issue of the god's activity, proving his divinity.

We have seen what was Aphrodite's action in the "Hippolytos," what was her motive, and how powerless Artemis was to thwart her. The best she could do was, after the harm was done, to expose the villainy of the goddess of love, undo what could still be undone by nullifying the false charge of Phaidra, and promise revenge in kind. Her helplessness to prevent the scheme against Hippolytos is explained as due to the customary law among the gods. "No one," she says, "wishes to oppose the desire of one who wills, but ever we withdraw; except for my fear of Zeus I never would have come to that degree of shame, permitting the death of one most dear to me."

If Euripides has taken anything in this kind from earlier playwrights, it is only the bare fact, belonging to the earliest traditions, of making divine beings *dramatis personae;* his gods themselves and their acts and motives belong to a different order from those of Aeschylus. Against Zeus himself the worst charge brought by these divine activities is that he permits the rest of the Olympians to be what they are. And they seem to be a society, outwardly polite, among whom malice, jealousy, lust, and other ignoble passions, along with mere caprice, are frequent motives, making havoc among mankind. We found no villain in our seven plays of Sophokles; we find several pretty villainous deities in those of Euripides. Aphrodite's intrigue against Hippolytos, because he is unduly chaste and slights her worship, is quite worthy of a jealous "maid of honor" at the court of a great monarch. That her intrigue involves the ruin of Phaidra, who is blameless, Aphrodite says expressly will not matter. The scheme whereby Dionysos proves his divinity and recommends his worship, if taken seriously, would imply a strange religion. The person most severely punished for the unbelief of Pentheus—who is punished with death—is his mother, one of the god's earliest and most enthusiastic worshipers. And what a glimpse of Olympian society we get from the scene in the "Herakles." For some reason called fate or divine law ($\chi\rho\acute{\eta}$) Hera could not get at Herakles before; yet it was she whose trickery had brought on him all his previous troubles. But now she is permitted to drive him mad that he may kill his wife and children. And her agent, Frenzy, dislikes to do so mean a thing; she warns Iris and Hera that they will repent. Contrast this with Athena's action in bringing insanity on Aias—an action that humiliates the pride of one who had offended, yet is beneficent to all concerned. In fact, the most striking thing about the "Herakles" on the moral side—a fact of the first importance for estimating Euripides—is the demonstration in the final scene, by Theseus and Herakles, that mortals may by loyalty and fortitude rise to a moral plane far above such gods as the play has exhibited. The traditional doctrines about power and goodness of the gods and their providential care of the righteous often recur in Euripides; their own acts, as

presented by him, often completely contradict the doctrine. The net impression is one of moral confusion in
celestial society itself and in the divine government of
the world. To believe that divine influence on human
life is what these plays attribute to the gods would be to
lose all faith in a moral order—to believe that the confusion in human affairs is not merely allowed by the gods
but is directly due to them.

What then was Euripides' point of view? What was
his aim? Was he deliberately preaching disbelief in the
old gods, covertly saying to his countrymen, "These be
the gods of your faith, what think ye of them?"

It has been maintained that just this was his purpose.
No one has put this more flatly than the late Mr. Verrall. In his edition* of the "Ion" he says: "That Euripides and those for whom he spoke hated and despised the
Olympian religion is written all over his work. Their
hate was chiefly moral, their contempt chiefly intellectual.
They detested the doctrine of the gods for its immorality;
they scorned it as resting ultimately upon the imposture
of prophecy and other fraud. Delphi was to them the
main position of the enemy. To Apollo in particular
Euripides seldom shows any mercy; to assail Apollo and
the authority of Delphi is a motive constantly present
with him, very strong in such works as the "Orestes" and
the "Andromache," dominant and absorbing in the "Ion."

The dictum is phrased with that uncompromising vigor
with which Verrall liked to maintain a paradoxical view.
This particular paradox, however, represents fairly a
whole school of interpreters, who agree on the essential
point, that Euripides was consciously undermining the

*Introduction, p. XVI.

orthodox religion. So Wilhelm Nestle* says: "Euripides wholly denied the gods of Greek popular belief. He rejects the entire anthropomorphism of the Greek pantheon." We see from Aristophanes that this view of his began with some of his contemporaries. For example, the comic poet makes a poor widow complain† that Euripides has ruined her business of selling wreaths, by persuading men that there are no gods.

But is such a view really credible? Assuming for a moment that his personal attitude was what Verrall and Nestle ascribe to him, is it credible that he could venture, at the greatest religious festival at Athens, to preach in this open way disbelief in the gods of the state? No doubt skepticism was widely current. Cruder features of the old myths are openly rejected by Pindar, as inconsistent with the fundamental belief that gods are wise and good. And Pindar was never charged with impiety. Sokrates did the same, if we can trust Plato. In Thucydides there is no hint that he personally believed in the Olympians or in oracles or divination, as Herodotus did. A purer and more rational religion, tending toward a philosophical monotheism, was gaining headway in thoughtful minds, as the primitive polytheism became less credible. Aeschylus and Sophokles in their way furthered this purifying tendency; Euripides went much farther than they in the same direction. He makes his characters utter with surprising freedom the current skepticism and contemporary philosophy. He thus offered occasion enough for such popular objurgation as Aristophanes' wreath-seller flings at him. But the prosecution of Anaxagoras and the death of Sokrates are

---

*Euripides, der Dichter der griechischen Aufklärung," p. 145.
†Thesm. 450 ff.

enough to indicate how dangerous it would have been for Euripides, if he had convinced any considerable part of his audience that he was not only an atheist but a public preacher of atheism. The Athenians, as Plato makes Sokrates remind Euthyphron, didn't mind what views a man held in private; but propagating ideas that tended to subvert the state religion stirred their quick and sharp resentment; the jury court of five hundred was a ready instrument for translating popular anger into action.

Nor is this difficulty met by alleging that Euripides managed his propaganda so cleverly that the multitude would not understand; that the stories he takes as the vehicle of his views are in fact traditional, so little changed that no charge could be based on his version, while the more intelligent would understand, would even sympathize and applaud. For in the first place there was no clear line dividing the more intelligent and the less, nor any dividing the more and less orthodox, nor were the orthodox and the unintelligent identical, any more than nowadays. To which class did Sokrates belong? Never were audiences more thoroughly mingled, more unified and intercommunicative, than those of Euripides. Evidence of what the Athenians would feel to be impiety, if distinct enough to convince the intelligent, would at once rouse the suspicion and anger of the many. Moreover, a tragic poet sought above all things popularity, approval of the many. A fit audience, though few, may satisfy a philosopher or a closet poet, but not a playwright. That universal law of drama has never been more compelling than it was in the Athens of Euripides. To win popular approval of such audiences for plays that aimed to overthrow the popular religion was beyond the skill of any playwright whatever.

Besides, there are other scenes and other plays where no atheistic spirit appears or can be read into them. The "Iphigeneia," either of the two, will serve as example. Nor is Athena, the special goddess of Athens, ever placed in a really unpleasant light, nor Zeus as a dramatic personage, although strange things are attributed to him and the traditional tales about him are taken for granted with little protest. Of the plays from which only fragments remain we know too little to enable us to use the fragments as evidence; but the inconsistencies in the plays we have are surely an additional count against the theory of an atheistic propaganda. That theory does not solve the problem of Euripides' religious attitude. The clue must be sought elsewhere.

But the thought may still recur that after all, in his treatment of traditional myths, Euripides is not so far from Aeschylus. In his "Agamemnon" also Artemis required the sacrifice of Iphigeneia, making it otherwise impossible for the Greeks to sail from Aulis, because she was offended at Agamemnon; the passion of Zeus for Io brought cruel suffering on her; Zeus tormented Prometheus for loving man, and the jealousy of Hera made endless trouble. That is all true. The task of the poet in showing a beneficent providence under the sufferings of Io, bringing good out of evil, not only for mankind but for her, is plainly very difficult. But the endeavor is equally plain. It is not unfair to compare that endeavor, and the faith that underlies it, with the religious attitude that still notes how God—or the moral constitution of the kosmos—brings good out of permitted or seeming evil. So with the punishment of Prometheus. To us

the play may not seem very satisfactory as an explanation of evil among men. But no reader can doubt the
religious seriousness of the poet's attitude toward the
gods, and toward Zeus above all. And we lack the rest
of the trilogy, in which as a whole we may be sure the
righteous rule of Zeus was exalted. Finally those actions
of Artemis and Hera are "outside the play," like Apollo's
passion for Cassandra—part of the mythological background from a ruder age, which no dramatist using the
tale could ignore. That is not the same as making them
integral factors in the plot, and in such a way as to
emphasize a deity's moral obliquity. The superficial
likeness is felt by a candid reader to disappear under a
wide divergence of religious attitude.

There can be no doubt that Euripides actively shared
the spirit of free inquiry about the traditional gods. He
was known to have a large library for his time. He was
said to be a pupil of Anaxagoras; remarks of a philosophical cast are often put in the mouths of his characters; reflections upon gods and religion are frequent
among these. A passage in "Iphigeneia among the Taurians" illustrates his continuation of Pindar's critical
spirit toward myths wherein traits are attributed to gods
which human morality rejects. Iphigeneia declines to
believe that Artemis, daughter of Zeus and Leto, can rejoice in human sacrifice, or that Tantalos served up the
flesh of his child at a feast to the gods. Men, she thinks,
being themselves the slayers of men, "attribute their vile-
ness to the goddess, *for no celestial can be wicked.*"
This no doubt states truly the poet's own attitude, and
a basic principle on which he was in harmony with
Sokrates, and with ourselves. It follows therefore, for
one who so holds, that he is bound to reject whatever

tale attributes to divinity anything that falls below our own highest ideal of morality. And that spirit must have been widely held as sound; criticism clearly based upon it was almost orthodox—was at least regarded, by large numbers, as not atheistic in itself. Many must have recognized that element as a large one in the Euripidean criticism of myth. "Euripides not merely shook the popular beliefs," says Henri Weil* but "he contributed powerfully toward spreading a higher conception of the divine, which was to be that of the future."

But remarks of a philosophical nature are often quoted without their context, in such a way as to give an entirely false impression. There is in the "Trojan Women" a striking passage of that kind: "O thou that carriest the earth and hast thy seat upon the earth, whoever thou art, hard for knowledge to guess out, O Zeus, whether thou be Necessity of Nature or the mind of mortals, I bow before thee; for all mortal things thou guidest, keeping thy silent path, in the way of justice." Without context this is a remarkable expression of faith in a supreme divine power, a faith stated in a philosophical form that far transcends the traditional view. In fact, however, it is the exclamation of the Trojan queen, captive in the Greek camp, on hearing Menelaos give orders to seize Helen by the hair and drag her away to be killed. It is her ejaculatory thanksgiving that the wicked cause of all this woe is now to get her deserts. And on Menelaos' remark at the strangeness of her prayer she gives him the wise advice to avoid seeing Helen, lest she change his purpose—which quickly comes to pass. The dramatic situation gives Hecuba's bit of philosophy a color far from purely philosophical.

*"Etudes sur le Drame antique," p. 105.

Even so, however, it is certain that the poet's attitude toward the traditional gods was neither that of the old religion nor that of Aeschylus, but that of one emancipated by the advanced thought of his time. Personally he might have been ready to drop the old names and ceremonials, so far as literal faith in them was concerned.

But no Greek could yet do that. Names and ritual were intertwined with all the events and memories of life. And religion was no private affair between the individual soul and the deity; it was above all an affair of the community, and that in all the steps of its organization, from which no one could detach himself and still live among Greeks. Especially, as I said, a tragic poet writing for the Dionysiac theater could not think either of dropping the old religion to make over the art of tragedy or of preaching disbelief in it by means of his art. The inherent contradiction was unthinkable. Several centuries had to elapse before a Lucian could arise—before one could publicly scoff at the gods and at the beliefs of the many. It is true that Aristophanes did something like it; Old Comedy was granted that license in jesting at the Lenaean festival, where it was part of the convention that everyone in heaven and earth might be turned to jest. And this feature of Old Comedy was continued in the mythological travesty of gods in New Comedy. But only in well-understood fun, not as propaganda of irreligion. And such fun had no place in tragedy.

We see the complexity of Euripides' position and the difficulty of stating it. We must recognize that he took the gods and the myths about them, primarily, as the traditional material for tragedy, which he made no attempt—so far as we can see, had no desire—to discard. He did not follow up the lead of Phrynichos and Aeschylus by drawing plots from what we distinguish as history; he did not follow the lead of Agathon by wholly inventing a plot. Like other tragic poets he took such parts of the old myths as he thought would furnish the best tragedies, changing details as best suited his immediate aim. Plenty of people doubted whether oracles had any basis but fraud and credulity, and whether diviners had any means of learning the will of heaven. When this doubt would yield a good dramatic turn, he let his characters utter the doubt. That was safe and would often waken a popular response. When, however, belief was inherent in the dramatic issue, his characters are orthodox enough. In the "Phoenician Women" the sacrifice of Menoikeus is essential to the story. Teiresias accordingly is an honored seer, whose directions are obeyed, with no protest against barbarity, to the salvation of the city. In the "Helen," from the failure of Kalchas and Helenos to recognize that Greeks and Trojans were fighting for a mere phantom of Helen, the slave-messenger is made to infer that divination is vain. Yet in the same play Theonoë is an infallible diviner. So of other doubts that were current. His mind is open to all criticism that detects absurdities and is shocked at immoralities; he lets his characters freely utter them, and so helps on the purification of religion, whenever this can be made dramatically effective. In the "Ion" a series of pointed situations is made possible by the fact, essential in the myth and fully accepted, that Ion is the son of Apollo by the Athenian princess Creüsa. All these opportunities the playwright uses, and with striking effect. But the solid basis of the play for every Athenian is that the god has all the while provided duly for his son's upbringing, and provides for his final settlement as lawful king of Athens, to the glory of Athens and the boy's mother as well. With that basis firmly settled beforehand, the youth, on partial knowledge, may chide his divine father, and Creüsa may reproach him, with dramatic piquancy and without giving serious offense. Xuthos, Creüsa's husband, is nothing to Athens; he is little more than a comic character, fooled awhile and then dismissed. We shall look again at this aspect of the play. For the poet's use of malevolent deities he had good warrant in Homer. Was not the hostility of Athena and Hera a factor in the ruin of Troy? Did not Poseidon relentlessly pursue Odysseus? Such cases Euripides takes as typical among the causes of human misfortunes, because that assumption yields excellent situations for dramatic portrayal. He hardly needed to invent cases. Well-known tales and popular speech offered enough. To ask whether he believed such tales, either literally or in some esoteric sense, or whether he disbelieved them, is beside the mark. In some cases the name but thinly veiled powers and influences of nature; in that sense there was truth in the tale; in any case, here was good dramatic material. Who asks whether Wagner believed the medieval myths on which he composed his music-dramas? They furnished him ready-made outlines on which, with minor changes that he thought would make them fitter for his purpose, he could construct, by his art as poet and musician, representations of life. That is what the Greek myths were to Euripides. He had the added advantage that the mass of his audience did believe in them, or at least did not distinctly recognize them as fictions, and that he was continuing an old tradition, universally accepted.

And it was really human life that all the tragic poets

painted, whatever names they gave their characters. They knew no other. No artist knows or can represent a higher, but only higher and lower phases of that. Euripides saw and desired to present in tragedy, now a settled, if still flexible, traditional form, other aspects and kinds of life than Aeschylus or Sophokles. He may have been hampered a little by the great number of existing tragedies from the same material; he had in a sense less freedom than his predecessors. But too much weight, I think, has been given to this. Was he more hampered by the work of his predecessors than Raphael was in his painting? I do not see how. Yet great Venetian painters could follow Raphael, even in painting the old religious subjects, producing works less simply religious, but hardly less great. Life itself remains for each new generation as various and fresh as ever. What we have to do is to make clear to ourselves, if we can, wherein Euripides' vision and presentation of life differed and was his own, and then take the wealth he offers, leaving the dross—as in some degree we have to do for every artist—and looking elsewhere for what he does not offer.

But it is clear that we must not ask from Euripides, with such a conception of religious myth, any consistent scheme of a society of gods, any consistent picture of divine action in the world. He could not on such a basis develop about the name of Zeus, as Aeschylus endeavored to do, a clear notion of a supreme and righteous rule, to which the other gods were subordinated on an intelligible plan. Nor could tragedy on such a basis offer any means of presenting a more rational religion dissociated from the old names. *Dramatis personae* may on occasion utter scraps of philosophy; they cannot even suggest a philosophical system. And Euripides was and wished to remain, not a philosopher, but a playwright. He must have been aware that his dramatic use of philosophical ideas and of questions about gods would go to strengthen and spread such ideas and questions. So much of intention we cannot deny. That is far from admitting, however, that a skeptical propaganda was a leading motive. It was an incident of his main purpose—to portray as effectively as he could the life he saw.

IV

Character-drawing of the static type we found highly developed in Aeschylus, to which in Sophokles was added the portrayal of growth of character under trial and stress. How about this element of tragic art in Euripides? As with other elements of his art, the answer is not easy nor simple.

Iphigeneia among the Taurians all would accept as a portrait well drawn, consistent, lifelike. A princess, offered by her father in sacrifice to Artemis that the fleet might sail, saved by the goddess to be her priestess in a barbarian land, officiating now many years at the sacrifice of shipwrecked Greeks, ever hoping that some happy chance may bring her home to Argos, all her strange experiences have conspired to give her a peculiar dignity, strength, and sweetness of spirit. Her creator was accused of being a woman-hater. I could never see any evidence to support the charge; one such figure is ample defense, and she is not alone. Romantic love— what we take as normal and happy love—is not portrayed in Greek tragedy, and she has about her none of that special glamour of youth in which the most winning of

Shakspere's heroines move. Her qualities are those of maturity, are fundamental and lasting. The recognition scene between her and Orestes is the finest that has come down to us, and it is she—her mingling of caution, eagerness, good sense, and sisterly affection—that makes it so charming. Goethe, to make his Iphigenie, added some modern traits, but he dropped off more than he added. The German princess is more sentimental, less simple, less gracious and attractive.

The picture of devoted friendship between Orestes and Pylades deserves the fame that has made it proverbial; the two young men also are drawn fully enough to make them distinct, yet are kept duly subordinate to the heroine.

Herakles, too, apart from the attack of madness, which has no relation to his real self, is clearly conceived and individual, and that in two aspects, of which the second grows out of the first, being the direct result of the suffering caused by Hera's cruelty. First he is the stout-hearted champion returning joyously to his wife and children from a dangerous enterprise and finding them at the point of death from an oppressor, whom it is his first duty to dispose of. Later, in the scene between him and Theseus, he is again sane and overwhelmed with despair at what Hera has driven him to do. It is the sustaining friendship of Theseus and his appeal to the native strength of Herakles, to his great deeds and his deserved fame, that win him back to life and courage. For this one scene, in which alone Theseus appears, he, too, is distinct and fine. Here is a second picture of friendship, this time between older men.

Ion is also a lifelike portrait of a youth, not unworthy in its way to be put beside that of Neoptolemos in

"Philoktetes," although the two are very unlike—unlike as personalities and unlike in that Ion is not subjected, like Neoptolemos, to a crucial test that forces character to a quick maturity. Knowing no tie of kinship, the foundling has grown up in the temple service, to which he is devoted and in which he has been content. He is frank and innocent, kindly to the birds that with his arrows he must drive away from the sacred place, and courteous to the visiting women, the chorus. To Creüsa, their mistress, he is mysteriously drawn. Surprised at her involuntary tears, an unwonted sight in the temple-precinct, he frankly questions her about her home and about the tales of Athens, as interesting to him as Delphi is to her. His curiosity, which might be too bold in another, befits his nature and situation. And Creüsa returns his interest in kind, herself mysteriously drawn to him. So it is brought about that each learns the other's greatest lack and desire, Creüsa prudently putting her case as that of a friend. Incredulous at the story that Apollo can so have wronged a mortal woman, Ion suggests that perhaps the god himself has taken and seen to rearing her friend's infant. He shrewdly observes that to inquire of the oracle is not likely to bring a response; from shame the god must desire not to be found out. Questions that might incriminate the god we should not put to the oracle, seeking to force an unwilling blessing; only from what the gods grant willingly do we get benefit.

At this point one may ask, Is this properly characterization, or rather a piquant situation, drawn out in several phases? It is properly both, very skillfully interwoven. The youth is ingenuously chiding his unknown father, a god, for a sin of youthful passion, and to his mother, the god's victim; mother and son, unaware of the tie between them, each wishing the tie were theirs, are seemingly close upon discovering the truth. And both are displaying in the most natural way their several personalities. Creüsa, plaintive, but gentle and womanly, is a fitting mother for her stronger son, to whom, from beginning to end, she is dramatically subordinated. When later she learns what her husband has concealed, that the god has given Ion as a son to Xuthos, jealousy and fear of the future impel her to a plot for killing her unknown son, whose natural indignation at the attempt, frustrated by the god's care, procures his mother's condemnation to death. The successive complications renew suspense continually, till at last the difficulties are solved by the Delphian priestess, Ion's foster-mother, and by Athena. The priestess produces the closed wicker cradle in which the child had been found at the temple door, and in it still the tokens put there by Creüsa, whereby the relationship is proved; Athena "from the machine" completes the revelation and foretells the future. Incident and the plot of surprise are far more highly developed than in Sophokles; yet both characters are consistently drawn, that of Ion more fully, and he is always the more prominent.

Gilbert Murray calls the "Ion" cynical, ironical, "of all the extant plays the most definitely blasphemous against the traditional gods." One hesitates to differ from Gilbert Murray about a poet whom he knows so well. But I am unable to believe that his view was at all that of the Athenian audience. Apollo Ancestral (πατρῷος), as father of Ion by Creüsa, was a corner stone of national Ionian sentiment and belief. In itself that story shocked no Athenian in the least. And in the play the god has not for a moment abandoned his child, who was miraculously conveyed to his temple and reared under the god's own care, saved from the danger of a plot conceived in ignorance, and restored at the right moment to his mother, as heir to a throne and leader of a people. It was against this permanent background of belief that an Athenian heard the chidings of the tearful mother and the high-minded son—chidings humanly natural and dramatically striking. To the popular conception of a Greek god it was no serious derogation that he should himself recognize with some shame the moral error of a passion so complimentary to the princess who inspired it. It is not very long since Englishmen, and our ancestors, readily condoned irregular liaisons of their kings; more than one noble family is unashamed, if not proud, of an unconsecrated descent from a monarch.

Both Verrall and Gilbert Murray make much of the alleged falsehood of the oracle's response to Xuthos. "The god had certainly used, in speaking to Xuthos," says Verrall, "the unlucky expression 'son by birth.'" That is not quite so clear. The word which Verrall insists on so rendering (πεφυκέναι, 536) is to Ion himself so ambiguous that he at once inquires (in Verrall's own version), "Son of thy loins, or given thee?" No doubt Xuthos had understood the god as meaning that the first person he should meet would be the son of his loins, and there is a bit of comedy in this, to which we shall return. But the Greek language made easy here one of those ambiguities for which the oracle was famous, even among believers. That comic bit at the expense of Xuthos—who, as I said, was nothing to the Athenians, and who drops out of the play soon after—is justification enough for introducing the ambiguity. That motive for a misunderstanding is quite

Euripidean. The assumption that the poet meant to discredit Apollo Ancestral, or was understood by his audience to have done so, is incredible. And for Athena's part we must not forget the invariable convention that a "god from the machine" never offers any credentials. Conventionally, the miraculous entrance is evidence enough of divinity, accepted without question by *dramatis personae* and audience alike.

And finally, what can Gilbert Murray possibly mean by saying* that Creüsa, after Athena's revelation, "forgives the god; Ion remains moodily silent"? He seems to intimate that the youth still doubts—that the play ends with a bitter innuendo against Apollo Ancestral. On the contrary, instead of remaining moodily silent, Ion in response to the revelation says in three trochaic tetrameters, "Not in disbelief, O Pallas, daughter of supreme Zeus, do we receive thy words; I believe that I am son of Apollo and this woman; and even before was this not incredible." To which Creüsa adds her praise of the god's care and a complete retraction of her chiding. There is no innuendo. What fuller acceptance could one ask?

Of another type of character, a distinctly Euripidean type, are Phaidra and Medea. Under the passion of Hippolytos which Aphrodite has inspired,, Phaidra has been wasting away and is now starving herself. Her old nurse at length succeeds, under promise of secrecy, in drawing from her the hidden cause of her disease; and then, on the pretext of a love-charm which will cure her, reveals it to Hippolytos. In shame at this—also in anger at the youth's loudly expressed horror of the nurse's proposal—Phaidra hangs herself; and for revenge—as

*"Euripides and his Age," p. 123.

Aphrodite had planned—she leaves a note accusing him of attempting her honor. From the Greek point of view, her rôle was secondary, not that of the protagonist; but to Euripides the study of her passion was apparently the chief interest. Certainly that has been the chief interest in the play since his time. Racine's "Phèdre" is closely modeled on it. Taking the same liberty which every Greek dramatist exercised, Racine has modified details and simplified the plot, reshaping it to his peculiar type. But the essence is the same, and "Phèdre" is admittedly one of the great French tragedies. No one now contests the originality of Racine, as no one denies his debt to Euripides. The close relation between the two plays is one token of Euripides' greatness.

Medea, as we saw in an earlier chapter, is a powerful study of a wronged wife's revenge. It has been often said that a Greek poet would have been unwilling to represent a Greek wife in such a storm of conflicting passions. But Medea is no Greek; the unrestrained violence of the Kolchian sorceress was a subject after Euripides' heart. And in Medea and Phaidra he created the tragedy of passion, which has filled so large a place in the annals of the later stage. Fierce personal vengeance was a passion that especially attracted him. It is a prominent motive in the "Bacchants"; Aphrodite makes Theseus and Phaidra her instruments to inflict it on Hippolytos; it is Hera's motive in the "Herakles," Hecuba's in blinding Polymestor. Vengeance might be called a passion of strength, or at least one simulating strength, Phaidra's passion rather one of weakness. Both passions are alike, however, in leaving no room in the soul, during their sway, for better qualities.

This aspect of Euripides has been concisely described

by Patin:* "He was fond of representing the soul given over, almost without defense, to overmastering inner impulse; the seductions of desire, confusion of mind, failure of will, the intoxication of passion; remorse, despair. He was the painter of human weakness, as before him Aeschylus and Sophokles had been painters of heroism." In this direction his originality and his genius are beyond dispute; and this is also made a heavy count in the indictment against him. As we have to do with weaker souls, the part of the body in the tragic spectacle becomes more important.† Hence the prominence of sex, old age, physical pain, delirium. Shall our admiration of the poet's power outweigh the considerations that Plato stated so strongly in the "Republic"? The dramatist must win sympathy for his characters. The sympathetic contemplation of moral weakness, admirably painted, must have another effect on the soul than the sympathetic contemplation of moral strength, in heroic struggle.

If we find in Euripides a group of dramatic portraits that stand high in the art of characterization, we have to note failures also. Passing over minor figures, what shall we call Hippolytos? The breath of life is not in him, as it is in Racine's Hippolyte. We cannot conceive him as real—one combining a healthy love of horses and hunting, more than maidenly purity, an outspoken pride in his own moral perfection, and a saintly spirit of forgiveness toward the father who had without hesitation accepted Phaidra's false charge, and condemned him to death. His extravagant denunciation of women is one of the passages that are absurdly cited to show that the poet himself was a woman-hater. That is as palpably

*"Etudes sur les tragiques grecs." Eschyle, p. 48 f.
†Croiset, "Hist. de la litt. grecque," III, p. 327.

unfair as it was to cite his line, "My tongue has sworn, my mind remains unsworn," to show that the poet condones perjury. In that line the youth is protesting against the deceit which has elicited an oath of secrecy on false pretenses; yet he dies rather than break the oath. Keeping the oath, to his own hurt, and the tirade against women, are both in character, so far as we can speak of a character for him. The fault in characterization is not there, but lies deeper. If we felt him to be real, his fate would be painful rather than tragic. If we could suppose that Euripides wished to point a moral by the young man's fate, it could only be this, that young men should not be too chaste. That doctrine hardly needs promulgation; we will not slander Euripides by attributing to him such a moral.

But in truth Hippolytos, like Aphrodite, is not a person; he is simply part of the machinery by which the playwright combined in an acceptable plot the kind of scenes he wanted for his effects, the passion of Phaidra being the most prominent note. It is enough if the youth serves that purpose and is not too obviously artificial.

The whole play is remarkable for the interlacing of dramatic contrasts. Aphrodite and her malice in the prologue are balanced by Artemis and her sympathy in the *exodos;* fierce virginity in a young man is contrasted with mad sexual impulse in a mature matron; the latter's passion, for which she is not responsible, contends with her moral resistance; her virtuous resolve not to yield gives place at the point of death to the base lie of a woman scorned. Then there is the quick shift in the nurse's attitude, from voluble horror at Phaidra's reluctant confession to eager furtherance of the aphrodisiac impulse; there is the grave warning of the old slave, with his prudent prayer to Aphrodite, balancing the young man's scorn; the father's instant acceptance of his wife's false accusation, and his rash prayer that means a dreadful death for his son, followed by remorse when Artemis tells him the truth. Such contrasts, especially such rapid transitions, added to the regular tragic reversal for the youth himself from princely prosperity to undeserved suffering and death, are among the effects that Euripides most valued. To attain them some departure from natural truth, even a wide departure, seemed a minor matter.

In short, what Euripides paints with fullest success is not character, still less growth of character, but mood. The backbone of a strongly marked character is moral principle; or in lack of that, then settled habit and resolute will. What he sees and portrays best is emotion; he likes a plot that offers occasion for shifts of emotion. Hence his cleverness in constructing a plot with more complication and surprise and renewals of suspense— with ingenious concatenation of knowledge and ignorance and conflicting motives, with unforeseen and capricious intervention of superhuman agents—intervention not referred to any theory of moral government, because that would allow less play for the effects he liked. Hence also his fondness for the pathetic, without too nice regard for the sources of the pathos. Hence his feeble old men dwelling weakly on their physical weakness, his suffering women dwelling on their suffering, and the series of ragged and wretched heroes whom Aristophanes laughs at so unmercifully. Hence, in the "Orestes," the feeble and delirious prince, anxiously tended by his sister, soon rising from his sick bed for vigorous action in restored health. Hence the larger place he gives to children, and to those pathetic groups of women, children, and old men, assembled about an altar, appealing to divine protection because they have no other. Hence, finally, those maidens—Makaria in the "Children of Herakles," Polyxene in the "Hecuba" and "Trojan Women," Iphigeneia at Aulis, with the youth Menoikeus in the "Phoenician Women"—all of whom, after full expression of their natural horror of untimely death, unexpectedly rise above this into the heroic mood and devote themselves freely to sacrifice. Aristotle cites the case of Iphigeneia as an evident departure from consistency of character and truth to life. If it stood alone, we might hesitate to agree with his judgment, the episode is so well done. It is a touching example of the self-forgetting devotion which many women have shown. But the series as a whole must be referred to the poet's general tendency. The case of Euadne in the "Suppliants," who throws herself upon the funeral pyre of her husband, is not the same in motive, and is more sensational, because consummated before our eyes; but it belongs with the others as an unexpected turn of emotion and a free choice of death. With Medea also one may doubt whether her alternations of mood, the will to punish her husband wrestling with love for her children and finally prevailing, is not rather a sensational theatrical stroke than a human possibility. But it makes a powerful scene.

If these generalizations are sound, they throw light on much that was at first puzzling. The poet's use of the supernatural fits into place without assuming either positive belief or aggressive skepticism. The plot of the "Bacchants" yielded a chorus that is steeped in wild emotion, in the Bacchic enthusiasm to which the relaxed

Ionic rhythms were by tradition appropriate. The devotees are contrasted with the scornful Pentheus, who is later shown with mind and sense perturbed, while for Agaue the wakening from Bacchic frenzy is a strikingly Euripidean scene. I see not the slightest hint of a return to orthodoxy in the author's old age; but the play is a succession of effective situations of his peculiar type. It may well be that his residence in Macedonia while composing it, and the Macedonian enthusiasm for Dionysiac worship, influenced his choice of the subject. The lack of congruity in the plot, if one looks at it from a religious point of view, is a minor matter, which probably troubled him not at all. There is, however, a suggestion that he recognized an incongruity. To Agaue's agonized question, why they also are included in the punishment of Pentheus, he makes Kadmos answer by falling back on the old principle of the solidarity of a house.* The guilt of the king had involved his believing mother and grandfather along with himself in the god's anger. The god's own house had rejected him. If slighted or offended a god might take vengeance in mysterious and dreadful ways. There is no likelihood that Euripides himself accepted this application of the principle as just or godlike; but the belief was ancient and was dramatically convenient. The "riddle" of the play is a modern invention.†

*Lines 1249 f., 1303 f., 1340-1350.

†In view of the deserved popularity of Gilbert Murray's translations, perhaps those who do not read the original should be reminded that his version brings into this play some modern spiritual meanings that are not in the Greek. From his frank account of his method and aim we may understand that this addition is deliberate—of course it is neither inadvertent nor

EURIPIDES AND NEW AIMS

We can now see what Sophokles may have meant by saying, as Aristotle reports him, that he had painted men as they should be, while Euripides painted them as they are. More of the latter's characters give way under stress, are in every way nearer to average humanity. Usages of his own time are carried back to the heroic age; the common things of life appear more. So in reading the Euripidean "Elektra," for example, we must forget the other versions of the story if we would judge this one fairly. The princess is outwardly married to a peasant, who refuses to regard her as a wife, but treats her as a princess under his protection. He must in his poverty accept her labor as if she were a peasant. Homely details of their housekeeping are shown. She fetches water from the spring, and chides him for inviting visitors to dinner when they have nothing fit to set before guests. They send to a neighbor, who is an old slave of Agamemnon, the *paidagōgos* of the Sophoklean "Elektra," who is now less poor than they; he brings a lamb and wreaths and some cheese and some treasured old wine, to help them out. Thus he is brought into the action to effect the recognition of Orestes. And in connection with this recognition scene occurs that curious criticism—very unfair—of the Aeschylean recognition scene in the "Libation-pourers." In the "Orestes" a new turn is given to the myth by assuming that the government of Argos rests with the popular assembly, as in the Athens of Euripides. The people bring their lawful prince to trial and condemn him to death, because he has killed Klytaimestra, who had murdered their former lawful prince, Agamemnon, and shared her

intended to deceive—to avoid another kind of misleading that a more exact version would involve.

usurped power with her paramour. Seemingly they had made no objection to the initial murder and usurpation, but are horrified at the crime of the avenger, returning to resume his right. This absurdity is a fitting prelude to the comedy of the latter part of the play; but it affords new and striking situations.

Ancient audiences and modern readers have somehow agreed in finding in the plays of Euripides more of the author's own opinions than in the plays of his rivals. Why should that be, since all are alike dramatists? Precisely because his characters are in general less clearly conceived, less distinctly drawn. One feels that these are not real persons, existing outside of the playwright's mind, merely depicted by him, uttering their own thought; they may at any moment be the poet himself, only partly concealed behind a mask. Not all, as we have seen; only, his character-drawing is not sure or consistent. A thought or a sentiment that presses for utterance, if suitable to the situation, he puts in the mouth of someone, not considering always whether it is also suitable to the speaker or singer. The method of reconstructing the author from his dramas has been carried much too far, but his dramas justify the method.

V

Besides giving a new direction to tragedy itself, Euripides expanded the comic element, creating tragi-comedy, foreshadowing melodrama.

In Aeschylus and Sophokles the comic touches are brief and restricted to slaves or common people and barbarians. But Xuthos in the "Ion" is king of Athens, with a considerable part in the plot. When the oracle has given Ion to him as a son and the youth questions his god-given father, the latter is comically unable to guess which can have been the boy's mother. His mis-interpretation of the oracular terms of gift adds to the humor of the situation—a situation for a Restoration comedy. The audience know that he is welcoming effusively, not his own illegitimate son, but his wife's. He finally recalls an occasion of about the right date, a torch-light festival of Dionysos at Delphi, which may account for Ion as the child of a Delphian maenad. Accepting that as probable, he realizes the difficulty of telling his wife what turn their search for a son has taken. He hopes they may in time find the mother for whom the young man yearns; but for the present they will conceal from Creüsa the newly discovered relationship and will celebrate it together, without her knowledge, by an elaborate banquet. Going off to develop this fatuous plan, Xuthos now disappears from the play, except as a messenger subsequently narrates the details of the affair, and Athena includes him briefly in her revelations of the future. Here is a distinct strain of comedy, not of the Aristophanic kind, but in our sense of the word, going much beyond the touches which we found in the other tragedians.

In the "Andromache" the scene of recrimination between Peleus and Menelaos departs radically from the tragic tone. In a way it is like other angry disputes in all three tragedians, only this goes much farther. In Euripidean fashion it is nearer to everyday life. Peleus says, "Shall I break your head with this staff?" To which the other retorts, "Touch me and you'll find out!" Whereupon Peleus proceeds in a long tirade to remind Menelaos that he lost his wife to a Phrygian—a fair specimen of Spartan girls with their naked thighs, who race and wrestle with young men! He should have thought himself well rid of her,—and so on. The cleverness of Menelaos in reply no doubt amused the audience, and his complete discomfiture was a pleasing sauce to the release of his victims. And then Hermione and her rapid shifts of mood! Malice against the captive slave and rival who has escaped her, fear of her husband, extravagant and voluble despair, plans of suicide, all melt into a cheerful readiness to elope with Orestes, who is clearly a fool to desire such a wife. The emotional elements which Euripides could combine endlessly are here combined to what is almost a farce.

In the "Helen" the entire fable is intrinsically comic, although diction, rhythm, and the general tone of much of the dialogue and choral song are kept in the tragic style. The device of a phantom Helen who went to Troy, an exact duplicate of the real one, who was a model of virtue, was taken from the Palinode of Stesichoros. It is the most striking illustration of a general principle; a conception of a mythical personage adopted in one play never hindered an author from adopting a radically different conception for a personage called by the same name in another play. The bare outline of a myth might thus furnish a great number of plots. This Helen is for this plot only. While Greeks and Trojans were fighting for this phantom, "that Zeus might lighten mother earth of her surplus of mortals," the real Helen was safe in Egypt, until Menelaos should find her there on his way home. King Theoklymenos has demanded her in marriage, to avoid which she has taken sanctuary at the tomb of Proteus, in front of the palace. To her comes Teukros, exiled from Salamis, on his way to found a new Salamis in Cyprus. His open amazement at seeing one so exactly resembling Helen does not draw from her any revelation of her identity; but she learns from him that Troy is taken and that Menelaos and Helen are still wandering, in the seventh year after the fall of Troy, if they are alive. Teukros hastily withdraws on being advised that the king Theoklymenos kills all Greeks who land here. At the advice of the chorus Helen goes into the palace, and the chorus with her, to learn from the seer Theonoë, sister of the king, whether her husband is living or not. While they are within, Menelaos himself comes, escaped from shipwreck, wretchedly clad, wishing to learn where he is. An old portress answers his knock and warns him away, as Helen had warned Teukros away for the same reason. The altercation, already comic, becomes more so when he learns that Helen is within. He had left Helen in a cave by the shore. His amazement increases when Helen herself comes out, with the chorus. While they are trying to come to an understanding, a messenger reports that the other Helen has vanished. After these mysteries are cleared up the problem of getting away confronts them. The fooling of Theoklymenos offers a new comic motive, making a scene to which the fooling of Thoas in "Iphigeneia among the Taurians" bears a rather close resemblance. The whole play is a tragi-comedy, in which the tragic element is but slight. The people are in serious trouble at the beginning, but the foundation is comic, and the issue happy.

The "Orestes" goes a step farther. The opening is pathetic—Orestes lying in a sleep of exhaustion, his sister at the foot of his bed watching tenderly over him. The first eleven hundred lines are tragic enough, once we accept the incongruity before noted—a popular assembly in the heroic age formally trying and condemning their prince for resuming his rightful position in the only possible way. But what attracts Euripides, in contrast with his predecessors, is a new aspect of the story. They had painted Orestes and Elektra as devotedly loyal to their great father, resolutely performing a painful duty, an act at once of righteous vengeance and of public justice, although one of the criminal pair was their mother. Euripides will paint the moral and physical sufferings of a brother and sister who have killed their mother. Her criminality is kept in the background. Physical exhaustion, not caused by remorse but supernaturally inflicted, with the misery of moral isolation and popular horror, assuaged by mutual affection—that is the leading theme in the tragic part of the play. There was a slight touch of comedy when Helen took such care to cut, for offering at Klytaimestra's grave, only the very end of a lock of hair, so as not to impair her beauty. But soon melodrama begins. Orestes, after five days of starvation and delirium, has risen from his bed in full vigor; he now prepares, with Pylades, to kill Helen and seize her daughter Hermione as a hostage. One of Helen's eunuchs escapes from within the palace, exhibits his abject fear, reporting the cause of it with plenty of comic detail, and Orestes plays with him in that state as a cat plays with a mouse. Presently the two young men are seen on the roof, ready to kill Hermione and set fire to the palace. Suddenly Apollo appears on "the machine," with Helen, miraculously rescued, because, forsooth, she is a daughter of Zeus, destined to immortality. He directs Menelaos to get another wife and Pylades to marry Elektra; Orestes, after a year of exile in Arcadia, and acquittal at Athens for his matricide, is to marry Hermione and reign over his father's realm. In some way not specified Apollo will make it up with the Argive assembly, who had condemned both brother and sister to death. Of course everybody accepts without demur the god's command.

We are definitely told that this play was very successful and often given; it is frequently quoted in later antiquity. Most moderns are repelled by the incongruities and not much attracted by the melodrama. Yet it contains in striking form some of the playwright's peculiar merits—unexpected turns of an old story, or rather of several stories, pathos, acute observation of morbid life, rapid shifts of emotion, ingenious plot, a great deal of action, a happy ending. The Greek language had no other name for it than *tragoidia;* but it was quite unlike the older fashion of tragedy.

With such unmistakable examples before us, incidents in other plays are seen to resemble them. In the "Children of Herakles" Iolaos goes out to battle, a feeble old man requiring the support of his attendant, who must carry for him the panoply taken from the temple wall. The attendant on his return tells how marvelously his master had in battle become young again, had overtaken the fleeing Eurystheus, and was bringing him captive. In Homer such rejuvenescence would have an air of epic *naïveté*. Here it is not in the least naïf; if we do not call it melodrama, that is because it is only narrated.

About the position of Achilles in "Iphigeneia in Aulis" perhaps not all would agree. But if it is not unmistakably comic, it is certainly compromising to his dignity. Agamemnon has secretly used his name to lure Iphigeneia to the camp under her mother's charge, pretending that his daughter is to be married to Achilles. On that very ground Klytaimestra appeals to him for protection. He promises that the sacrifice shall not be consummated, and exerts himself to save the maiden. But from the nature of the case his exertions are futile; he is compelled to break his promise. His own troops threaten rebellion, Iphigeneia herself accepts her fate. There are tragic grounds for his failure; yet, though there is no place where we can be sure that the poet meant us to laugh, Achilles himself, we cannot but feel, is no tragic figure.

And finally, in the "Trojan Women," the episode between Menelaos and Helen must have been intended as a bit of comic relief in a somber tragedy. The weakness of the uxorious king, the confidence with which Helen relies on her charms to subdue him, and her complete success, as foreseen by Hecuba, make a naturally comic combination.

So there is ample ground for the feeling, ancient as well as modern, that New Comedy derived from Euripides at least as much as from Aristophanes and his fellows of the Old Comedy. This is not to be turned to the reproach of Euripides. It is one of the ways in which he was preparing the future. To speak of him as breaking down the old conception of tragedy is true enough, but is only half of the truth. No less true is it to say that in his hands tragedy grew and expanded until, by natural biological process, it became two or three new kinds of drama, and not tragedy alone. One may prefer the strength, massive simplicity, and soaring imagination of Aeschylus, with his occasional obscurity and occasional turgidity; one may admire the full-rounded dramatic art and profound character-drawing of Sophokles; from either one gains a greater unity of impression. But there is a certain fascination about the very miscellaneousness of Euripides. Between his monotonous prologues and his closing scenes, too little varied, along with dramatic faults and lapses of taste, there is more that is unexpected, there are more beginnings of future development. One more such beginning, a very remarkable one, we have still to consider.

VI

The "Alkestis" is the oldest play of Euripides preserved, with possible exception of the "Cyclops," the satyr-play. It was brought out in 438 B. C. as the fourth play of a tetralogy—in the place therefore that was always assigned to the satyr-play, if a satyr-play was included in the tetralogy. The same notice informs us that Euripides was second in the contest, Sophokles first. Apparently all the other plays of this festival are lost. But the "Alkestis" is no satyr-play, for there is no satyr-chorus. Also it is longer than a satyr-play. In external form, as in length, it is a tragedy. There is a prologue by a god, a chorus of men of Pherai, whose songs are of the tragic type, and at the end—if not a "god from the machine"—a hero, Herakles, effects a happy and a miraculous issue. But neither is it a true tragedy, although the poet and his contemporaries had no other name for it that was more descriptive. Browning's mingled translation and paraphrase in "Balaustion's Adventure" is deeply dyed with Browning, in the version itself as well as in the interspersed comments, but is not the less interesting for that. But Browning's error is that he takes it too seriously, missing the romantic and playful air of the whole. He plays a minuet as if it were a march. The notes are all there but there is no dance.

Coming as it does in the place where a satyr-play was to be expected, the audience would look for a change of sentiment and subject, approaching more or less that of the usual fourth play. This expectation of the audience, due to setting and time of day and what had gone before, is an important clue for interpreting what might otherwise be doubtful.

Apollo, for the prologue, comes out from the house of Admetos, whom he has served for a year as shepherd, and explains that he is leaving because he may not look upon one dying, and the day has come when Alkestis, who has consented to die in her husband's place, must meet her fate. At this moment comes Thanatos (Death) to perform his office, of cutting with sacrificial knife the lock of hair whose severance consecrates to the lower world. He hails Apollo suspiciously, taunts him with having saved Admetos by deceiving the Fates, and asks if he intends to repeat his trick. Apollo tries—not very seriously—to induce Thanatos not to fulfill his office, which Thanatos insists on doing. Apollo assures him—and the spectator—that one is coming, on an errand for Eurystheus, who will nevertheless force him to yield his prey, and Thanatos with a scornful reply enters the house.

To spectators disposed as we have said, this Thanatos, about to be foiled, is no grim monster, but a semi-humorous embodiment, whom nobody need fear. The calm good nature of Apollo, the knowledge of the coming hero, the assurance of Death's defeat, enable people to enjoy the pathos of the self-sacrifice, with a suggestion of humor in it, and the beauty of the choral songs, without being distracted in the least by any tragic fear; the humorous scenes need lose none of their intended effect. The ambiguities by which Admetos conceals from Herakles the nature of his loss, the readiness of Herakles to accept them, would be incredible in a tragedy but are in place here. They harmonize with the *prologos* and with the rôle of Herakles, which would have been impossible without them. The whole is a sort of rebirth, in drama, of the romantic spirit of the Odyssey. Not that any single episode of the Odyssey is quite like it. I only mean that one might imagine the marvels and the pathos and adventure and grotesquerie and the domestic affection and happy ending of the Odyssey all fused together, and then recast, with some addition to the humorous element, in a fifth-century form. In this atmosphere, from this predisposition, no one inquires how Thanatos got out of the house, which we saw him enter, to be ready at the grave for the encounter with Herakles; nor how Herakles on his way to the grave could miss the funeral procession returning. No one asks just how the personal prowess of Herakles could by overcoming Thanatos restore a corpse to life. Allegory and imaginary fact can be treated as one, and we are quite ready to accept wonders. It is true that a mortal hero—Herakles is not yet immortal—is represented as able to help a friend and restore to life, in easy disregard of fate, when Apollo, the god, for all his affection and his divine power, is confessedly helpless. But to see in this a bitter satire and a fling at the old theology is to miss the playful spirit, taken over from the satyr-play.

It is this air of romance that in the death-scene softens tragic poignancy to a delicate pathos. One may almost—

I do not say quite—compare it to a death-scene in a fairy tale; instead of heart-rending it is charming—not a real death-scene but a pretty imitation of one. Incidentally, whatever the poet's own mishaps in marriage, this whole piece, without a trace of personal disappointment, is a delicate encomium of a devoted wife. When she exacts from her husband the promise not to marry again, if the question that rises tends to assume a cynical tinge, the tendency is rebuked in the sequel. The question is answered dramatically, and humorously, when Admetos is shown converted from his selfishness, rejecting the custody of his restored wife, offered him as a stranger. He recognizes that her lot is happier than his own; the romantic fancy is what saves the moral lesson from being unpleasantly obtrusive.

In like manner the altercation between Admetos and his father is saved—barely saved—from being intolerably painful. We needn't take it too seriously; the selfishness of both is sufficiently exaggerated to appear unreal rather than realistic. All the while there is that thought of a satyr-play in the background. The part of Herakles is clear and has not been misunderstood; nearly all else has been, because that satyr-play in the background was forgotten. That was the presupposition on which the play was built. The poet seems to give free play to his fancy in this delightful substitute, as if in a spirit of revolt against the coarse tone that the satyrs almost demanded. What is needed for its interpretation is not philological acumen so much as dramatic imagination.

The "Alkestis" is often the first Greek play read, and is in some ways well adapted to be read first. But for proper understanding one should read it after reading several tragedies and then the "Cyclops." The "Trackers," the large fraction of a satyr-play by Sophokles, recovered in Egypt a few years ago, is far nearer than the "Cyclops" to the general tone of the "Alkestis."

VII

Although Sophokles outlived him a few months and both left plays that were brought out after their death, it is Euripides who marks, for us, the close of Athenian tragic art. Contemporary rivals were sometimes preferred by the Athenian public to both, but we can form no definite conception of them. The one exception is Agathon, who is a living figure only because Plato has pictured him for us as the brilliant and genial host of the "Symposium." There was no farther development of the old type, only the progressive decay that follows the culmination of every great art. Of Greek successors, who were many, nothing is left but allusions and insignificant fragments. Comedy was to have a new lease of life, to which Euripides, and in his later phase Aristophanes, pointed the way. But for tragedy, decay and stagnation in decay were to last many centuries before a rebirth and new growth on other soil could follow.

NOTE.

Some Translations and Imitations

Lyric poetry, which is so large a factor in Athenian tragedy, offers peculiar difficulties to the translator, and no version of the choral parts is quite satisfactory. Yet if one reads attentively and makes due allowance for the inevitable loss, a fair notion of all three tragedians may be obtained from the English alone. A comparison of different versions will often clarify things. Only what seem to me the least defective translations are here mentioned.

Aeschylus and Sophokles entire in English verse, by E. H. Plumptre, Dean of Wells, were published by George Routledge and Sons, London and New York, and have been reissued in a cheaper but good form by D. C. Heath and Co., Boston, U. S. A. The choral parts are given in two versions, one with rime and the other without. The translation is good, though not inspired. Mrs. E. B. Browning's rendering of "Prometheus Bound" retains more of the poetic fire, and that compensates amply for a few of Mrs. Browning's mannerisms. Robert Browning's "Agamemnon" is perversely bad, and more obscure than Aeschylus. Edward Fitzgerald's "Agamemnon, a Tragedy taken from Aeschylus," treats the text of the choral parts with great freedom, so that he declines to call his play a translation; yet he retains all of the plot, most of the character-drawing, and the real heart of the original.

NOTE

Sir Richard Jebb's prose translation of Sophokles (Cambridge University Press) is perhaps on the whole the best of that poet. The vigor of the original is often toned down by using the Latin element of our language where the Saxon element would have given a truer impression. Barring this, the accuracy, taste, and literary judgment of the distinguished scholar are beyond praise. The translation of Sophokles into English verse by R. Whitelaw (Rivingtons, London) is good to compare with that of Jebb. That by Lewis Campbell (Kegan Paul and Co., London) may also be recommended.

Euripides is well translated in verse by A. S. Way (Macmillan and Co., London and New York) and by Gilbert Murray. The latter version is deservedly popular, though not yet complete. The separate plays are published mostly by G. Allen (London), the "Iphigenia in Tauris" by the Oxford University Press. The footnote about his version of the "Bacchants" (p. 270) applies in a general way to all. It should in fairness be added that the liberty he takes has much to do with his success in maintaining the interest of the reader, which was precisely his aim.

Modern dramatic poems that follow more or less the ancient model are Milton's "Samson Agonistes," the most successful in English, Matthew Arnold's "Merope," Swinburne's "Atalanta in Calydon" and "Erechtheus." The latter two contain beautiful choral songs, but are wholly undramatic. In "Merope" the lyrics have little suggestion of song, but the dialogue conveys admirably the effect of Sophoklean trimeters. Racine's "Esther" and "Athalie" employ a chorus, but not at all in the Greek manner. Leconte de Lisle's "L'Apollonide" is a slight variation on the plot of Euripides' "Ion," "Les

285

Erinnyes" recasts in more modern form the plot of the "Agamemnon" and the vengeance of Orestes. In these also the Greek chorus is not wholly naturalized; to any modern audience a chorus, on the Greek model, can be only an exotic.

INDEX

The titles of plays are in italics, those of each tragedian under his name.

INDEX

288

INDEX

Character-drawing, limited, 184; static, 186; in Homer, 189, 190; in Euripides, 259-261, 268, 272.

Choral odes, indeterminate time of, 90; only ode to Dionysos extant, 97; not affecting action, 98; emotional reflex of action, 98.

Chorēgos, 66.

Chorus, 56-58; why felt to be central, 65, 66; always of men, 66; often gave name to play, 66; always of amateurs, 66; essential, and singing as one, 77; participants in story, 78, 79; motives for their presence, 78, 79; leading character in Aeschylean *Suppliants,* 78, 97, 186, 187; also in *Eumenides,* 78, 97; central in *Persians,* 187; rarely leave orchestra, 82; continuation of old dithyramb, 94, 95; dominates tragic form, 97; in action usually subordinate, 97; as mediator and confidant, 97; extra chorus, 99.

Chorus-leader, as actor, distinct from chorus as whole, 97.

Clarinet, 54.

Comedy, imitates men as worse, 53; from phallic songs, 56; Old and New, 56, 255; Aristophanic, 59.

Complication, see *desis.*

Conflict, tragic, 121-123.

Contest, dramatic, 60, 61; four plays of each author, 67; change in order of, 68.

Convention in art, 22.

Costumes, 69, 70.

Cox, K., quoted, 16.

Crisis, dramatic and non-dramatic, 130, 131.

Curiosity about outcome, 63-65.

DANCE, mimetic, 29, 30; in dithyramb, 55; Greek associations with, 65; essential for chorus, 76, 77; in Shakespere an interlude only, 77.

Dancing-place, 56, 57.

Decharme, P., on *Hecuba,* 243, 244.

Demeter, 54.

Desis, complication, 162, 172.

Dialogue, germ of future development, 97.

Dionysiac festival, 57, 58, 60.

Dionysos, 54, 56.

Dithyramb, 52, 54-60.

289

INDEX

INDEX

Hecuba, prologue by ghost of Polydorus, 235; falls into two sections, 243; an aside in, 44; self-devotion of Polyxene, 269.

Helen, intrinsically comic, 274, 275; inconsistency about seers in, 256.

Herakles, version by R. Browning, 238, 239; not divided, 244; Hera, Iris, and Frenzy in, 245, 246; final scene, 248; hero well drawn, in two phases, 260.

Hippolytos, action of Aphrodite in, 247; extra chorus in, 86; hero a lay figure, 266, 267; series of contrasts in, 267, 268; prologue by Aphrodite, 235; Phaidra, a characteristic type, 264-266.

Ion, prologue by Hermes, 235; chorus reveals a secret, 98; stage whisper in, 44, 45; pointed situations in, 256, 257, 261; hero characterized, 260-262; G. Murray quoted on, 262, 264; Murray's and Verrall's views criticized, 262-264; Creüsa characterized, 262; Xuthos largely comic, 272, 273.

Iphigeneia among the Taurians, plot analyzed, 145-149; heroine characterized, 259, 260; Orestes and Pylades in, 260.

Iphigeneia in Aulis, prologos of, 236, 237; self-devotion of heroine, 269; position of Achilles in, 277, 278.

Medea, plot analyzed, 170-178; *parodos* of, 179; "god from the machine," 116; heroine a characteristic type, 264, 265; the great scene rather a sensational stroke than true, 269.

Orestes, new turn given the myth, 271, 272; sudden return of the hero's vigor, 268, 269; new aspect of the story, 276; merits, 277.

Phoenician Women, not unified, 242, 243; chorus of, 242; sacrifice of Menoikeus, 256, 269.

Rhesos, begins with *parodos,* 100; only tragedy extant on plot from the Iliad, 100.

Suppliants, extra chorus, 99; Euadne's suicide, 106, 269.

Trojan Women, prologos, 236, 241; a series of episodes, 241, 242; episode of Helen and Menelaos comic, 278; self-devotion of Polyxene, 269.

Exodion, 103.

Exodos defined, 102, 103.

Exposition, see *archē.*

FATE, in Greek tragedy, 134-138.

Fictive beginning and end, 35, 36.

Flute, 54, note.

INDEX

INDEX

INDEX

Play, defined, 32; subject of, 32; how the subject is recast, 33, 35-37; text only the musician's score, 50; written to fit actors, 211.

Playwright, his material limited, 40, 41.

Plot, before characters, 119, 120; nature of dramatic and tragic plot, 121, 123; as technical term, 120.

Plots, dramatic, why not draw from Iliad and Odyssey, 139, 140; from myths, advantages of, 65; from non-Dionysiac myths, 62.

Poet Laureate, Dr. Bridges, on Homer's character-drawing, 190.

Poetry, its wide range, 30; its material, words, 30, 31; rhythm in, 31; the intermediary, 31, 32; the common speech in Attic tragedy, 42.

Portraiture, Greek, 183, 184; Roman, 184.

Prologos, defined, 101.

Proportionality, in time and space, 26.

Protagoras of Plato, double time in, 91.

Racine, his *Phèdre* and Euripides, 265.

Raphael, 62.

Recognition, ἀναγνώρισις, 148, 158.

Religious atmosphere of Attic tragedy, 60, 61.

Religious attitude of Homer, 202; of Aeschylus, 202, 203; of Pindar, 202; of Sophokles, 202; of Sokrates and Plato, 203.

Rembrandt, 47.

Reversal, περιπέτεια, 158.

Rhythm, in arts of time, 26, 27.

Ridgeway, Wm., on the origin of tragedy, 113, 114.

Ridiculous, defined by Aristotle, 53.

Saint-Gaudens, "artificer of beauty," 16.

Satyrs, 56.

Satyr-play, 54, 59; fourth in order, 67; connected with trilogy or not, 68.

Scene, change of, 82-89.

Scene of the action, Greek convention and ours, 79-81; in Corneille and Racine, 81.

Scène or *Eintritt,* 96; *scènes,* one to five in a division, 107.

Scene-painting, 52, 117, 118.

Sculpture, how far imitative, 21, 22.

Selection in art, 22.

Self-devotion, of maidens and Menoikeus, 269.

INDEX

INDEX

Oedipus at Kolonos, on local myths, 63; scene of, 206; fourth actor in ?, 108; change in Oedipus, 213; *stasimon* on old age, 216.

Philoktetes, Odysseus narrates their abandonment of hero, 106; "god from the machine" in, 116, 206; scene of, 206; *parodos* of, 179, 180; third speaker in, 208; stage whisper in, 44; Odysseus and Philoktetes unchanged, 213, 214; *kommos,* 215; change in Neoptolemos, 213-215.

Trackers, 59.

Women of Trachis, plot analyzed, 226, 227; Herakles scene, *exodos,* 232; messenger in, 103, 104; chorus, 205; moment of hope before catastrophe, 219; Deianeira characterized, 226, 227.

Stage utterance, 38; stage whisper, 44, 45; stage not raised, 71, 72; stage question, 71-73, 114, 115.

Stasimon defined, 101, 102.

Stichomuthia, 239.

Students in female parts, 70.

Suicide, the act seen, result hidden, 106.

Symmetry in space, 25, 26.

Symphony, executants of, joint creators, 28.

TELOS, 162, 164, 168-170, 177, 178.

Terence, 56.

Terry, Ellen, quoted, 50.

Theater at Athens, 69, 71.

Theatrical production at Athens, 60, 61.

Thespis, 57, 58.

Third actor, introduced by Sophokles, 52.

Time, double standard of, 89.

Titian, 62.

Tolstoi, his definition of art, 17.

Tragedy, Greek conception of, and ours, 74-76; choice of stories for, 76; Attic, always in verse, 76, 77; no set scheme of, 112; relation to vegetation-ritual, 112.

Trilogy, one extant, of Aeschylus, 67.

Trochaic tetrameter, 52.

UNITY of time, 93; of action, what makes it, 132.

VEDDER, ELIHU, quoted, 16, 17.

Verse, required for Attic tragedy, 76.

296

INDEX

297

g